沥青混合料荷载效应分析与抗疲劳设计

吕松涛　刘宏富　郑健龙　著

科学出版社

北京

内 容 简 介

本书分 8 章。第 1 章总结国内外关于沥青混合料疲劳试验方法与疲劳方程研究的现状及存在的问题。第 2 章通过对比分析国内外现行常用的沥青混合料不同疲劳试验方法，选出本书开展研究的主要疲劳试验方法，同时便于读者了解不同疲劳试验方法。第 3 章介绍传统的 S-N 疲劳方程，肯定其贡献也分析其不足，并在此基础上提出真实应力比概念，建立基于真实应力比的沥青混合料疲劳方程，提出抗拉强度结构系数。第 4 章通过引入材料刚度参数，以模量为损伤因子，考虑在疲劳加载过程中模量的衰变，建立基于模量衰变的沥青混合料疲劳损伤模型。第 5 章通过引入材料强度参数，考虑疲劳加载过程中强度的衰变，建立基于强度衰变的沥青混合料疲劳损伤模型。第 6 章基于沥青路面中沥青混合料层真实的应力状态——同时承受拉与压应力，以及拉、压模量的差异性，提出沥青混合料拉压模量同步测试方法，并建立考虑拉压差异性的沥青混合料疲劳损伤模型。第 7 章通过开展不同应力状态下沥青混合料的疲劳试验，对试验结果进行归一化分析处理，建立不同应力状态下沥青混合料疲劳损伤归一化模型。第 8 章为结论与展望。

本书既适合于道路工程领域的研究人员和技术人员阅读，又可供相关专业研究生学习参考。

图书在版编目(CIP)数据

沥青混合料荷载效应分析与抗疲劳设计 / 吕松涛，刘宏富，郑健龙著. —北京：科学出版社，2018.6
ISBN 978-7-03-057618-7

Ⅰ.①沥… Ⅱ.①吕… ②刘… ③郑… Ⅲ.①沥青拌和料-载荷效应-分析 ②沥青拌和料-疲劳强度-设计 Ⅳ.①U414.7

中国版本图书馆 CIP 数据核字(2018) 第 111405 号

责任编辑：赵敬伟 / 责任校对：邹慧卿
责任印制：张 伟 / 封面设计：耕者工作室

科学出版社 出版
北京东黄城根北街 16 号
邮政编码：100717
http://www.sciencep.com

北京盛通商印快线网络科技有限公司 印刷
科学出版社发行 各地新华书店经销

*

2018 年 6 月第 一 版　开本：720×1000 B5
2019 年 11 月第二次印刷　印张：11 3/4
字数：230 000
定价：79.00 元
(如有印装质量问题，我社负责调换)

前　　言

沥青路面具有优越的使用性能，是我国目前高等级公路主要采用的路面结构类型，沥青混合料作为路面的主要建筑材料之一，在道路工程中得到了广泛应用。疲劳开裂是沥青路面结构的主要破坏形式之一，因此，研究沥青混合料的疲劳特性，建立准确的疲劳损伤预估模型非常重要，这项工作一直受到国内外道路工作者的高度重视。

常见的沥青混合料疲劳试验方法主要有弯拉疲劳、间接拉伸疲劳、直接拉伸疲劳、压缩疲劳等，国内外道路工作者根据不同的疲劳试验方法与试验条件建立了相应的疲劳预估模型。为了客观地揭示沥青混合料的抗疲劳性能，有必要对不同疲劳试验方法、试验条件等进行系统的比较分析，建立不同疲劳试验条件下能客观反映材料抗疲劳性能的预估模型，并合理地测定沥青混合料的抗疲劳设计参数，从而为科学地建立沥青路面的预防性养护决策模型提供依据，对提高沥青路面的路用性能、延长沥青路面的使用寿命将起到积极的作用。

本书的作者一直从事耐久性沥青路面结构设计与沥青混合料疲劳损伤特性的研究，主持了国家自然科学基金项目"老化沥青路面荷载效益非线性分析与抗疲劳设计关键技术研究"(51578081)、"弯剪组合作用下沥青混合料非线性疲劳损伤特性研究"(51208066)、"沥青混合料宏细观损伤变量及非线性疲劳损伤模型研究"(51608058)等科研课题。本书在调研国内外关于沥青混合料疲劳试验方法与疲劳寿命预估模型的基础上，系统地介绍了十多年来，作者所在的科研团队关于沥青混合料疲劳特性表征方面的研究成果，具体包括沥青混合料真实应力比下的疲劳方程、基于刚度衰变的沥青混合料疲劳损伤模型、基于强度衰变的沥青混合料疲劳损伤模型、考虑拉压差异性的沥青混合料疲劳损伤模型以及不同应力状态下沥青混合料疲劳损伤模型的归一化等。

本书内容在注重基础理论知识的同时，又强调理论与试验相结合。本书上篇分8章。第1章概论，总结国内外关于沥青混合料疲劳试验方法与疲劳方程研究的现状及存在的问题。第2章沥青混合料疲劳试验方法，介绍并比较现行的沥青混合料不同疲劳试验方法。第3章沥青混合料疲劳方程，在传统的疲劳方程的基础上，提出真实应力比概念，并建立基于真实应力比的沥青混合料疲劳方程，提出抗拉强度结构系数。第4章基于刚度衰变的沥青混合料疲劳损伤模型，通过引入材料刚度参数，考虑在疲劳加载过程中刚度的衰变，建立基于刚度衰变的沥青混合料疲劳损伤模型。第5章基于强度衰变的沥青混合料疲劳损伤模型，通过引入材料强度参数，考虑在疲劳加载过程中强度的衰变，建立基于强度衰变的沥青混合料疲劳损伤模型。第 6 章考虑拉压差异性的沥青混合料疲劳损伤模型，基于沥青路面中沥青混合料层真实的应力状态——同时承受拉与压应力，以及拉、压模量的差异性，提出沥青混合料拉压模量同步测试方法，并建立考虑拉压差异性的沥青混合料疲劳损伤模型。第 7 章不同应力状态下沥青混合料疲劳损伤模型的归一化，通过开展不同应力状态下沥青混合料的疲劳试验，基于屈服准则思想，对疲劳试验结果进行归一化处理，建立不同应力状态下沥青混合料疲劳损伤的归一化模型。第 8 章为结论与展望。

本书内容在研究过程中得到国家自然科学基金项目（51578081，51208066，51608058）、交通运输部建设科技项目（2015318825120）、中国工程院咨询研究项目（2017-XY-17）的大力支持，在此表示由衷的感谢。长沙理工大学刘宏富主要撰写了第 1、2、4、5 章，长沙理工大学道路与铁路工程专业博士刘超超和樊喜雁参与本书中试验数据的整理及论文的整理汇总。

本书所涉及的部分内容仍为目前国内外道路工程界研究的热点与难点问题，尽管提出了一些疲劳分析方法，仍存在不小差距与问题。鉴于作者水平有限，书中的缺点和不足在所难免，恳请各位专家、学者和读者批评指正。

吕松涛

长沙理工大学

2017 年 11 月

目 录

前言
第1章 概论 ··· 1
　1.1 问题的提出及研究意义 ··· 1
　1.2 国内外研究现状 ·· 2
　　1.2.1 沥青混合料疲劳损伤特性研究 ·· 2
　　1.2.2 沥青路面轴载换算方法研究 ··· 8
　参考文献 ·· 14
第2章 沥青混合料疲劳试验方法 ·· 17
　2.1 沥青混合料疲劳试验方法确定 ·· 17
　　2.1.1 目前国内外沥青混合料主要疲劳试验方法 ···························· 17
　　2.1.2 对主要疲劳试验方法的评述 ··· 17
　参考文献 ·· 21
第3章 沥青混合料疲劳方程 ··· 22
　3.1 原材料试验及配合比设计 ·· 22
　3.2 不同加载速率下直接拉伸强度试验 ······································· 24
　3.3 直接拉伸疲劳试验结果及传统疲劳方程的建立 ······················· 28
　　3.3.1 疲劳试验方法及方案设计 ·· 28
　　3.3.2 疲劳试验结果及传统疲劳方程的建立 ·································· 29
　3.4 真实应力比疲劳方程的建立 ·· 31
　3.5 沥青面层抗拉强度结构系数计算新方法 ································· 34
　参考文献 ·· 35
第4章 基于刚度衰变的沥青混合料疲劳损伤模型 ·························· 36
　4.1 以模量定义的疲劳损伤变量 ··· 36
　4.2 直接拉伸疲劳变形特性分析 ·· 38
　　4.2.1 循环应力应变滞回曲线 ··· 39
　　4.2.2 应变随循环寿命比变化曲线 ··· 43
　4.3 直接拉伸疲劳动模量衰变模型的建立 ···································· 46
　　4.3.1 动模量初始值的确定 ·· 47
　　4.3.2 破坏时动模量的确定 ·· 47
　　4.3.3 动模量衰变模型的建立 ··· 48

目 录

- 4.4 基于刚度衰变的疲劳损伤模型的建立 ···52
  - 4.4.1 临界疲劳损伤的计算 ···53
  - 4.4.2 疲劳损伤修正模型的提出及验证 ···56
- 4.5 疲劳损伤非线性累计的试验验证 ···62
  - 4.5.1 两级荷载疲劳试验设计 ··62
  - 4.5.2 两级荷载疲劳试验结果分析 ···63
- 参考文献 ···65

第 5 章 基于强度衰变的沥青混合料疲劳损伤模型 ·······································67
- 5.1 疲劳剩余强度试验设计和试验结果 ··67
- 5.2 疲劳剩余强度衰变模型的建立 ···70
- 5.3 基于剩余强度衰变的损伤模型的建立及验证 ··74
  - 5.3.1 以剩余强度定义的损伤变量 ···74
  - 5.3.2 基于剩余强度的损伤失效的判断 ···77
  - 5.3.3 基于剩余强度衰变损伤模型的建立 ··78
- 5.4 刚度和剩余强度定义的损伤变量比较 ··81
- 5.5 刚度和剩余强度定义的损伤变量的统一 ··83
- 5.6 本章小结 ··86
- 参考文献 ··87

第 6 章 考虑拉压差异性的沥青混合料疲劳损伤模型 ···································89
- 6.1 沥青混合料四点弯曲疲劳试验拉、压模量衰变规律 ································89
  - 6.1.1 拉、压模量初始值随应力水平变化规律 ··89
  - 6.1.2 拉、压模量临界值随应力水平变化规律 ··95
  - 6.1.3 临界疲劳损伤随应力水平变化规律 ···96
  - 6.1.4 基于拉、压模量衰变规律的沥青混合料疲劳损伤特性 ·····························97
- 6.2 疲劳试验过程中沥青混合料拉、压、弯模量差异性分析 ························99
- 6.3 沥青混合料拉、压、弯模量衰变特性对比分析 ···································100
- 6.4 基于沥青路面各点实际应力状态确定结构设计参数的新思想 ···············104
- 6.5 本章小结 ··105
- 参考文献 ··105

第 7 章 不同应力状态下沥青混合料疲劳损伤模型的归一化 ·······················107
- 7.1 基于屈服准则强度屈服面的建立 ···108
  - 7.1.1 Desai 强度屈服面模型 ···108
  - 7.1.2 不同加载速率下不同应力状态的沥青混合料强度试验及结果 ················109
  - 7.1.3 不同加载速率下强度屈服面的建立 ···110
- 7.2 基于屈服准则思想不同应力状态下沥青混合料疲劳特性的归一化 ···111

7.2.1 不同应力状态下沥青混合料疲劳试验 ·· 111
  7.2.2 不同应力状态下沥青混合料疲劳试验结果及基于 $S\text{-}N$ 疲劳方程的结果
       分析 ··· 112
  7.2.3 基于屈服准则与真实应力比思想的不同应力状态下沥青混合料疲劳特性
       的归一化模型的建立 ·· 114
 7.3 与真实应力比疲劳方程的比较 ·· 120
 7.4 结论 ·· 121
 参考文献 ·· 121
第 8 章 结论与展望 ··· 123
 8.1 主要结论 ··· 123
 8.2 创新点 ·· 125
 8.3 不足与进一步工作构想 ·· 125
附录 ·· 126

第 1 章 概　　论

1.1 问题的提出及研究意义

交通运输部统计公报显示：截至 2011 年底，我国公路通车里程已达 408 万公里，其中高速公路 8.5 万公里。沥青路面是我国目前主要采用的路面结构类型，沥青混合料作为沥青路面的主要建筑材料，其疲劳性能是非常重要的，直接影响路面的使用性能和使用寿命。疲劳开裂是沥青路面结构的主要破坏形式之一，在道路运营过程中，受外界环境和交通荷载的反复作用，沥青路面结构内部将会出现损伤；随着荷载作用次数的增加，损伤将不断演化累计，疲劳损伤导致路面材料和结构性能的退化直至最终破坏。沥青路面常常远没达到设计寿命就出现大范围疲劳破坏，不能简单地归因于施工质量和超载重载，现有沥青路面设计方法中以路面疲劳特性作为基本设计原则，而基于传统疲劳方程经典的分析方法，在描述沥青路面结构和材料的疲劳破坏时其作用是有限的，还需要进一步地研究并认识沥青混合料的疲劳损伤过程，建立较好的数学模型来描述复杂的疲劳破坏现象。

以疲劳设计为主的沥青路面设计方法存在的一些问题还没有得到解决：

一是现有设计方法中沥青面层抗拉强度结构系数推导过程中，规范将传统疲劳方程后延到 $N_f = 1$，并认为此时的拉应力就是极限抗拉强度，缺乏足够的论据和试验验证；将极限抗拉强度引入疲劳方程，这表明在疲劳试验过程中，沥青混合料的极限抗拉强度是个常数，不随环境温度和加荷速率变化，不能反映沥青混合料黏弹性材料的本质特征。因此现行设计方法中沥青面层抗拉强度结构系数的推演不合理，有必要建立一种新方法。

二是经典的疲劳分析，对准确描述沥青路面结构与材料的疲劳性能劣化是有限的，损伤力学的发展为材料在重复荷载作用下的力学行为研究提供了新的手段，首要和最基本的问题是要选择恰当的损伤定义来描述材料的损伤状态。基于等效应变假说的经典损伤定义的弹性模量法，尽管具有计算方便和测量简单等优点，但用于研究沥青混合料具有黏塑性变形的非弹性损伤，理论上不完善，并且基于弹性模量衰变的定义难以表示损伤对材料组织敏感特性的影响。因此有必要针对沥青混合料开展损伤定义方法的研究，以期提出一种普适性、可靠性更好的损伤变量表示方法。

三是现有对不同交通荷载进行标准化处理过程中的模型太过简单，在考虑交通荷载的重复作用效应时也是一直沿用 Miner 线性疲劳损伤理论和方法,没有考虑交通荷载历史和非线性累计对路面结构破坏的影响,可能低估了交通荷载特别是重载车辆的破坏作用。在此举一个例子更能说明问题,一台后轴重 150kN 的重车在一条新建路面上行驶一百次与在使用末期破损严重的路面上行驶一百次,两种状态下对路面造成的损伤和破坏明显是不一样的。而现有设计方法一直沿用 Miner 线性疲劳损伤理论和方法,认为两种状态下使用初期和使用末期得到的标准轴载作用次数是相同的,这显然是不合适的,没有考虑交通荷载历史和材料在疲劳作用下性能的时变损伤衰减对轴载换算的影响。因此需要建立能考虑加载历史或损伤历史影响的、基于非线性疲劳损伤的沥青路面轴载换算新方法。

针对上面提出的三个问题,本章在调研国内外已有研究成果的基础上,以损伤力学为理论基础,结合沥青混合料室内直接拉伸疲劳试验和剩余强度试验,分别选择刚度和剩余强度为损伤变量,开展沥青混合料非线性疲劳损伤特性的研究,建立基于非线性疲劳损伤的沥青路面轴载换算新方法。研究内容对于推进沥青路面轴载换算方法的发展,完善沥青路面设计方法,提高沥青路面耐久性和设计水平有重要意义。

1.2 国内外研究现状

针对以上提出的需要研究的问题,本节主要涉及沥青混合料疲劳损伤特性和沥青路面轴载换算方法两方面的内容。在查阅国内外大量相关参考文献和调查的基础上,现对这两方面研究现状分别综述如下。

1.2.1 沥青混合料疲劳损伤特性研究

在每次车辆通过时沥青路面材料遭受短期荷载作用,随着重复荷载作用的累计,沥青路面逐渐疲劳,沥青混合料的刚度和强度不同程度地衰减,直至最后导致破坏。路面结构的疲劳性能是非常重要的,世界各国沥青路面设计方法均以路面材料的抗疲劳特性作为确定设计寿命的依据。因此,国内外一直十分重视沥青混合料疲劳特性的研究,已经发表了大量关于试验方式、试验条件、材料组成、荷载特性、环境因素等对于沥青混合料疲劳寿命影响的专门著作[1,2]和研究报告[3],并把这些成果用于沥青路面结构设计理论与设计规范[4,5]。

由国际材料与结构研究实验联合会 (RILEM) TC 101-BAT 和 TC 152-PBM 分会组织进行的沥青及沥青混合料疲劳性能联合试验研究,于 1996 年完成。研究结论指出,经典的疲劳分析对准确描述沥青路面结构与材料的疲劳性能劣化是有限的,并一致认为,为了认识沥青混合料疲劳损伤现象并对其复杂的疲劳损伤过程建立数学模型,还需进一步的研究[6]。

1.2 国内外研究现状

损伤力学的发展为材料在重复荷载作用下的力学行为研究提供了新的手段。在重复荷载作用下材料内部分布的缺陷也将不断演化导致材料破坏,这类损伤可以称为损伤累计,在广义条件下也称之为疲劳损伤。疲劳损伤主要注重研究损伤的过程与损伤失效的判断标准[7]。

用损伤力学理论分析材料受力后的力学行为时,首要和最基本的问题是要选择恰当的损伤定义来描述材料的损伤状态。损伤变量 $D(*)$ 作为描述材料劣化状态的参数,其自变量 $(*)$ 常是一些材料响应参量,如弹性模量、损伤面积等,其中有的是宏观性能参量,有的是细观状态参量。据此,可将损伤变量分为宏观损伤变量和细观损伤变量[8]。

沥青混合料是一种典型的黏弹性材料,在重复荷载作用下的疲劳损伤过程是一个能量耗散的过程。因此很多道路工作者从耗散能的角度分析了沥青混合料的疲劳损伤过程。Carpenter 和 Jansen 利用能量耗散率的概念研究沥青混合料的疲劳问题,这种方法认为不是所有的能量都对材料的损伤产生作用。对每个荷载循环,由材料的机械功和环境的影响导致的能量耗散将保持不变。因此,如果能量耗散开始显著变化,则说明损伤在发展[9]。Ghuzlan 和 Carpenter 检验了该方法并进行了修正。他们发现能耗率 (DER) 与疲劳寿命之间有很强的相关性,而且与荷载水平、荷载模式、混合料类型没有关系[10,11]。Shen 和 Carpenter 后来进一步发展了该方法,并将能量率重新定义为能量耗散变化率 (RDEC)[12,13]。Bhasin 等 2009 年应用能量耗散的方法去评估沥青混合料的疲劳开裂,提供了关于能量方法论上的关键性解析:① 对相同材料的应变控制和应力控制模式试验的结果进行统一;② 准确地预估不同材料的疲劳开裂寿命[14]。

Kim 和 West 2010 年基于 Schapery 的相关原则和连续损伤原理发展建立了黏弹性连续疲劳损伤模型,但是由于这个模型基于单轴拉伸试验,因此在现场的应用受到了限制。根据开发的一种可将此模型适用于间接拉伸试验的解析方法论,此方法在间接拉伸试验中能够利用黏弹性连续疲劳损伤模型评价沥青混合料的损伤演化[15]。

Bodin 等 2002 年为了预测路面疲劳开裂,建立了疲劳损伤模型来预测路面的疲劳开裂,用循环疲劳试验评估沥青混合料的疲劳性能。在加载正弦曲线的试验中,材料复合模量的演化被定义为与微观裂缝形成机理相关的损伤变量。在疲劳试验中它的演化被描述为基于弹性基础的非局部损伤模型。这个损伤模型的参数是通过单轴疲劳试验确定的。在试件局部损伤之前的破裂过程中,数值模拟结果和试验数据有很好的相关性[16]。Zhi 和 Wong 利用三种不同类型的沥青混凝土材料进行间接拉伸疲劳试验,建立疲劳损伤模型和破坏准则;利用基于连续损伤的方法,用疲劳损伤模型描述了微裂纹的形成和裂纹的扩展;结合疲劳损伤模型进行了有限元分析,模拟路面结构层的裂缝贯穿[17]。

同时，在疲劳损伤过程中，由于缺陷的聚集与扩展，伴随有材料宏观物理量的变化，如模量、韧性、强度、密度等量值的降低；可以使用这些物理力学参数的变化来度量材料的损伤。

Lundstrom 等 2004 年通过对三种不同针入度的沥青混合料在三种温度下进行圆柱体拉压疲劳试验发现：随着疲劳损伤的发展，模量逐渐衰减，并且在低温条件下的沥青混合料的模量衰减幅度要小，针入度较小的沥青混合料的模量衰减幅度也较小；还对传统的控制应变疲劳试验中以模量衰减到初始模量的 50% 作为疲劳失效提出了质疑，并对疲劳破坏的确定提出了修正方法[18]。

法国里昂大学的 Benedetto 教授等总结了不同的疲劳试验方法，并用同一种沥青混合料进行了比对试验，疲劳试验方法及参数见表 1.1[19]。选择用动态模量衰变分析了沥青混合料的疲劳损伤特性；综述了几种不同的损伤模型，介绍了各自在分析沥青混合料疲劳损伤规律时的特点，如 ENTPE 模型[20]、LCPC 模型[21]、Partial Healing 模型[22]、Work Potential Theory 模型[23]。

ENTPE 模型假定疲劳过程中的一段时间内，模量的衰减随疲劳次数呈线性变化规律，这种方法的特点是确定了每个疲劳循环过程中"真实"损伤所占比例，剔除了"伪应变"的疲劳损伤，不再以线性损伤为假定，基于刚度衰减提出了一种非线性疲劳损伤模型：

$$\mathrm{d}D/\mathrm{d}N = B[A(1-D)]^{(B-1)/B} \big/ A^{(B-1)}, \quad D = (E_0 - E_N)/E_0 \tag{1.1}$$

式中，D 表示疲劳过程中的损伤，A 和 B 是应变幅值的线性函数，E_0 和 E_N 分别是初始刚度和在循环次数 N 时的刚度。

LCPC 模型是基于损伤力学而形成的，其特点是能描述疲劳试验的性能劣化的全过程。损伤增长率定义为关于等效应变率的一个函数：

$$\mathrm{d}D/\mathrm{d}N = f(D)\tilde{\varepsilon}^\beta \langle \dot{\tilde{\varepsilon}} \rangle \tag{1.2}$$

其中

$$f(D) = \frac{\alpha_2}{\alpha_3 \alpha_1} \left(\frac{D}{\alpha_2}\right)^{1-\alpha_1} \exp\left(\frac{D}{\alpha_2}\right)^{\alpha_1} \tag{1.3}$$

式中，α_1、α_2、α_3 和 β 为材料参数，β 与疲劳曲线的斜率相关。$f(D)$ 是疲劳试验中基于模量分三阶段的衰变模型。

Partial Healing 模型能描述疲劳试验过程的刚度演化规律，在不同荷载、试验条件下能预测刚度衰变规律，基于刚度衰变的损伤变量 D 与疲劳损伤耗散能有关：

$$\mathrm{d}D/\mathrm{d}t = \mathrm{d}\delta \cdot \Delta W_\mathrm{dis}/\mathrm{d}t \approx \delta \frac{\Delta W_\mathrm{dis}}{T} \tag{1.4}$$

式中，D 为基于刚度衰变的疲劳损伤，ΔW_dis 为耗散能，T 为循环周期。

1.2 国内外研究现状

表 1.1 疲劳试验方法及参数

疲劳试验方式	加载方式	应力状态/应力区	幅值/(10^{-6}m/m 或 MPa)
拉/压		单轴拉压/"均匀"	应变水平：80, 100, 140, 180 应力水平：0.9
梯形悬臂梁两点弯曲		单轴向/"不均匀"	应变水平：140, 180, 220 应力水平：1.4
三点弯曲		单轴向/"不均匀"	应变水平：140, 180, 220 应力水平：1.4
四点弯曲		单轴向/"均匀"	应变水平：140, 180, 220 应力水平：1.4
间接拉伸		双轴向/"不均匀"	应变水平：25, 40, 65 应力水平：1.4

基于 Work Potential Theory 的损伤模型可描述为

$$\mathrm{d}D/\mathrm{d}t = \left(-\frac{\mathrm{d}W^R}{\mathrm{d}D}\right)^\alpha \tag{1.5}$$

其中，W^R 是伪应变能密度函数，$W^R = W^R\left(\varepsilon^R, D\right)$，$\varepsilon^R$ 为伪应变，D 为损伤变量，α 为材料常数。

Benedetto 教授等研究认为，通过建立连续损伤力学的模型能更好地描述疲劳损伤特性的本质，并指出关于连续损伤模型还需进一步的研究，建立一个合理的疲劳损伤特性力学模型，对于未来进行更有效的沥青路面设计是非常重要的。

国内沥青混合料疲劳损伤研究起步相对较晚，但是逐渐认识到研究重复荷载作用下的疲劳破坏的重要性，近年来相关研究单位对沥青路面的疲劳损伤更加关心，其中沥青混合料非线性疲劳损伤演化和累计是研究的热点。

长沙理工大学从20世纪80年代以来，开展了大量的沥青混合料疲劳损伤方面的研究。郑健龙教授在国内外率先开展沥青混合料的黏弹性损伤特性的研究，1995年率先应用损伤力学的原理，研究了沥青混合料的黏弹性损伤特性，通过引入损伤因子，建立了等应力疲劳和等应变疲劳的相互关系[24]。在后续研究中创建了沥青混合料非线性疲劳损伤理论与分析方法[25]。唐雪松教授等克服了经典弹性损伤理论存在的缺陷，直接由热力学第二定律出发，建立了完整的各向同性弹性损伤理论，采用损伤力学方法研究了沥青混合料的疲劳失效问题[26]。周志刚针对现有沥青混合料疲劳损伤试验时直接依据刚度或模量计算损伤值而无法真实反映材料微观损伤特性的不足，提出了应用反分析方法以得到沥青混凝土的疲劳损伤演化规律。疲劳寿命的数值模拟结果与试验结果较吻合，证明了所提出的沥青混凝土疲劳损伤模型的合理性和有效性[27]。吕松涛建立了基于Burgers模型的老化沥青混合料黏弹性疲劳损伤模型，通过直接拉伸试验确定了沥青混合料的黏弹性参数，求出了损伤演化方程，提出了一种考虑疲劳过程中老化程度对疲劳损伤影响的累计疲劳损伤计算的理论与方法，为沥青混合料在不同老化过程下的疲劳寿命预估提供了依据[28]。杨毅进行了不同加载频率下的沥青混合料动态拉伸模量衰变规律的研究[29]。

东南大学黄卫与邓学钧教授研究了应变控制下沥青混合料的能耗与荷载作用次数的关系，建立了基于能耗的新型疲劳响应模型[30]。孙志林运用疲劳损伤有限元方法分析半刚性基层沥青路面在交通荷载与温度荷载下的疲劳损伤行为与疲劳寿命的关系，揭示了半刚性基层沥青路面的疲劳破坏机理[31]。

吴旷怀和张肖宁教授通过相同条件下一组大样本沥青混合料应变控制小梁弯曲疲劳试验，将弯曲疲劳循环次数和对应循环次数的模量无量纲化后，拟合得到了一组疲劳损伤和对应循环次数比的关系曲线，发现各曲线之间非常相似，尽管各试件的疲劳寿命相差较大。对曲线族进一步分析，归纳得到了沥青混合料疲劳损伤的非线性演化的统一模型[32]。

重庆交通大学严恒等针对AC-13沥青混合料进行了不同试验条件下的疲劳试验；分析了每次加载下的耗散能与荷载作用次数之间的关系；利用数理统计的方法研究了试验条件对总累计耗散能与疲劳寿命的影响。结果表明：总累计耗散能和疲劳寿命之间的关系与荷载作用模式有关，与试验温度及加载频率无关[33]。

重复荷载作用下材料和结构的刚度衰变规律，是研究内部损伤演化特性的重要手段之一。长安大学沙爱民和武建民教授研究了半刚性材料动态弯拉模量的衰变[34,35]；刘业敏等通过控制应变的小梁疲劳试验，研究了沥青混合料疲劳过程中弯拉劲度模量随应变水平的变化情况，应变水平的变化模拟了实际路面厚度变化对层底拉应变的影响。结果表明：当应变水平较高时，弯拉劲度模量随荷载作用次数的增加而急剧减小；随着应变水平的降低，衰减趋势逐渐变缓；通过研究发现，弯拉劲度模量可以用于表征应变疲劳过程中沥青混合料试件力学状态变化，并由此推算混合料的疲劳寿命[36]。

损伤理论中的"弹性模量法"是一种基于应变等效性假说，以损伤前后材料弹性模量的变化来定义或量度损伤的方法。值得注意的是，等效性假说和以此为基础的"弹性模量法"实质上是一种弹性损伤描述方法。但在描述或测量具有不可逆塑性变形特征材料的损伤行为时，多数研究也利用"弹性模量法"，并将材料受力过程中的卸载刚度取作受损材料的瞬时弹性模量，去描述或测量此类材料的损伤演化行为并建立理论模型。严格讲，这种处理方法是不完全正确的，用此种近似方法来描述和测定具有塑性变形特征材料的损伤过程将显著简化或掩盖材料真实的损伤行为。实际上，一些弹塑性材料的损伤试验研究已发现了用这种方法刻画损伤演化时所存在的问题，并得出了"弹性模量法"并不总是有效等类似性结论，出现了材料损伤描述方法的不确定现象。

损伤不是材料的一种独立的物理性质，它只能作为一种"劣化因素"被结合到弹性、塑性和黏性介质中。谢和平等从等效应变假说的基本原理出发，研究了弹性模量法损伤定义中材料弹性模量的物理概念，指出了弹性模量法的局限性和适用条件，以及用于描述弹塑性材料损伤行为时存在的问题，并通过损伤实验结果，分析了由此造成对材料真实损伤行为的误判。弹性模量法描述损伤演化过程，其实质为弹性受损材料的卸载模量不断减小的过程，但具有弹塑性变形及弹黏塑性变形的材料的损伤演化过程，其卸载模量的变化与材料特性、加载条件有密切关系。许多试验结果表明，一定加载条件下，只有当内部损伤积累至一定程度后，测得的卸载模量才开始衰减，而此前某损伤状态下的卸载模量可能不低于材料的初始弹性模量。

肖建清等利用再生混凝土的疲劳试验结果，分析了常用的几种损伤变量定义法的优缺点；超声波速法、弹性模量法、最大应变以及残余应变法都能够反映再生混凝土的疲劳损伤演化规律，而残余应变法由于概念明确，考虑了疲劳初始损伤，拟合得到的损伤演化方程与试验数据高度相关，而理论分析得出的疲劳寿命的变化规律与试验结果也一致，因此肖建清等认为采用残余应变法定义损伤变量描述再生混凝土的疲劳损伤更为合适[37]。

Guan等通过沥青混合料高频和低频的疲劳试验，采用应变幅值、残余应变、动模量和耗散能四种不同损伤变量定义方法，分析了沥青混合料的疲劳损伤演化规律，结果表明不同定义方法所描述的疲劳损伤演化过程和临界损伤值均不相同，基于耗散能的定义方法得到的疲劳损伤演化曲线与其他三种十分不同，认为基于耗散能的疲劳损伤定义方法是最合适的[38]。

迄今，已有不少研究人员根据具体情况选用不同的损伤变量来研究损伤，但所选变量的普适性、可靠性等方面的研究还很有限，各损伤变量之间的相关性研究就更少见了。具体损伤过程的损伤规律是确定的，描述该过程的几个损伤变量的变化规律在理论上应是一致的，据此，为了更好地定义、筛选损伤变量，从不同角度对同一损伤过程进行定义，观测其损伤发展规律并进行分析对比。

总结沥青混合料疲劳损伤方面的研究，虽然有很多道路研究者已经开展了大量工作，也各自通过损伤力学理论和疲劳试验提出了相应的疲劳损伤模型，但是这些研究成果也表明，由于沥青混合料的疲劳破坏行为极其复杂，影响因素较多，因此，沥青混合料疲劳特性试验研究尚有许多困难需要克服。

由于损伤演化通常伴随材料某些物理力学性能的退化，常采用一些表征材料宏观物理力学性能的状态变量描述损伤程度，目前应用最多的损伤定义是基于模量的衰变；模量衰变可在疲劳试验过程中连续测量而不会影响材料的性能，它随着材料内部损伤的不断演化与累计而下降，因此模量是一个常用的宏观检测参数，能够描述沥青混合料疲劳过程中的损伤状态。由于疲劳过程中沥青混合料强度的衰减是造成结构疲劳破坏的直接原因，测量剩余强度也是一种分析疲劳损伤的手段，其优点在于剩余强度的工程测量十分简便，精度也较高，并且强度模型的破坏准则非常简明，便于破坏失效的判断；但是由于剩余强度试验不能连续测量，不同疲劳次数后的剩余强度需要大量的试件，耗时耗力；对于不同损伤状态下沥青混合料的剩余强度衰减规律的研究，在国内外文献中鲜有报道。基于这两种定义的损伤变量在描述材料的疲劳损伤特性上的差异，需要提出一种普适性好、可靠性高的损伤变量定义方法，以更好地描述沥青混合料的疲劳损伤特性。本书拟开展沥青混合料的直接拉伸疲劳试验和剩余强度试验研究，建立以刚度和剩余强度为损伤变量的沥青混合料非线性疲劳损伤方程，为更合理地描述沥青混合料非线性疲劳损伤特性奠定基础。

1.2.2 沥青路面轴载换算方法研究

交通量即荷载重复作用次数是路面设计的重要因素。由于轴载和交通量变化很大，且其对路面的影响难于处理，目前所用的设计方法是将不同轴载换算成标准轴载下的重复作用次数。在设计年限内，所有轴载当量作用的总和用累计当量轴次 N_e 表示，该值是沥青路面设计需要的交通参数。

下面对国外沥青路面设计中的轴载换算方法作一归纳小结[39]：

美国 AASHTO 的轴载换算公式是当今世界大多数路面结构设计方法的基石，AASHTO 方法根据试验路结果回归分析确定当量轴载系数 (EALF)，当量系数取决于路面类型、厚度或结构性能及认为路面破坏时的最终状况。计算公式为

$$\lg\left(\frac{W_{tx}}{W_{t18}}\right) = 4.79\lg(18+1) - 4.79\lg(L_x + L_2) + 4.33\lg(L_2) + \frac{G_t}{\beta_x} - \frac{G_t}{\beta_{18}} \quad (1.6)$$

其中

$$\beta_x = 0.40 + \frac{0.081 \times (L_x + L_2)^{3.23}}{(\text{SN}+1)^{5.19} \times L_2^{3.23}}, \quad G_t = \lg\left(\frac{4.2 - P_t}{4.2 - 1.5}\right)$$

式中，L_x 为单轴或复轴 (10^3lb)；L_2 为轴号 (单轴为 1，复轴为 2)；SN 为结构数；P_t 为路面服务指数允许最低值。

通过对 AASHTO 轴载换算计算公式 (1.6) 的分析和对 AASHTO 给定的换算系数表的统计，将其简化归纳为

$$\frac{N_1}{N_2} = \left(\frac{L_2}{L_1}\right)^4 \tag{1.7}$$

式 (1.7) 与式 (1.6) 有等效性且形式简单，因此被很多路面设计法所采用。

澳大利亚设计方法确定的标准轴载为单轴双轮、轴重 80kN 的荷载，造成与标准轴载同样损伤的不同轴型的轴重见表 1.2，不同路面结构形式的破坏类型不同，相应的轴载换算公式的指数也不同，不同指数值见表 1.3。标准轴载重复作用次数 SAR_m 的计算公式为

$$\text{SAR}_m = \left(\frac{L_{ij}}{\text{SL}_i}\right)^m \tag{1.8}$$

式中，SAR_m 即造成 m 类损伤等于 i 型轴载 L_{ij} 作用一次相对于标准轴载的作用次数；SL_i 即 i 型轴组的标准荷载，其大小见表 1.2；L_{ij} 为轴组总荷载；m 对应于 K 种破坏类型的指数见表 1.3。

表 1.2 造成与标准轴载同样损伤的不同轴型的轴重

轴组类型	SAST	SADT	TAST	TADT	TRDT
轴组荷载/kN	53	80	90	135	181

表 1.3 对应于不同破坏类型的损伤指数

设计方法	路面类型	破坏类型	幂指数 m
力学方法	含一层或多层整体性材料路面	沥青层疲劳	5
		无机结合料稳定材料层疲劳	12
		路面变形和车辙	7
经验方法	薄沥青层粒料路面和罩面层	综合破坏	4

日本沥青路面结构设计经验法和理论计算法轴载换算方法相同，都是计算时将不同轮重换算为 49kN 标准轮重，求出一天单向 49kN 换算轮数 (N_{49})，然后计算设计年限内的累计 49kN 换算轮数。轴载换算公式为

$$N_{49} = \sum_{j=1}^{m}\left[\left(\frac{P_j}{49}\right)^4 \times N_j\right] \tag{1.9}$$

式中，N_{49} 为一天单向 N_{49} 换算轮数；P_j 为第 j 类轮重范围内的轮重代表值；m 为轮重范围数，$j=1\sim m$；N_j 为 P_j 的通过数。

法国沥青路面结构设计以单轴双轮组 130kN 为标准轴载，沥青路面轴载换算系数按式 (1.10) 计算，K 为两联轴或三联轴系数，对传统柔性结构和补强为 1，新建半刚性结构为 12，复合结构为 1.5。

$$d = K\left(\frac{P}{130}\right)^5 \tag{1.10}$$

南非沥青路面设计方法中标准轴次的获得方法为：通过动、静态观测得到的信息是各种确定轴载及其重复次数，它们具有不同的荷载等效系数 (F)，与路面组成和类型、材料类型、边界条件、破坏模型及道路可靠度有关。荷载等效系数计算公式为

$$F = (P/80)^n \tag{1.11}$$

式中，P 为各种确定轴载大小；n 为相关破坏指数。水泥稳定类基层的沥青路面 n 的范围为 2~5，通过重车模拟试验研究得到的沥青路面建议破坏指数为 4，但路面结构对超载敏感，特别是较薄水泥稳定基层路面的 n 值大于 4。

俄罗斯沥青路面设计方法中轴载计算对不是给定的运输工具类型以及与 A 类或 B 类标准荷载有区别的计算荷载，则其轴载换算式为

$$S_{McyM} = \sum S_n \tag{1.12}$$

式中，n 为需要确定 S_{McyM} 的运输工具的轴数；$S_n = (\theta_n^{(\vartheta)}/\theta_{pa\mu}^{(\vartheta)})^{4.4}$，即相当于 $S_n = (P_i/P_s)^{4.4}$，系数 S_n 用于实际荷载不超过标准轴载，或不超过标准轴载的 20% 的情况。

德国高等级沥青路面设计中是以 100kN 为标准轴载，轴载换算的公式为

$$\text{EDTA}_{i-1}^{(SV)} = \sum_K \left[\text{DTA}_{(i-1)K}^{(SV)} \cdot \left(\frac{L_K}{L_0}\right)^4\right] \tag{1.13}$$

式中，$\text{EDTA}_{i-1}^{(SV)}$ 为在使用第 $i-1$ 年，重车当量转换轴载日平均数量；$\text{DTA}_{i-1}^{(SV)}$ 为在使用第 $i-1$ 年，重车轴载日平均数量；K 为轴载种类根据单个轴载进行划分；L_K 为在轴载荷载种类中的一般轴载；L_0 为 100kN 标准轴载。

美国沥青协会 (AI) 沥青路面设计方法对交通量的预测以 80kN 为标准轴载。相对应的当量轴载系数 F 计算公式为

$$\lg(1/F) = \lg\left(\frac{W_{tx}}{W_{t18}}\right) = 4.79\lg(18+1) - 4.79\lg(L_x+L_2) + 4.33\lg(L_2) + \frac{G_t}{\beta_x} - \frac{G_t}{\beta_{18}} \tag{1.14}$$

1.2 国内外研究现状

其中

$$G_t = \log[(4.2-2.5)/(4.2-1.5)]$$

$$\beta_x = 0.4 + 0.081(L_x+L_2)^{3.23}/[(5+1)^{5.19}L_2^{3.23}]$$

式中，L_x 为作用在一组单轴、一组双轴、一组三轴上的荷载，单位为 10^3lb；L_2 为轴的编号，单轴为 1，双轴为 2，三轴为 3。

F_i 即 i 荷载组的当量轴载系数 (EALF)，是根据最终服务能力指数 $p_t = 2.5$，路面结构数 SN=5 时的 AASHTO 当量系数。

壳牌沥青路面设计方法采用标准轴载为 80kN，单轴双轮。各轴组的轴次换算为当量标准轴次，换算系数式为

$$n_{e,i} = 2.4 \times 10^{-8} \times L_i^4 \tag{1.15}$$

式中，L_i 为第 i 组的轴载 (kN)；$n_{e,i}$ 即等效轴载系数。

我国《公路沥青路面设计规范》(JTG D50—2006) 规定，选用 100kN 单轴双轮组为标准轴载，推荐了以弯沉和沥青层底弯拉应力为指标的轴载换算公式：

$$N = \sum_{i=1}^{K} C_1 \cdot C_2 n_i \left(\frac{P_i}{P}\right)^{4.35} \tag{1.16}$$

式中，N 为标准轴载的当量轴次 (次/日)；n_i 为各种被换算汽车的作用次数 (次/日)；P 为标准轴载 (kN)；P_i 为各种被换算车型的轴载 (kN)；C_1 为被换算车型的轴数系数；C_2 为被换算车型的轮组系数，双轮组为 1，单轮组为 6.4，四轮组为 0.38；K 为被换算车型的轴载级别。

将我国和国外沥青路面设计轴载换算方法进行比较，汇总于表 1.4 中。

由各国轴载换算方法汇总可见，除日本轮载为 49kN、法国标准轴载为 130kN 外，标准轴载取值大部分为 80kN 或 100kN，根据《重载沥青路面设计规范》研究报告，国外资料表明"世界上采用 100kN 为标准轴载的国家最多，占 34%；以 80kN 为标准轴载的国家次之，占 28%；标准轴载大于 100kN 的国家占 26%；标准轴载为 60kN 或 90kN 的国家各占 6%[40]"。由表 1.4 可见，标准轴载换算公式的幂指数集中在 4~5 变化；各种设计方法轴载换算公式形式类似，可发现均受 AASHTO 法影响较大。

近年来，针对公路运输出现的重载、超载的现象，国内道路工作者开展了大量的重载、超载条件下的轴载换算方法研究；除此之外，还有些研究者从不同角度开展了轴载换算的研究工作，有的针对钢桥面铺装开展了不同结构和材料的轴载换算，有的提出以车辙等效的轴载换算，有的对弯沉等效的轴载换算作了进一步的研究，有的尝试用疲劳损伤力学开展了轴载换算方法研究。

表 1.4 各国沥青路面设计轴载换算方法汇总

名称	标准轴载/kN	沥青路面轴载换算公式	公式编号
中国	100	$N = \sum_{i=1}^{K} C_1 \cdot C_2 n_i \left(\dfrac{P_i}{P}\right)^{4.35}$	(1.16)
AASHTO 法	80	$\lg\left(\dfrac{W_{tx}}{W_{t18}}\right) = 4.79\lg(18+1) - 4.79\lg(L_x + L_2)$ $+ 4.33\lg(L_2) + \dfrac{G_t}{\beta_x} - \dfrac{G_t}{\beta_{18}}$	(1.6)
澳大利亚	80	$SAR_m = \left(\dfrac{L_{ij}}{SL_i}\right)^m$，沥青层疲劳 m 取 5	(1.8)
日本	49	$N_{49} = \sum_{j=1}^{m}\left[\left(\dfrac{P_j}{49}\right)^4 \times N_j\right]$	(1.9)
法国	130	$d = K\left(\dfrac{P}{130}\right)^5$	(1.10)
南非	80	$F = (P/80)^n$，重车模拟试验建议 n 取 5	(1.11)
俄罗斯	$\theta_{pa\mu}^{(\vartheta)}$	$S_n = (\theta_n^{(\vartheta)}/\theta_{pa\mu}^{(\vartheta)})^{4.4}$	(1.12)
德国	100	$\text{EDTA}_{i-1}^{(SV)} = \sum_{K}\left[\text{DTA}_{(i-1)K}^{(SV)} \cdot \left(\dfrac{L_K}{L_0}\right)^4\right]$	(1.13)
AI 法	80	$p_t = 2.5$，SN=5 时的 AASHTO 当量系数	(1.14)
壳牌	80	$n_{e,i} = 2.4 \times 10^{-8} \times L_i^4$	(1.15)

长安大学在"重载交通沥青路面设计研究"中提出，当考虑路面材料的非线性时，大于 130kN 轴载沥青层弯沉和层底拉应力等效的当量轴次应按下式计算[41]：

$$\frac{n_s}{n_i} = \left(\frac{P_i}{P_s}\right)^5 \quad (1.17)$$

姚祖康等 2000 年应用动态称重仪测定了上海市干线公路的轴载谱和超重情况，采用当量损坏系数概念分析了超限行驶和不同限载水平对路面损坏的影响程度[42]。李海军等 2004 年依据调查的重轴载作用特点和有关文献资料，提出了适于重载的容许弯沉公式修正式 $l_R = A_0 N^{-0.20}(\delta/\delta_0)^{0.72}$，重载交通条件下，针对高等级公路结构形式的轴载换算公式，$N_i/N_0 = (P_i/P_0)^{5+(P-P_{0i})/130}$[43]。彭波等 2001 年应用有限元计算求解各类轴型更大范围内的荷载应力关系，按等效疲劳损耗原则进行不同轴载间的换算，提出适用于超限范围的轴载换算公式 $\eta_i = (\alpha \cdot P_i)^\beta$，认为根据现在的车辆荷载条件，采用原有规范公式低估了超限轴荷载的疲劳损坏作用[44]。

陈忠达 2006 年首次提出了轴载换算季节修正和温度修正的概念[45]。黄卫等 2005 年遵循疲劳和车辙等效轴载换算原则，推导出基于疲劳等效的钢桥面铺装体系轴载换算公式。根据室内疲劳试验及力学分析结果，确定该公式中的换算指数和其他轴型与轮组轴载换算为单轴双轮组的轴载换算系数。对于钢桥面浇注式沥青

1.2 国内外研究现状

混凝土铺装体系的轴载换算指数为 4.35,对于钢桥面改性沥青 SMA 铺装体系的轴载换算指数为 5.30,对于钢桥面环氧沥青混凝土铺装体系的轴载换算指数为 6.25,在钢桥面铺装设计与验算中,经换算其结果较为精确、可行[46]。

颜利等 2006 年通过对 3 种典型的沥青路面结构进行直线式加速加载足尺试验,用等形变法建立了基于路面车辙等效的重载轴载换算公式[47]。何兆益等 2007 年基于运动车辆与不平整路面的相互耦合作用,建立了车辆动力作用下沥青路面车辙计算与预估方法,提出了以车辙等效的轴载换算及轴载累加作用时间计算方法[48]。

邱欣等 2005 年应用疲劳损伤力学基本原理的轴载换算新方法,计算结果要比规范大,规范低估了设计年限内累计当量标准轴载作用次数;揭示弯沉等效表征的是路面结构的瞬间刚度性质,代替不了路面结构的长期疲劳强度特性[49]。元松 2010 年采用疲劳断裂理论,根据完好路面结构半刚性基层底部弯拉应力等效原则,对三维与平面应变模型荷载进行近似的等效转换。以裂缝扩展速率为等效原则,给出不同轴型和级位下荷载型反射裂缝的轴载换算系数。基于裂缝扩展速率等效原则的轴载换算系数当轴重小于标准轴载时,比现有沥青路面设计规范中轴载换算系数略微偏大,当轴重大于标准轴载时要偏小一些[50]。

关宏信等 2010 年采用与我国路面结构设计时轴载等效换算类似的方法,按照抗滑指标衰减量等效的原则建立了沥青路面轴载抗滑等效换算公式,并提出了轴数系数和轮组系数的确定方法;基于轴载抗滑等效换算公式,提出了沥青路面抗滑寿命预测方法;以某高速公路为算例,开展不同轮压下 SMA16 的抗滑性能衰变试验,建立了 SMA16 基于 BPN 值的抗滑疲劳方程,以此为基础,应用所提出的抗滑性能预测方法预测了该高速公路路面的抗滑寿命;结果表明:轴载抗滑等效换算方法用于高速公路沥青路面抗滑性能分析是可行的[51]。

王辉等 2003 年采用单轴双轮弯沉测试车,实测了不同轴载、轮压与路面强度下的弯沉,分析表明半刚性基层沥青路面轴载换算指数主要与路面结构强度、公路等级和轴重有关,轮压的影响并不明显;轴载换算采用轴重比比轮压比更准确、方便。分析得到了半刚性基层沥青路面按弯沉等效单轴双轮组轴载换算公式和轴载下界,是对沥青路面设计规范关于重载 $(P > 130kN)$ 换算的补充完善[52]。孙志林等 2007 年计算了基于路基顶面压应变的不同路面结构在不同轴重、不同胎压下的轴载换算指数,得到基于路基顶面压应变的轴载换算系数为 4.93[53]。

以弯沉为指标的轴载换算公式的推导过程中,一个明显的隐含概念是通过弹性层状体系理论建立的弯沉与轴载比的关系是理想状态,与路面结构所处的不同强度状态无关,可以认为是在路面结构使用初期,也可以认为是在路面结构使用过程中的任意状态;实际上路面结构从新建到临界状态,代表结构整体强度的弯沉是不断变化的,现在建立的轴载换算公式则忽略了这种过程。

综上所述，无论是以弯沉或车辙，还是以弯拉应力或应变等效的轴载换算，往往在轴载换算理论中，并没有考虑车辆轴载对路面结构和材料性能的损伤过程的影响，简单地应用 Miner 叠加损伤疲劳准则，难以准确地描述路面结构和材料的疲劳损伤过程。特别是在重型轴载作用时，重型轴载对软弱路面比对坚实路面更容易造成破坏，换算系数必然随路面的服务能力或结构强度的减小而增加。然而目前现有轴载换算公式均未考虑当前损伤状态的影响，因此有必要建立以非线性疲劳损伤为基础的新轴载换算方法，为沥青路面设计提供更准确的交通量数据。

参 考 文 献

[1] 张肖宁. 沥青与沥青混合料的粘弹力学原理及应用 [M]. 北京：人民交通出版社，2006

[2] 郑健龙，周志刚，张起森. 沥青路面抗裂设计理论与方法 [M]. 北京：人民交通出版社，2002

[3] 沥青路面疲劳损伤特性及抗疲劳破坏的措施与方法研究鉴定文件 [R]. 长沙交通学院，2002

[4] 交通部公路规划设计院. 公路沥青路面设计规范（JTJ014—97）[S]. 北京：人民交通出版社，1997

[5] 中交公路规划设计院. 公路沥青路面设计规范（JTG D50—2006）[S]. 北京：人民交通出版社，2006

[6] Castro M, Sa'nchez J A. Estimation of asphalt concrete fatigue curves—A damage theory approach[J]. Construction and Building Materials, 2008, 22(6):1232-1238

[7] 徐灏. 疲劳强度 [M]. 北京：高等教育出版社，1988

[8] 余寿文，冯西桥. 损伤力学 [M]. 北京：清华大学出版社，1997

[9] Carpenter S H, Jansen M. Fatigue behavior under new aircraft loading conditions[J]. Proceedings of Aircraft Pavement Technology in the Midst of Change, 1997, 4(2): 259-271

[10] Ghuzlan K A, Carpenter S H. An energy-derived/damage-based failure criteria for fatigue testing[J]. Transportation Research Record (TRR), 2000, 1723: 131-141

[11] Carpenter S H, Ghuzlan K A, Shen S H. A fatigue endurance limit for highway and airport pavement[J]. Journal of Transportation Research Record (TRR), 2003, 1832: 131-138

[12] Shen S, Carpenter S H. Application of dissipated energy concept in fatigue endurance limit testing[J]. Journal of Transportation Research Record: Transportation Research Board, 2005, 1929: 165-173

[13] Shen S, Airey G D, Carpenter S H, et al. A dissipated energy approach to fatigue evaluation[J]. International Journal of Road Materials and Pavement Design, 2006, 7(1): 38-51

[14] Bhasin A, Veronica T F, Branco C, et al. Quantitative comparison of energy methods to characterize fatigue in asphalt materials[J]. Journal of Materials in Civil Engineering,

ASCE, 2009
- [15] Kim J, West R C. Application of the viscoelastic continuum damage model to the indirect tension test at a single temperature[J]. Journal of Engineering Mechanics, ASCE, 2010
- [16] Bodin D, Pijaudier-Cabot G, de La Roche C, et al. A continuum damage approach of asphalt concrete fatigue tests[J]. ASCE, 2002
- [17] Zhi S, Wong W G. Analysis of fatigue crack growth behavior in asphalt concrete material in wearing course[J].Construction and Building Materials, 2009, 23: 462-468
- [18] Lundstrom R, Benedetto H D, Isacsson U. Influence of asphalt mixture stiffness on fatigue failure[J]. Journal of Materials in Civil Engineering, 2004, 16(6): 516-525
- [19] Benedetto H D, de La Roche C, Baaj H, et al. Fatigue of bituminous mixture[J]. Journal of Materials and Structures, 2004, 37: 202-216
- [20] Benedetto H D, de la Roche C. State of the art on stiffness modulus and fatigue of bituminous mixtures in bituminous binders and mixtures: State of the art and interlaboratory tests on mechanical behavior and mix design[J]. E&FN Spon, Ed. L. Francken, 1998: 137-180
- [21] Bodin D. Modèle d'endommagement cyclique: Application à la fatigue des enrobé bitumineux[D]. PhD thesis, EC Nantes, 2002
- [22] Pronk A C. Partial healing model—Curve fitting[R]. Report WDWW-2000-047, DWW, Delft, The Netherlands, 2000
- [23] Lundstr6m R, Isacsson U. Asphalt fatigue modeling using viscoelastic continuum damage theory[J]. Accepted for Publication in International Journal of Road Materials and Pavement Design, 2003
- [24] 郑健龙. Burgers 粘弹性模型在沥青混合料疲劳特性分析中的应用 [J]. 长沙交通学院学报，1995，11(3)：32-42
- [25] 郑健龙, 吕松涛. 沥青混合料非线性疲劳损伤模型 [J]. 中国公路学报, 2009，22(5)：21-29
- [26] 唐雪松, 蒋持平, 郑健龙. 沥青混合料疲劳过程的损伤力学分析 [J]. 应用力学学报, 2000, 17(4)：92-99
- [27] 周志刚. 交通荷载下沥青类路面疲劳损伤开裂研究 [D]. 中南大学博士学位论文, 2003
- [28] 吕松涛. 老化沥青混合料粘弹性疲劳损伤特性研究 [D]. 长沙理工大学博士学位论文, 2008
- [29] 杨毅. 不同加载频率下沥青混合料疲劳损伤特性研究 [D]. 长沙理工大学硕士学位论文, 2009
- [30] 黄卫, 邓学钧. 沥青混合料疲劳响应新模型研究 [J]. 中国公路学报, 1995, 8(1)：56-62
- [31] 孙志林. 基于损伤力学沥青路面疲劳损伤研究 [D]. 东南大学博士学位论文, 2008
- [32] 吴旷怀, 张肖宁. 沥青混合料疲劳损伤非线性演化统一模型试验研究 [J]. 公路, 2007, (5)：125-130
- [33] 严恒, 朱洪洲, 唐伯明, 等. AC-13 沥青混合料疲劳能耗模型分析 [J]. 重庆大学学报 (自然科学版), 2010, 29(4)：559-563

[34] 沙爱民, 贾侃, 陆剑卿, 等. 半刚性基层材料动态模量的衰变规律 [J]. 中国公路学报, 2009, 22(3): 1-6
[35] 武建民. 半刚性基层沥青路面使用性能衰变规律研究 [D]. 长安大学博士学位论文, 2005
[36] 刘业敏, 韩森, 徐鸥明, 等. 疲劳试验中沥青混合料的弯拉劲度模量 [J]. 广西大学学报 (自然科学版), 2010, 35(1): 127-131
[37] 肖建清, 丁德馨, 骆行文, 等. 再生混凝土疲劳损伤演化的定量描述 [J]. 中南大学学报 (自然科学版), 2011, 42(1): 170-177
[38] Guan H X, Zheng J L, Tian X G. Comparing of fatigue damage defining ways of asphalt mixtures[J]. ICTE, 2009: 2749-2755
[39] 沈金安. 国外沥青路面设计方法汇总 [M]. 北京: 人民交通出版社, 2004
[40] 交通部公路科学研究所. 重载沥青路面设计规范研究报告 [R]. 2003
[41] 长安大学. 重载交通沥青路面设计研究 [R]. 2005
[42] 姚祖康, 彭波, 田波, 等. 超限车辆对路面损坏的影响分析 [J]. 中国公路学会 2000 年学术交流论文集, 2000: 217-221
[43] 李海军, 黄晓明. 重载条件下沥青路面按弯沉等效的轴载换算 [J]. 公路交通科技, 2004, 21(7): 5-8
[44] 彭波, 姜爱锋. 半刚性基层沥青混凝土路面的轴载换算关系探讨 [J]. 华东公路, 2001, 2(6): 50-53
[45] 陈忠达. 沥青路面交通参数的研究 [D]. 长安大学博士学位论文, 2006
[46] 黄卫, 刘振清, 钱振东, 等. 基于疲劳等效的钢桥面铺装体系轴载换算方法 [J]. 交通运输工程学报, 2005, 5 (01): 14-18
[47] 颜利, 周晓青, 李宇峙, 等. 基于直道足尺车辙试验的沥青路面重载轴载换算方法研究 [J]. 公路交通科技, 2006, 23(3): 35-39
[48] 何兆益, 雷婷, 王国清, 等. 基于动力问题的高等级公路沥青路面车辙预估方法 [J]. 土木工程学报, 2007(03): 104-109
[49] 邱欣, 张敏江, 何桂平, 等. 应用线弹性疲劳损伤理论的沥青路面轴载换算 [J]. 公路交通科技, 2005, 22(6): 6-9
[50] 元松. 基于应力强度因子的面层反射裂缝轴载换算方法研究 [J]. 公路交通科技, 2010, 4(9): 89-95
[51] 关宏信, 张起森, 徐旸, 等. 沥青面轴载抗滑等效换算方法 [J]. 公路交通科技, 2010, 5(9): 37-42
[52] 王辉, 武和平. 沥青路面按弯沉等效轴载换算的研究 [J]. 中国公路学报, 2003, 16(1): 19-21
[53] 孙志林, 黄晓明. 基于路基顶面压应变的沥青路面轴载换算方法 [J]. 公路交通科技, 2007, 24(7): 28-30

第 2 章　沥青混合料疲劳试验方法

2.1　沥青混合料疲劳试验方法确定

2.1.1　目前国内外沥青混合料主要疲劳试验方法

疲劳破坏是沥青路面的三大破坏形式之一，人们对其试验研究方法给予了很大的关注，归纳起来可以分为四类：一是实际路面在真实行车荷载作用下的疲劳破坏试验，如美国的 AASHO 试验路，历时三年才完成；二是足尺路面结构在模拟行车荷载作用下的疲劳试验，包括环道试验和加速加载试验，如南非的重型车辆模拟车 (HVS)、澳大利亚和新西兰的加速加载设备 (ALF)、美国华盛顿州立大学的室外大型环道、中国长沙理工大学的亚洲最大的路面直道实验中心和交通运输部重庆公路科学研究所的室内大型环道疲劳试验等；三是试板试验法；四是室内小型试件的疲劳试验。由于前三类试验研究方法耗资大、周期长，开展得并不普遍，多采用的是周期短、费用少的室内小型试件的疲劳试验[1]。

但是，沥青混合料的室内小型疲劳试验方法繁多，北美大多数国家采用梁式试件进行反复疲劳试验；欧洲的研究者多采用悬臂梯形梁试件，在其端部施加正弦波荷载；而采用圆柱试件进行间接拉伸疲劳试验近年来在日本开展得比较多。总之，各研究者所采用的试验方法不尽相同，呈现出一种百家争鸣的现象。迄今为止，各国均没有将疲劳试验作为标准试验方法纳入规范。

2.1.2　对主要疲劳试验方法的评述

间接拉伸法在早期的沥青混合料疲劳试验研究中开展得较为普遍[2]。由于其试验方法相对简单，因而许多研究者都曾经使用该方法进行沥青混合料疲劳性能的评价。国内早期开展的疲劳试验也以间接拉伸为主，其中的一些研究成果被现行《公路沥青路面设计规范》(JTG D50—2006) 所采纳。间接拉伸法的主要优点如下：

(1) 试验方法简单。

(2) 从总体上来说，基本满足沥青路面疲劳设计分析的要求，疲劳试验结果与实际路面性能有一定的相关性。

(3) 其试验设备还适用于开展其他的一些试验，如回弹模量、间接抗拉强度试验等。

(4) 从线弹性理论角度分析，在试件开裂破坏区域所受到的拉应力作用相对比较均匀。

(5) 能够方便地评价路面芯样的疲劳性能。

而作为一种室内小型疲劳试验方法，间接拉伸疲劳试验由于其试验模式本身的一些不足，也正在逐渐被沥青混合料疲劳研究人员所放弃。间接拉伸法的主要缺点和不足表现为：

(1) 虽然圆柱体试件中心点处于双轴向受力状态，但其加载方式与实际路面受力状态有较大的差别。

(2) 相对于其他试验方法，在同样受力水平下，用间接拉伸法所得到的疲劳寿命要小于其他的试验方法，从而可能低估沥青混合料的疲劳性能。

(3) 采用劈裂加载方式，在试件受力两端会产生明显的局部变形，这直接影响试件受力模式，也使得在较高温度情况下进行沥青混合料疲劳试验会十分困难。

(4) 试件实际开裂模式与理论开裂位置经常不一致。理论要求裂缝出现的位置应在试件中央或附近，而实际上有许多试件会首先在加载条边缘产生开裂，还有的试件直至达到垂直变形的极限也不发生开裂。

(5) 通过间接拉伸疲劳试验方式，难以从耗散能角度进行沥青混合料的疲劳特性分析。

(6) 到目前为止，尚无法用间接拉伸加载方式进行控制应变方式的疲劳试验。

梯形悬臂梁弯曲和四点弯曲疲劳试验是目前国外较为流行的小型试件疲劳试验方法。前者主要在欧洲开展得比较普遍，而后者在美国、南非以及澳大利亚等国家有大量的试验研究与应用。梯形悬臂梁弯曲和四点弯曲两种疲劳试验方法存在着许多共同的特性，主要表现在如下几个方面：

(1) 两者均以重复弯拉作为疲劳试验的主要加载方式，这更接近实际路面在交通荷载作用下的真实受力状态。

(2) 除了劲度模量、疲劳寿命等常规试验结果外，两者均能提供滞后角和耗散能的数据。

(3) 两者均能较好地避免由重复加载引起的试件局部变形对试验结果产生的误差。

(4) 两者均能进行控制应力模式和控制应变模式的疲劳试验。

然而，相对于梯形悬臂梁弯曲疲劳试验方式，四点弯曲疲劳试验方法有其一定的优越性，主要表现在：

(1) 梯形悬臂梁弯曲加载模式下，试件最大应力点位于距试件底部 1/3 处，而该位置也即试件发生疲劳开裂的理论开裂位置。而在四点弯曲加载模式下，试件中央 1/3 区域均承受着最大应力作用，使得疲劳裂缝产生位置由一具体的位置扩展为一个理论开裂区域，这对于评价非均质的沥青混合料性能更为合理。

(2) 梯形悬臂梁弯曲疲劳试验的试件制作过程要相对复杂，由于梯形悬臂梁试件受弯拉作用的四面均为等腰梯形，这给试件的切割成型带来了一定的难度。而四点弯曲梁疲劳试验方式所采用的试件为长方体试件，采用双面平行切割技术时，可以将试件的尺寸控制得非常精确。

(3) 梯形悬臂梁弯曲疲劳试验在试验过程中需要将试件的两端进行粘结固定，而四点弯曲疲劳试验则采用夹具夹持固定的方式，无需对试件进行粘结操作，试验操作更为方便。

美国 SHRP 研究计划对上述三种试验方法进行过详细的评价，SHRP 研究计划主要对上述三种试验方式进行了影响因素敏感性、试验可靠性及合理性三方面的评价与分析，由于该方面的研究工作量比较大，要占用较大的设备资源和较长的试验时间，因此在此将引用 SHRP-A-404 报告的研究成果，为本书试验方法和试验方案的确定提供参考。

影响因素敏感性分析主要用于评价试验方法对沥青混合料各试验影响因素变化的敏感程度，即反映各试验方法区分试验参数变化的能力。在 SHRP 研究计划中，考虑的试验影响因素包括沥青种类、沥青含量、集料类型、空隙率、温度和应力水平，所选参数均按两水平考虑。敏感性分析评价结果列于表 2.1，各参数间的敏感程度用百分比表示[3]。

表 2.1 不同试验方法影响因素敏感性分析结果

评价指标	影响因素	四点弯曲	梯形悬臂梁弯曲	间接拉伸
劲度模量变化百分比/%	沥青种类	51	29	43
	沥青含量	0[a]	0[b]	0[a]
	集料类型	11	5[b]	27
	空隙率	33	24	18
	温度	84	44	67
	应力水平	8	4	0[a]
疲劳寿命变化百分比/%	沥青种类	56	58	53
	沥青含量	50[b]	0[a]	0[a]
	集料类型	67	49[b]	45[b]
	空隙率	85	80	67
	温度	99	98	99
	应力水平	88	80	76

注：上标 a 表示主效应与两水平交互作用结果均统计不显著；上标 b 表示主效应统计不显著，但两水平交互作用结果统计显著。

从劲度模量和疲劳寿命变化百分比来看，四点弯曲疲劳试验和间接拉伸疲劳试验对沥青类型变化的敏感程度大致相当。对于其他影响因素，总体上四点弯曲疲劳的敏感程度最好，其次依次为梯形悬臂梁弯曲疲劳和间接拉伸疲劳。

试验可靠性分析主要用于评价试验方法在重复试验条件下的可靠程度，即反映各试验方法的数据离散程度。在 SHRP 研究计划中，主要采用了变化系数和采样方差两个指标进行试验可靠性程度的评价，其评价结果列于表 2.2[4]。

表 2.2　不同试验方法试验可靠性分析结果

评价指标		四点弯曲	梯形悬臂梁弯曲	间接拉伸
劲度模量	变化系数/%	12.3	11.4	19.7
	采样方差 (ln psi)	0.01	0.014	0.015
疲劳寿命	变化系数/%	98.7	171.8	65.5
	采样方差 (ln N_f)	0.282	1.696	0.213

可靠性分析结果表明，对于劲度模量的可靠性，四点弯曲疲劳和梯形悬臂梁弯曲疲劳基本相当，而从疲劳寿命的可靠性来看，间接拉伸疲劳可靠性最佳，其后依次为四点弯曲疲劳和梯形悬臂梁弯曲疲劳。

合理性分析主要是评价各试验方法所获得的试验结果是否合理，即试验结果是否与先前经验所期望的一致。在 SHRP 研究计划中，主要通过比较不同温度下的平均劲度模量和平均疲劳寿命值进行各试验方法的合理性评价，具体评价结果列于表 2.3[5]。

表 2.3　不同试验方法平均劲度模量和平均疲劳寿命值

评价指标		四点弯曲	梯形悬臂梁弯曲	间接拉伸
平均劲度模量/psi	0℃	2454700	1978100	3712400
	20℃	425100	1063100	1211300
平均疲劳寿命	0℃	5834000	488800	214900
	20℃	24500	245600	108100

注：1psi=6.895kPa=0.0689476bar=0.006895MPa。

上述试验结果表明间接拉伸疲劳与四点弯曲疲劳的试验结果相差非常大。通过间接拉伸方式获得的平均劲度模量要比四点弯曲高出 51%，而四点弯曲疲劳试验所得的平均疲劳寿命却是间接拉伸疲劳的 27 倍。造成这一现象的主要原因可能是间接拉伸疲劳试验过程中，在试件受力两端产生了明显的永久变形，从而显著地缩短了沥青混合料的疲劳寿命。而梯形悬臂梁弯曲疲劳试验所得的平均劲度模量和平均疲劳寿命似乎对温度不太敏感，这有可能是梯形悬臂梁弯曲疲劳加载速度过快所引起的，而 SHRP A-003A 研究计划的早期调查表明沥青混合料实际的温度敏感性要比梯形悬臂梁疲劳试验结果高。

参 考 文 献

[1] Shen S, Airey G D, Carpenter S H, et al. A dissipated energy approach to fatigue evaluation [J]. International Journal of Road Materials and Pavement Design, 2006, 7(1):38-51

[2] Bhasin A, Branco V T F C, Masad E, et al. Quantitative comparison of energy methods to characterize fatigue in asphalt materials [J]. Journal of Materials in Civil Engineering, ASCE, 2009, 21(2): 83-92

[3] Daniel J, Kim Y R. Simplified fatigue modeling of asphalt concrete using viscoelasticity and continuum damage mechanics [J]. Presented at Fatigue Damage Prediction Symposium Laramie, Wyoming, July 18-21, 2001

[4] Lytton R L, Chen C W, Little D N. Microdamage healing in asphalt and asphalt concrete. Volume IV: A viscoelastic continuum damage fatigue model of asphalt concrete with microdamage healing [J]. Asphalt Pavements, 2001: 178

[5] Scarpas A, AI-Khoury R, Gurp C A P M, et al. Finte element simulation of damage development in asphalt concrete pavements [J]. Eighth International Conference on Asphalt Pavements, 1997: 673-692

第3章 沥青混合料疲劳方程

常规的疲劳试验先确定试样的静载强度，即在固定的较慢的加载速率 (准静载条件) 下进行强度试验，一方面检验材料的静强度是否符合要求，另一方面根据静强度 σ_b 选定疲劳试验时的各级应力水平。由高应力到低应力逐级进行疲劳试验，记录试样破坏时的循环数，通过应力水平与疲劳寿命间的关系，建立传统的 S-N 疲劳方程。现行沥青路面设计规范在确定沥青面层抗拉强度结构系数计算方法时，是通过传统疲劳方程后延到 $N_f=1$，由疲劳方程得到此时的拉应力就是极限抗拉强度，所以认为沥青混合料的极限抗拉强度是个常数。这与沥青混合料本身的黏弹性性质不相符，其刚度指标与强度指标均受到加载速率和温度的显著影响，沥青混合料抗拉强度是随加载速率和温度不同而变化的。一方面，传统疲劳方程后延得到沥青混合料的极限抗拉强度，缺乏充分的论据和试验验证；另一方面，极限抗拉强度不能反映沥青混合料的黏弹性特性[1]。因此依据传统的疲劳方程建立的沥青面层抗拉强度结构系数计算方法是不合适的，有必要提出一种更合理的新方法以解决上述问题。

本章首先开展不同加载速率下的强度试验，分析沥青混合料强度的速度特性；引入动载强度和真实应力比的概念，通过不同应力水平下的疲劳试验，建立基于真实应力比的疲劳方程，并与传统疲劳方程进行对比分析；依据真实应力比疲劳方程建立一种确定沥青路面抗拉强度结构系数的新方法。

3.1 原材料试验及配合比设计

选用细粒式沥青混合料 AC-13C 作为研究对象，原材料为东海石油 SBS 改性沥青和湖南株洲产玄武岩集料，沥青检测结果见表 3.1，集料密度和力学指标试验结果分别见表 3.2 和表 3.3。

上面的检测结果表明，原材料东海石油 SBS 改性沥青和玄武岩集料各项指标均满足《公路沥青路面施工技术规范》(JTG F40—2004) 的技术要求。

选用 AC-13C 沥青混合料矿料级配见表 3.4，级配曲线见图 3.1。

通过马歇尔试验控制目标空隙率为 4.5% 来确定最佳油石比，最佳油石比及马歇尔试验结果见表 3.5。

3.1 原材料试验及配合比设计

表 3.1　SBS(I-D) 改性沥青试验结果

试验项目	试验结果	技术要求
针入度 (25℃,100g,5s)/0.1mm	50.9	30~60
针入度指数 PI	0.533(r=0.997)	⩾0
延度 (5cm/min, 5℃)/cm	36.0	⩾20
软化点 TR&B/℃	72.5	⩾60
运动黏度 135℃/(Pa·s)	2.31	⩽3
弹性恢复 (25℃)/%	77	⩾75
储存稳定性离析，48h 软化点差/℃	1.5	⩽2.5
溶解度/%	99.9	⩾99
闪点/℃	267	⩾230
薄膜加热试验 (TFOT)(或旋转薄膜加热试验 (RTFOT)) 后残留物　质量变化/%	0.29	⩽±1.0
残留针入度比 (25℃)/%	78.0	⩾65
残留延度 (5℃)/cm	24.3	⩾15

表 3.2　玄武岩集料密度试验结果

编号	粒径规格/mm	表观密度/(g/cm³)	毛体积密度/(g/cm³)	表干密度/(g/cm³)	吸水率/%
1	16~13.2	2.670	2.578	2.612	1.34
2	13.2~9.5	2.672	2.568	2.607	1.51
3	9.5~4.75	2.663	2.571	2.606	1.34
4	4.75~2.36	2.650			
5	2.36~1.18	2.641			
6	1.18~0.6	2.607			
7	0.6~0.3	2.594	—	—	—
8	0.3~0.15	2.584			
9	0.15~0.075	2.617			

表 3.3　玄武岩集料压碎值、磨光值及磨耗值试验结果

集料类型	压碎值/%	磨光值 (BPN)	磨耗值/%
玄武岩	15.8	57	19.2
规范要求	⩽28	⩾45	⩽30

表 3.4　AC-13C 密级配沥青混合料矿料级配

筛孔尺寸/mm	16	13.2	9.5	4.75	2.36	1.18	0.6	0.3	0.15	0.075
级配上限	100	100	85	68	50	38	28	20	15	8
级配下限		90	68	38	24	15	10	7	5	4
通过率/%	100	95	74	48.5	34	23.5	15	11	8.5	6

AC-13C矿料级配图

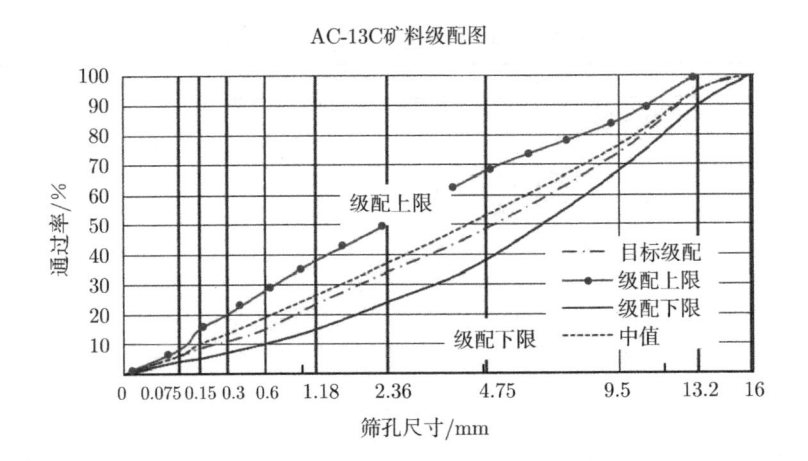

图 3.1 AC-13C 密级配沥青混合料矿料级配曲线

表 3.5 最佳油石比及马歇尔试验结果

最佳油石比/%	毛体积相对密度/(g/cm³)	空隙率 VV/%	矿料间隙率 VMA/%	饱和度 VFA/%	稳定度/kN	流值/0.1mm
5.2	2.455	4.5	16.1	67.2	12.7	27.9

3.2 不同加载速率下直接拉伸强度试验

目前,研究者较多地从影响沥青混合料强度的因素角度进行研究,对影响沥青混合料强度的内部因素(材料的组成、结构以及材料的性能)和外部因素(温度、荷载大小及速率)进行分析,李立寒等借助劈裂强度试验,探讨了泡沫沥青混合料强度增长规律及其影响因素、生产工艺条件对泡沫沥青混合料强度的影响以及泡沫沥青混合料的储存特性。孟岩等分析了纤维增强沥青混合料强度形成机理,与无纤维沥青混合料试验结果进行对比。沥青混合料是一种典型的黏弹性材料,其强度指标受到加载速率与温度的显著影响,强度随加载速率的变化规律还有待进一步研究[2]。

将沥青混合料拌合成长×宽×高为 30cm×30cm×5cm 的车辙板试件,然后将其切割成 25cm×5cm×5cm 的小梁试件备用。由于切割时的误差,试件面积以三个不同横截面积的实测平均值为准。本节试验共成型了 30 块车辙板,切割了 150 根小梁试件,分别用于直接拉伸强度、直接拉伸疲劳和疲劳剩余强度试验。

试验采用 MTS-810 材料试验系统,通过内置编程程序编制好加载程序并设置好相应荷载和数据采集参数,强度试验可以自动采集到破坏时最大荷载及相应位移,疲劳试验过程中可以由数据采集系统自动采集每个加载周期的力、位移

3.2 不同加载速率下直接拉伸强度试验

值,通过计算可求出对应的应力、应变,强度试验和疲劳试验数据采集频率分别为 1024Hz、204Hz。图 3.2 中给出了小梁试件直接拉伸试验图和受力示意图。

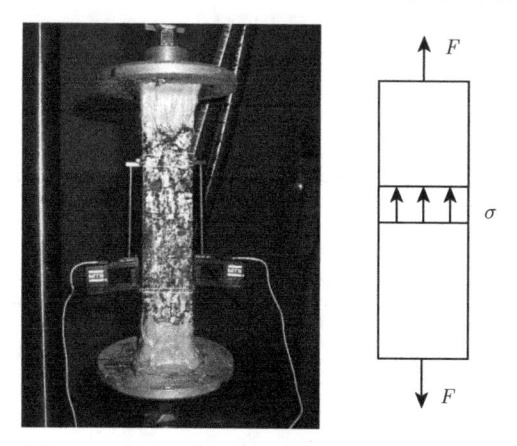

图 3.2　小梁试件直接拉伸试验及受力示意图

为了尽量减小偏心受拉的影响,一方面,在拉头上刻有细纹的同心圆,既可以增加摩擦、提高粘结强度,又可以保证粘贴试件时更好对中;另一方面,在拉头两端用球形阀连接 MTS,可以更好地保证试件轴心受拉。试件与拉头之间用环氧树脂粘钢胶粘结,环氧树脂粘钢胶按 A、B 组分 10:3 的比例拌合均匀,固化时间为1h,三天固结后的抗拉强度已能满足试验要求,粘钢胶粘结强度远大于沥青混合料抗拉强度且变形小,完全能保证直接拉伸强度和疲劳试验的顺利进行,粘钢胶的各项力学指标及性能见表 3.6。

表 3.6　粘钢胶性能技术指标检测结果 (武汉大筑公司提供)

序号		项目名称	技术指标 A 级	技术指标 B 级	检测结果
1	胶体性能	抗拉强度/MPa	$\geqslant 30$	$\geqslant 25$	57.41
		受拉弹性模量/MPa	$\geqslant 4.0 \times 10^3$	$\geqslant 3.0 \times 10^3$	$\geqslant 4.6 \times 10^3$
		伸长率/%	$\geqslant 1.3$		1.65
		抗弯强度/MPa	$\geqslant 45$ 且不得呈脆性 (碎裂状) 破坏	$\geqslant 35$	88.04,且不呈脆性 (碎裂状) 破坏
		抗压强度/MPa	$\geqslant 65$	$\geqslant 65$	97.17
2	粘结能力	钢–钢拉押抗剪强度/MPa	$\geqslant 15$	$\geqslant 12$	23.69
		钢–钢不均匀扯离强度/(kN/m)	$\geqslant 16$	$\geqslant 12$	18
		钢–钢粘结拉强度/MPa	$\geqslant 33$	$\geqslant 25$	40.64
		与砼正拉粘结强度/MPa	$\geqslant 2.5$	$\geqslant 2.5$	5.7

按常规疲劳试验要求,首先用 3 个试件进行准静载条件下的直接拉伸强度试

验，加载速率为 5mm/min。小梁破坏时的直接拉伸强度 S 计算公式如下 [3]：

$$S_{\mathrm{j}} = F_{\max}/A \tag{3.1}$$

式中，S_{j} 为试件准静载条件下破坏时的直接拉伸强度，MPa；$F_{\max}$ 为试件破坏时的荷载，N；A 为试件 3 个不同断面面积的平均值，mm^2。

准静载条件下的直接拉伸强度试验结果见表 3.7。准静载条件下 3 次平行试验结果的平均值为 1.228MPa。

表 3.7 准静载条件下的直接拉伸强度试验结果

序号	试件截面积 A/mm^2	破坏荷载 $F_{\max}/N$	静载强度 S_{j}/MPa	平均值/MPa	标准偏差/MPa	变异系数/%
1	2646.5	3244	1.226			
2	2581.9	3172	1.229	1.228	0.002	0.16
3	2644.3	3252	1.230			

沥青混合料通常采用等应变方式测定强度，但是本节主要考虑推导沥青面层抗拉强度结构系数，采用的是以应力表示的疲劳方程，通过对应力形式表示的疲劳方程反推得到沥青路面的极限拉应力，由此来推导沥青路面的抗拉强度结构系数；并且沥青混合料疲劳试验采用的也是应力控制方式，保证疲劳试验半个周期内的荷载加载速率与强度试验的加载速率保持一致；基于以上两点，为了掌握不同加载速率下直接拉伸沥青混合料强度的变化规律，故本节采用应力方式设计了强度试验加载速率为 0.0037~37MPa/s (10N/s~100kN/s)，14 种不同速率的直接拉伸破坏试验，试验结果见表 3.8。

将表 3.8 中不同加载速率下的直接拉伸强度绘于图 3.3，不同加载速率下直接拉伸强度试验的荷载–变形曲线见图 3.4。

沥青混合料是典型的黏弹性物质，其破坏形态受加载速率影响。在不同使用条件下，菅原提出了沥青混合料的三种破坏模式：脆性破坏、柔性破坏及过渡区破坏。由图 3.4 可见，随着加载速率的增大，荷载–变形曲线位置逐渐由低到高，曲线的峰值逐渐增大，荷载–变形曲线说明随加载速率的增大强度逐渐增大，当加载速率较高时，如直接拉伸试验加载速率 100kN/s 时，荷载–变形近似呈线性关系，沥青混合料呈脆性破坏，破坏表现为突然的脆断，一到破坏点立即丧失承载能力，破坏断面中往往可见粗集料的断裂破坏。当加载速率较低时，如直接拉伸试验的加载速率 0.1kN/s，荷载–变形关系图呈曲线形式，沥青混合料发生流动变形时的柔性破坏，荷载达到最大值时，试件已明显产生裂缝，实际上已经破坏，定义曲线的峰值为破坏点，过峰值后，试件仍有一定的承载能力，破坏方式以微裂缝的形式存在。当加载速率由高到低变化时，沥青混合料的破坏形式逐渐由脆性破坏向柔性破坏

3.2 不同加载速率下直接拉伸强度试验

过渡;介于脆性破坏和柔性破坏之间的为过渡区破坏模式。荷载-变形曲线在保持一段直线关系后在接近峰值时产生类似于屈服点的转折或微小的曲线,过了峰值后即使并非马上断裂也只能维持极短时间而破断。不同加载速率下的沥青混合料直接拉伸强度试验验证了菅原所提出的破坏模式。

表 3.8 不同加载速率下的直接拉伸破坏试验结果

序号	加载速率 v MPa/s	kN/s	试件面积 A/mm^2	破坏荷载 F_{max}/N	强度 S/MPa
1	0.0037	0.01	2695.7	2276	0.844
2	0.037	0.10	2688.2	3749	1.395
3	0.37	1.0	2727.2	5453	2.000
4	1.85	4.9	2662.8	7548	2.835
5	3.70	10.0	2676.6	7910	2.955
6	7.40	20.7	2799.6	10757	3.842
7	10.80	30.0	2778.3	11892	4.280
8	13.72	40.0	2915.4	13888	4.589
9	17.77	50.0	2813.1	13027	4.695
10	21.00	60.3	2869.8	13550	4.722
11	24.80	70.0	2818.7	13927	4.941
12	29.60	80.0	2703.0	13969	5.168
13	33.30	87.4	2625.1	13119	4.998
14	37.00	100.0	2703.1	14129	5.227

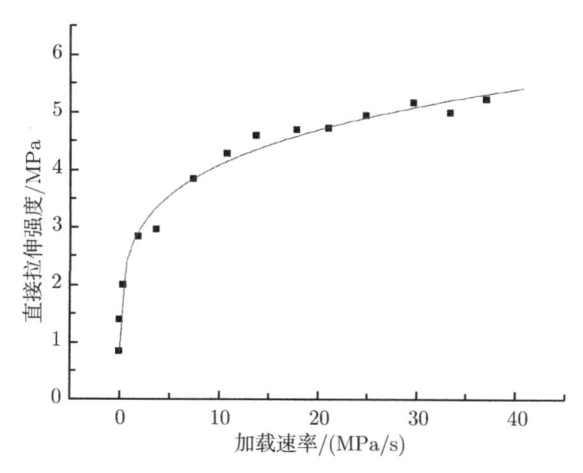

图 3.3 直接拉伸强度随加载速率变化曲线

不同加载速率下沥青混合料断面破坏特征表现为:在低加载应变速率时,破坏方式以微裂缝的形式存在,界面破坏的表现形式以沥青及胶浆内部的黏聚破坏居多，破坏断面由沥青砂组成，没有大骨料的破坏，相应强度试验结果较小；在高加载应变速率时，由于沥青混合料在瞬间承受较大的应力，界面破坏的主要表现形式为集料与胶浆间的破坏，破坏断面中往往可见粗集料的断裂，相应强度试验结果较大。

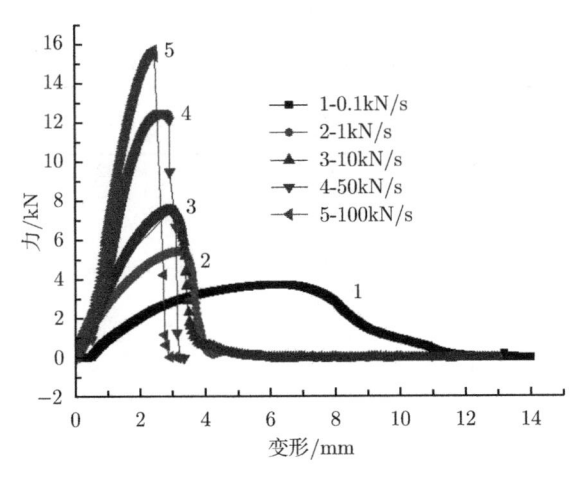

图 3.4 不同加载速率下直接拉伸强度试验的荷载-变形曲线

表 3.8 中的试验结果也证实了上述破坏特征，在试验的加载范围内，加载速率最大值 37MPa/s 下的强度 5.227MPa 是最小值 0.0037MPa/s 下的强度 0.844MPa 的 6.2 倍，说明加载速率对沥青混合料的强度影响非常显著。

由图 3.3 明显看出，直接拉伸强度随加载速率增加而增大，开始阶段强度急剧增加，随着加载速率的增大，增加幅度渐渐平缓。将加载速率与强度进行非线性拟合，可得二者的回归关系如下式所示：

$$S_{\mathrm{dz}} = 2.583 v^{0.2}, \quad R^2 = 0.984 \tag{3.2}$$

式中，S_{dz} 为不同加载速率下的直接拉伸强度，MPa；v 为加载速率，MPa/s。

静载强度平均值 1.228MPa 只相当于加载速率 0.024MPa/s 下的强度值。由拟合结果可知，加载速率对沥青混合料强度有显著影响，在本次试验一定温度和加载速率范围内，动载强度和加载速率可近似表示为幂函数关系。

3.3 直接拉伸疲劳试验结果及传统疲劳方程的建立

3.3.1 疲劳试验方法及方案设计

疲劳试验方法采用沥青混合料小梁试件直接拉伸疲劳，直接拉伸试验可以在试件的横截面上获得明确均匀的拉应力分布，是研究沥青混合料受拉疲劳性能理想的试验方法。

设计疲劳试验方案和主要控制标准如下，① 试件成型方法：轮碾压实成型车辙板，再切割成小梁；② 加载方式：直接拉伸应力控制疲劳；③ 加载波形和频率：10Hz 连续式半正矢波形；④ 应力水平：2MPa、1.5MPa、1MPa、0.5MPa 和 0.25MPa 五种；⑤ 试验温度：(20±1)℃，试验前试件在该温度下保温 24h 以上。疲劳试验方案及影响因素汇总于表 3.9 中 [4]。

表 3.9 疲劳试验方案及影响因素汇总

因素种类	因素名称	控制标准
外部因素	应力水平/MPa	2、1.5、1、0.5、0.25
	试验温度	20℃
	加载频率	10Hz
内部因素	沥青品种	SBS 改性沥青
	沥青用量	5.2%
	混合料级配	AC-13C
	空隙率	4.5%

3.3.2 疲劳试验结果及传统疲劳方程的建立

每个应力水平下疲劳试验平行试件不少于 4 个，按照疲劳试验设计方案获得的试验结果见表 3.10。名义应力比 t_m 是应力水平与静载强度的比值，其结果见表 3.10 中第 2 列，静载强度已由准静载条件下的强度试验测得为 1.228MPa。名义应力比、动载强度和真实应力比、疲劳寿命及其变异系数在表 3.10 中一并给出。

由表 3.10 中的试验结果发现：一是疲劳寿命随应力水平的减小而增大，且在双对数坐标上表现为线性关系，可用式 (3.3) 的方程拟合，见图 3.5。二是名义应力比与真实应力比明显不相等；当应力水平为 1.5MPa 和 2MPa 时，名义应力比已大于 1，但其疲劳寿命分别为 485 次和 206 次，说明基于名义应力比的疲劳方程不能涵盖一次作用下的强度破坏；在双对数坐标上名义应力比与疲劳寿命也表现为线性关系，可用式 (3.4) 的方程拟合，见图 3.6。三是疲劳寿命从不同应力水平的变异性来看，随应力水平的减小变异系数增大，说明应力水平越小疲劳寿命的离散性越大。相同应力水平下平行试件的变异系数由 10%增大到 60%[5]。

$$\lg \sigma = a - b \lg N_f \tag{3.3}$$

$$\lg t_m = c - d \lg N_f \tag{3.4}$$

式中，σ 为应力水平，MPa；t_m 为名义应力比，MPa/MPa；N_f 为疲劳寿命，次；a, b, c, d 为回归系数。

表 3.10　不同应力水平下的直接拉伸疲劳试验结果

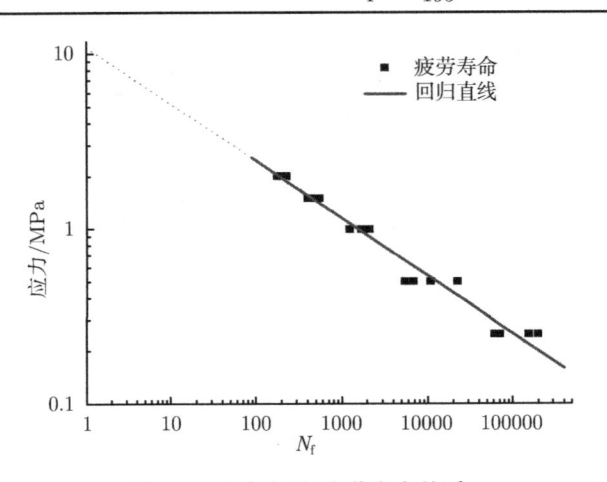

应力水平/MPa	名义应力比	速率/(MPa/s)	动载强度/MPa	真实应力比	编号	疲劳寿命/次	平均寿命/次	标准偏差	变异系数
0.25	0.20	5	3.56	0.070	1	154449	122131	66638	54.6%
					2	200337			
					3	61705			
					4	72032			
0.5	0.41	10	4.09	0.122	1	6874	11414	7711	67.6%
					2	5447			
					3	22454			
					4	10880			
1	0.81	20	4.70	0.213	1	1867	1719	374	21.8%
					2	1675			
					3	1225			
					4	2109			
1.5	1.22	30	5.10	0.294	1	552	485	62	12.9%
					2	406			
					3	469			
					4	511			
2	1.63	40	5.40	0.370	1	223	206	23	10.9%
					2	227			
					3	180			
					4	195			

图 3.5　应力水平-疲劳寿命关系

在双对数坐标上，对图 3.5 和图 3.6 分别用式 (3.3) 和式 (3.4) 线性回归得

$$\lg \sigma = 1.049 - 0.33 \lg N_\mathrm{f}, \quad R = 0.987$$

$$\lg t_\mathrm{m} = 0.966 - 0.33 \lg N_\mathrm{f}, \quad R = 0.987$$

即得到传统的和基于名义应力比的疲劳方程为

$$\sigma = 11.2 N_f^{-0.33} \tag{3.5}$$

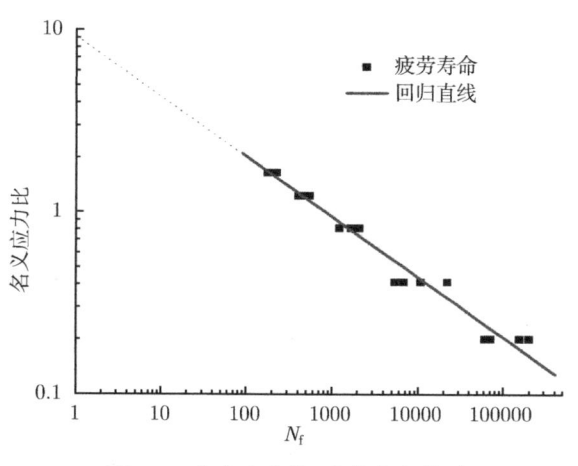

$$t_m = 9.25 N_f^{-0.33} \tag{3.6}$$

图 3.6 名义应力比-疲劳寿命关系

将图 3.5 中回归直线后延到 $N_f = 1$ 时相当于一次受拉强度破坏，得到极限强度为 11.2MPa，这显然与准静载条件下强度试验测得的 1.228MPa 不符合，说明建立的沥青混合料传统疲劳方程不可后延；传统疲劳方程是疲劳试验结果经过回归分析后得出的，它有一定的试验条件和适用范围。将图 3.6 中回归直线后延到 $N_f = 1$ 时名义应力比 t_m 并不等于 1，即疲劳次数为 1 时，疲劳荷载与一次破坏强度值并不相等，即说明传统疲劳方程不能反映一次强度破坏。

3.4 真实应力比疲劳方程的建立

由于基于名义应力比的疲劳方程不能将重复荷载作用下的疲劳和一次荷载作用下的强度进行统一，因此建立一种能同时反映沥青混合料重复荷载作用下的疲劳性质和一次荷载作用下的强度性质的疲劳方程，对更好地描述沥青混合料疲劳特性是非常有意义的。

由于静载强度试验加载速率远小于疲劳试验 1/2 周期内的加载速率 (与应力水平和加载频率有关)，所以静载强度与疲劳试验加载速率下对应的动载强度差别较大。在进行沥青混合料疲劳试验时，通常选择 10Hz 的加载频率，假如在 1MPa 的应力水平下进行疲劳试验，其加载过程中速率为 20MPa/s；而由不同加载速率下的直接拉伸强度试验结果及式 (3.2) 可反算得到，静载强度平均值 1.228MPa 只相当于加载速率 0.024MPa/s 下的强度值，二者加载速率相差 832 倍；由式 (3.2) 计算出加载速率 20MPa/s 所对应的强度为 4.703MPa，与静载强度的比值为 4.703/1.228=3.83，可见传统疲劳试验中所采用的名义应力比没有考虑加载速率对强度的影响。

为此通过引入疲劳动载强度和真实应力比的概念，考虑加载速率对沥青混合料强度的影响，将不同速率下的强度称为动载强度，由回归公式 (3.2) 可得，为了同静载强度区别用 S_{dz} 表示。根据动载强度，引入真实应力比的概念，即疲劳试验施加的应力水平与动载强度的比值，用 t_s 表示，计算式为 [6]

$$t_s = \sigma/S_{dz} \tag{3.7}$$

式中，t_s 为真实应力比，MPa/MPa；σ 为应力水平，MPa；S_{dz} 为疲劳试验中一定加载频率、应力水平对应加载速率下的动载强度，MPa。

根据疲劳试验中的加载频率 f 和应力水平 σ 可以求出对应的加载速率，见式 (3.8)，加载速率见表 3.10 中第 3 列；再由加载速率与强度的回归公式 (3.2) 可求出对应的动载强度值 S_{dz}，其结果见表 3.10 中第 4 列。

$$v = \frac{\sigma}{T/2} = 2f\sigma \tag{3.8}$$

式中，v 为加载速率，MPa/s；σ 为应力水平，MPa；T 为加载周期，s；f 为加载频率，Hz。

用表 3.10 中得到的真实应力比和疲劳寿命试验结果，在双对数坐标中用线性方程 (3.9) 拟合，拟合曲线见图 3.7 中直线 a。

$$\lg t_s = k \lg N_f + e \tag{3.9}$$

式中，t_s 为真实应力比，MPa/MPa；N_f 为疲劳寿命，次；k、e 为回归系数。

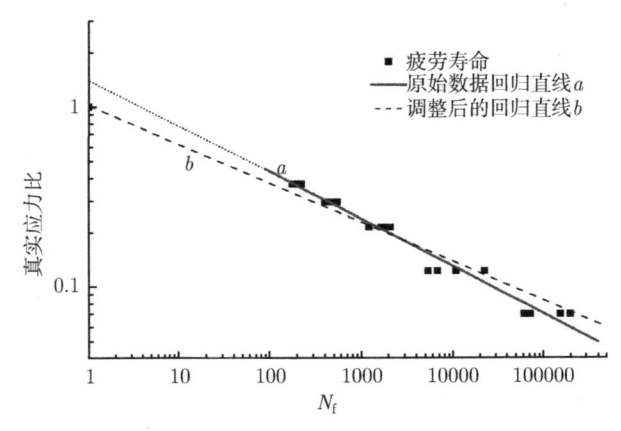

图 3.7 真实应力比–疲劳寿命关系

3.4 真实应力比疲劳方程的建立

通过在双对数坐标上用式 (3.9) 线性回归得

$$\lg t_s = -0.26 \lg N_f + 0.168, \quad R = 0.987$$

即得到基于真实应力比的疲劳方程为

$$t_s = 1.47 N_f^{-0.26} \tag{3.10}$$

由拟合直线 a 后延到 $N_f = 1$ 时 $t_s = 1.47$，真实应力比 t_s 接近于 1；说明按真实应力比的定义，当应力水平足够大、疲劳寿命为 1 次时，该应力水平与疲劳动载强度相等，即真实应力比疲劳方程满足极限条件当 $N_f = 1$ 时 $t_s = 1$。因此对拟合直线 a 进行微调，拟合直线过 (1,1) 点，得到线性拟合方程为

$$\lg t_s = -0.218 \lg N_f, \quad R = 0.971$$

调整后的拟合曲线见图 3.7 中直线 b。从相关系数来看，调整后的拟合直线仍具有较好的相关性，即调整后的真实应力比疲劳方程为

$$t_s = N_f^{-0.218} \tag{3.11}$$

将名义应力比–疲劳寿命和真实应力比–疲劳寿命关系进行比较，见图 3.8。

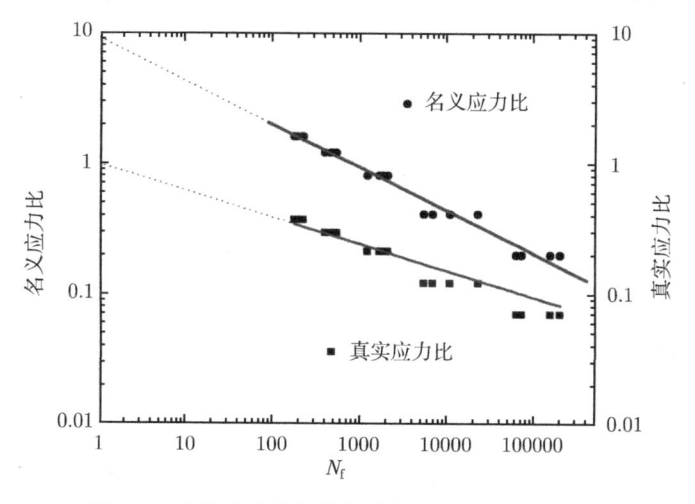

图 3.8 真实应力比与名义应力比疲劳方程的比较

由名义应力比疲劳方程 (3.6) 和真实应力比疲劳方程 (3.11) 比较可见，基于名义应力比的疲劳方程后延到 $N_f = 1$ 时 $t_m = 9.25$，名义应力比 t_m 明显大于 1；但基于真实应力比的疲劳方程后延到 $N_f = 1$ 时 $t_s = 1$，疲劳寿命为 1 次时真实应力比等于 1，对应疲劳动载强度下的一次破坏，说明真实应力比的疲劳方程可以统一重

复荷载作用下的疲劳破坏和一次荷载作用下的强度破坏，即基于真实应力比的疲劳方程不仅可以反映沥青混合料的疲劳性质，而且可以反映一次破坏的强度性质，因此基于真实应力比的疲劳方程揭示了一次荷载作用下强度破坏和重复荷载作用下疲劳破坏的内在联系。

3.5 沥青面层抗拉强度结构系数计算新方法

公路沥青路面设计规范中沥青面层抗拉强度结构系数是通过劈裂疲劳试验得到的，推荐的疲劳方程为 [7]

$$\sigma = 3.45 N_{\mathrm{f}}^{-0.22} \tag{3.12}$$

并令抗拉强度结构系数的计算式为

$$K_{\mathrm{s}} = \frac{\sigma_1}{\sigma_{\mathrm{R}}} = \frac{3.45}{3.45 N_{\mathrm{f}}^{-0.22}} = N_{\mathrm{f}}^{0.22} \tag{3.13}$$

式中，K_{s} 为抗拉强度结构系数；σ_1 为疲劳方程 (3.12) 中 $N_{\mathrm{f}} = 1$ 时的拉应力，并认为此时就是极限劈裂强度；σ_{R} 为容许拉应力，为作用 N_{f} 次疲劳破坏的拉应力，可由疲劳方程 (3.12) 计算得到。

考虑间歇时间、裂缝传播速度、交通量折减和轮迹横向分布等各种室内外试验条件的差异等因素的修正公式为

$$K_{\mathrm{s}} = 0.09 N_{\mathrm{e}}^{0.22} / A_{\mathrm{c}} \tag{3.14}$$

式中，N_{e} 为设计年限内一个方向上一个车道累计当量轴次；A_{c} 为公路等级系数。

姚祖康教授提出了公路沥青路面设计规范中抗拉强度结构系数计算存在的问题：① 将传统疲劳方程后延到 $N_{\mathrm{f}}=1$，并认为此时的拉应力就是极限劈裂强度，即式 (3.13) 中的极限劈裂强度 σ_1 为 3.45MPa，缺乏足够的论据和试验验证。而传统疲劳方程由不同名义应力比下的疲劳试验结果线性回归得到，往往有一定的适用范围。② 公路沥青路面设计规范通过上述方法将极限抗拉强度引入疲劳方程，并维持传统疲劳方程中的斜率 (−0.22) 不变。这表明，在疲劳试验过程中，混合料的极限抗拉强度是个常数，不随环境温度和加载速率变化。然而，这种情况只有采用水硬性结合料的混合料 (水泥混凝土或水泥稳定粒料等) 被试验所证实；而本章沥青混合料直接拉伸强度的速度特性试验，已证明直接拉伸强度随加载速率的不同而发生显著变化，在一定试验温度和加载速率范围内动载强度随加载速率近似呈幂函数增长规律。

针对上述问题，突破原有确定抗拉强度结构系数的思路，重新建立应用真实应力比疲劳方程确定沥青面层抗拉强度结构系数的新方法。由真实应力比疲劳

方程 $t_s = N_f^{-0.218}$ 和疲劳动载强度的定义，用应力形式表示的疲劳方程为 $\sigma = S_{dz} N_f^{-0.218}$；因为真实应力比疲劳方程可近似后延到 $N_f = 1$ 时 $t_s = 1$，当后延到疲劳寿命为 1 次时，用动载强度 S_{dz} 取代极限抗拉强度 σ_1，S_{dz} 是与疲劳试验的加载速率和温度相关的。将此特点应用到抗拉强度结构系数计算式 (3.13) 中，建立基于真实应力比疲劳方程确定沥青面层抗拉强度结构系数的新方法：

$$K_s = \frac{\sigma_1}{\sigma_R} = \frac{S_{dz}}{\sigma} = \frac{1}{t_s} = N_f^{0.218} \tag{3.15}$$

式中，K_s 为抗拉强度结构系数；原有方法中 σ_1 为 $N_f = 1$ 时的拉应力或极限抗拉强度，新方法用动载强度 S_{dz} 取代，S_{dz} 与疲劳试验的加载速率和温度相关；原方法中 σ_R 为容许拉应力，由传统疲劳方程 (3.12) 计算得到，新方法中直接用疲劳试验中拉应力水平取代，同样为作用 N_f 次疲劳破坏的拉应力；t_s 为真实应力比。

新方法提出了确定沥青面层抗拉强度结构系数的新思路，纠正了原有方法推导抗拉强度结构系数计算过程中的错误，应用真实应力比疲劳方程建立的抗拉强度结构系数计算新方法，较好地解决了前面提出的两个问题：一是通过沥青混合料直接拉伸疲劳试验数据，已验证了基于真实应力比疲劳方程可以近似后延到 $N_f = 1$ 时 $t_s = 1$；二是用动载强度 S_{dz} 取代极限抗拉强度 σ_1，动载强度 S_{dz} 是随加载速率和温度而变化的，符合沥青混合料本身的黏弹性性质。因此应用真实应力比疲劳方程建立的抗拉强度结构系数计算新方法更加合理。

参 考 文 献

[1] 公路沥青路面设计规范 (JTJ014—97) [S]. 北京：人民交通出版社，1997
[2] 公路沥青路面设计规范 (JTG D50—2006) [S]. 北京：人民交通出版社，2006
[3] 孟宪宏. 混凝土疲劳剩余强度试验及理论研究 [D]. 大连：大连理工大学，2006
[4] 公路沥青路面施工技术规范 (JTG F40—2004) [S]. 北京：人民交通出版社，2004
[5] 许金泉. 材料强度学 [M]. 上海：上海交通大学出版社，2009
[6] Pell P S. Fatigue characteristics of bitumen and bituminous mixes [J]. Proceedings, International Conference on the Structural Design of Asphalt Pavements, University of Michigan, 1962
[7] 姚祖康. 对我国沥青路面现行设计指标的评述 [J]. 公路，2003，(2): 44-49

第4章 基于刚度衰变的沥青混合料疲劳损伤模型

与疲劳断裂不同，疲劳损伤通常很难像材料内部裂纹扩展通过精确计算加以描述，而损伤力学更加关注受损物体重复荷载作用下宏观物理力学性能的衰变。最早的损伤定义由 Rabotnov 于 1963 年提出，用材料有效承载截面积减小的比例描述损伤的程度。虽然 Rabotnov 的损伤定义具有明确的物理意义，但却难以在试验过程中准确地测定有效承载截面积的减小及其演化。根据 Lemaitre 应变等效原理，假设损伤对于受损物体变形的影响只需通过有效应力来加以修正，应用本构关系有效应力等价原理，获得以模量定义的损伤变量，利用模量退化是测量损伤的方法之一，模量可在疲劳试验过程中连续测量而不会影响材料的性能[1]。

为了获得重复荷载作用下沥青混合料的损伤演化累计规律，本章重点基于刚度(模量)衰变分析沥青混合料的疲劳损伤演化、累计规律。首先介绍以刚度(模量)定义疲劳损伤变量的理论基础；其次分析单级等幅应力直接拉伸疲劳的变形特性，揭示疲劳过程中动模量衰变规律；接着计算不同应力水平下的临界疲劳损伤，提出一种能考虑临界损伤的非线性疲劳损伤修正模型，并通过直接拉伸疲劳试验数据验证模型的适用性，揭示不同应力水平下的疲劳损伤演化规律；最后通过设计两级等幅应力疲劳试验，验证沥青混合料疲劳损伤累计的非线性。

4.1 以模量定义的疲劳损伤变量

在力、温度、加载速率等因素影响下，材料内部将形成大量微细观缺陷，微缺陷的形核、扩展、汇合将造成材料逐渐劣化直至破坏，该过程即材料的损伤。为了研究材料内部微细观缺陷的特征变化引入损伤变量，以便建立较合适的损伤模型来描述受损材料的力学响应。

1963 年，著名力学家 Rabotnov 在研究金属的蠕变本构方程问题时建议用损伤因子 D 描述损伤[2]：

$$D = 1 - \frac{A'}{A} \tag{4.1}$$

式中，A' 为有效承载面积，即扣除了由于微缺陷而不能承载的部分面积后得到的面积；A 为名义面积(初始面积)，即无损状态下的面积。对于完全无损状态，$D=0$；对于完全丧失承载能力的状态，$D=1$。

将外加荷载 F 与名义面积(无损状态下的面积) A 的比值定义为名义应力 σ，

4.1 以模量定义的疲劳损伤变量

即

$$\sigma = F/A \tag{4.2}$$

式中，σ 为名义应力；A 为无损状态下的面积。

将外加荷载 F 与有效承载面积的比值定义为有效应力 σ'，即

$$\sigma' = F/A' \tag{4.3}$$

式中，σ' 为有效应力；A' 为有效承载面积。

联立式 (4.1)~ 式 (4.3)，有效应力 σ' 与损伤因子 D 的关系可表示为

$$\sigma' = \frac{\sigma}{1-D} \tag{4.4}$$

以刚度 (模量) 定义的疲劳损伤变量，是由应用最广泛的本构关系的有效应力等价原理推导而来，有效应力等价原理指出："对于任何受损材料，无论是弹性、塑性、还是黏塑性、黏弹性的，在单轴或多轴应力状态下的变形状态都可通过原始的无损材料本构定律来描述，只要在本构关系方程中用有效应力来替代寻常的名义应力即可。" 此原理在理论上未必完善，但具有简单、实用和便于工程应用等优越性。

本节沥青混合料小梁直接拉伸疲劳按弹性本构关系来考虑，根据损伤力学理论和应变等效原理 (即有效应力等价原理)，损伤后的本构关系仍可表示为

$$\varepsilon = \frac{\sigma'}{E} = \frac{\sigma}{E_0(1-D)} \tag{4.5}$$

显见式 (4.5) 中名义应力 σ 与应变 ε 的关系仍然具有胡克定律的形式，仅将弹性模量改用有效弹性模量 E 来代替，即有

$$E = E_0(1-D) \tag{4.6}$$

损伤变量可用有效弹性模量 E 和初始弹性模量 E_0 表示为

$$D = 1 - E/E_0 \tag{4.7}$$

式中，E_0 为初始动模量；E 为疲劳荷载作用 N 次后试件的动模量；D 为重复荷载作用过程中的疲劳损伤。

微分损伤本构关系式 (4.5) 得

$$\mathrm{d}\varepsilon = \frac{\mathrm{d}\sigma}{E_0(1-D)} + \frac{\sigma \mathrm{d}D}{E_0(1-D)^2} \tag{4.8}$$

由于卸载时损伤增量为零，则受损物体的有效弹性模量即为卸载模量：

$$E = \frac{\mathrm{d}\sigma}{\mathrm{d}\varepsilon} \tag{4.9}$$

在基于刚度衰变分析沥青混合料非线性疲劳损伤的过程中，选取疲劳重复荷载作用下卸载段的割线模量，即以动模量的衰变定义疲劳损伤变量。

模量可在疲劳试验过程中连续测量而不会影响材料的性能，它随着材料内部损伤的不断演化与累计而下降，因此模量是一个非常有潜力的宏观检测参数，能够描述沥青混合料疲劳全过程中的损伤状态。疲劳损伤研究的重要目的之一就是预测材料的疲劳特性，认识损伤的产生、演化及累计的过程，以便建立疲劳损伤方程，为材料疲劳寿命的计算和结构疲劳设计打下基础。

4.2 直接拉伸疲劳变形特性分析

本次试验选用 SBS 改性沥青和玄武岩配制的 AC-13 沥青混合料的小梁试件，用 MTS 试验机以应力控制方式，在 5 种应力水平 (2MPa、1.5MPa、1MPa、0.5MPa、0.25MPa)、20℃ 条件下进行直接拉伸疲劳试验，加载频率为 10Hz，加载波形为半正弦波，5 种应力水平下对应的疲劳荷载加载速率为 40MPa/s、30MPa/s、20MPa/s、10MPa/s、5MPa/s。疲劳试验加载过程中荷载控制精度较高，为了尽量减少试验中偏心的影响，在正式开始疲劳试验之前，进行了小应力水平的预压过程，并在半正弦波荷载卸载时，并不将其完全卸载为零，仍保持有 2%应力水平的拉应力 (一般为 20~100N，如此小的拉应力对疲劳试验结果的影响可以忽略)。疲劳试验数据采样频率为 204Hz，即每个周期采集 20 个点的试验数据，包括采样点的时间、荷载和位移。采样频率的确定一方面需能保证数据的精度，另一方面需便于疲劳试验数据的分析处理。如 0.5MPa 下直接拉伸疲劳加载波形见图 4.1。

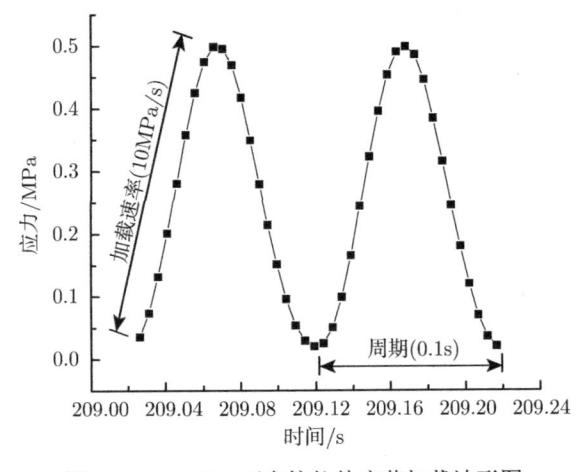

图 4.1　0.5MPa 下直接拉伸疲劳加载波形图

因刚度 (模量) 的变化用材料的应力应变关系表征，在分析疲劳过程刚度衰变

4.2 直接拉伸疲劳变形特性分析

的规律之前,需要掌握应力应变的变化规律。下面对单级等幅直接拉伸疲劳试验的变形特性的变化规律进行分析,为后续揭示模量衰变及损伤演化规律奠定基础。

4.2.1 循环应力应变滞回曲线

在交变荷载作用下,试件内产生交变的循环应力,并依据材料的本构关系,引起循环应变。在重复加卸载疲劳过程中,当材料发生应变能耗散时,加荷和卸荷时的应力应变曲线将首尾相接但具有不同的路径,由这一路径形成的封闭曲线称为滞回曲线,封闭曲线的面积代表了一定荷载状态下每一加卸荷过程中材料应变能的逸失。2MPa、1.5MPa、1MPa、0.5MPa 和 0.25MPa 五种不同应力水平下疲劳全过程的循环应力应变滞回曲线分别举例如图 4.2 所示。

由图 4.2 可见,随着循环次数的增加,循环应力应变滞回曲线朝着应变增大的方向不断蠕动,因为平均拉应力的存在产生了单向的塑性变形,即累计黏塑性应变。每一个周期半正矢波所消耗的能量可以用下式求得[3]:

$$w_i = \int_0^T \sigma(t) \cdot \varepsilon(t) \mathrm{d}t \tag{4.10}$$

式中,$\sigma(t)$、$\varepsilon(t)$ 分别为某时刻的应力、应变;T 为一个加卸载循环的周期;w_i 为每个周期的耗散能。

加载段曲线下的面积即外载对试件做功,卸载段曲线下的面积即释放的弹性能。加卸载段应力应变曲线并不重合,外载做功除了引起混合料弹性变形能的增加,还有一部分被耗散掉了,故卸载段低于加载段。每个周期滞回曲线的面积可以由 Origin 软件的积分功能计算得到,计算简单且准确。

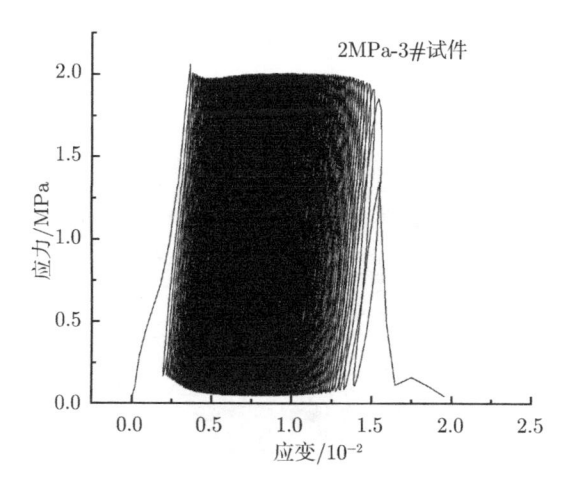

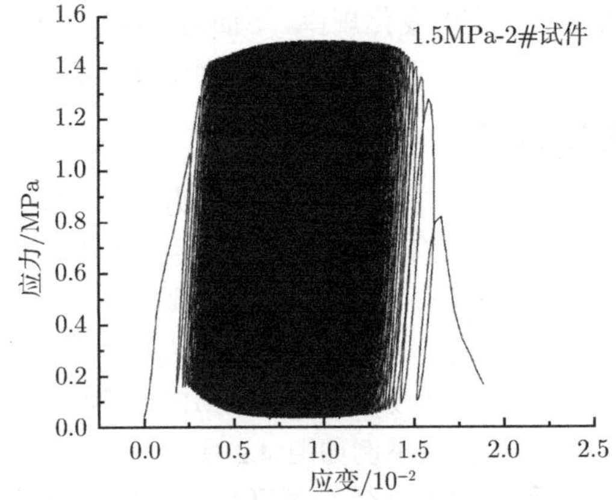
1.5MPa-2#试件
应力/MPa
应变/10⁻²
0.0
0.2
0.4
0.6
0.8
1.0
1.2
1.4
1.6
0.5
1.5
2.0
2.5

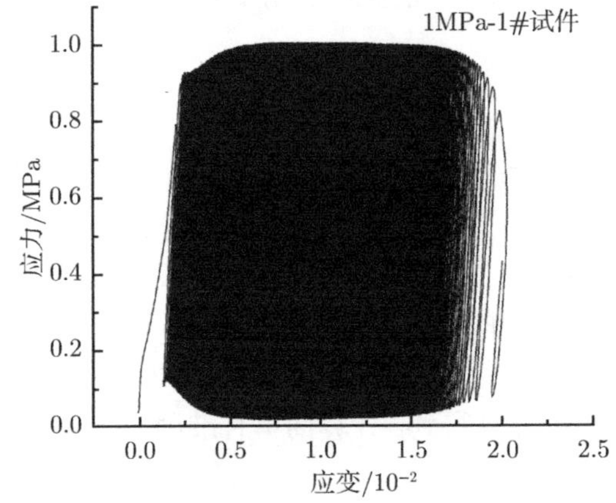
1MPa-1#试件
应力/MPa
应变/10⁻²
0.0
0.2
0.4
0.6
0.8
1.0
0.5
1.5
2.0
2.5

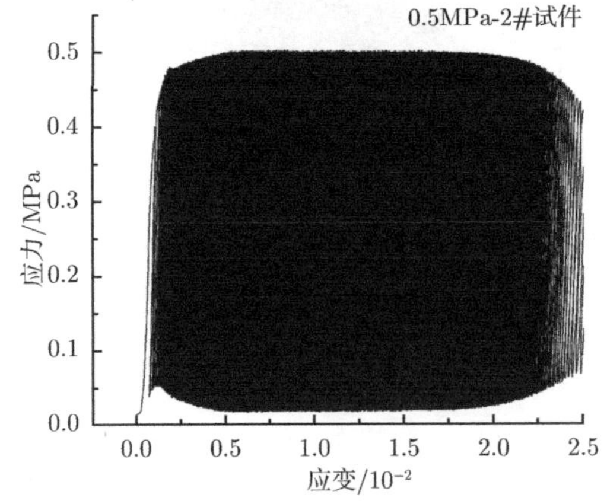
0.5MPa-2#试件
应力/MPa
应变/10⁻²
0.0
0.1
0.2
0.3
0.4
0.5
1.0
1.5
2.0
2.5

4.2 直接拉伸疲劳变形特性分析

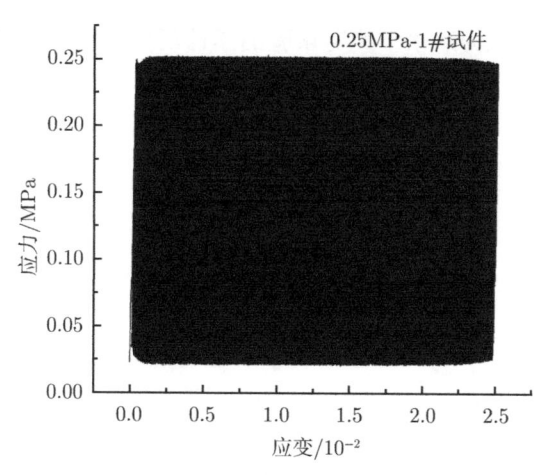

图 4.2 不同应力水平下疲劳全过程的循环应力应变滞回曲线

在整个疲劳过程中,达到破坏时的总能耗即累计耗散能 W_f 可以表示为

$$W_\mathrm{f} = \sum_{i=1}^{N_\mathrm{f}} w_i \tag{4.11}$$

式中,W_f 为达到破坏时的总能量,即累计耗散能;w_i 为每个周期的耗散能;N_f 为达到破坏时的重复荷载作用次数,即疲劳寿命。

不同应力水平下疲劳试验的累计耗散能结果汇总于表 4.1 中。

表 4.1 不同应力水平下疲劳试验的累计耗散能

σ/MPa	序号	N_f/次	W_f/kPa	σ/MPa	序号	N_f/次	W_f/kPa
0.25	1	154449	1009.8	1.5	1	552	193.6
	2	200337	1360.3		2	406	163.3
	3	61705	384.5		3	469	164.1
	4	72032	494.5				
0.5	1	6874	225.2	2	1	223	157
	2	5447	198.8		2	227	157.1
	3	22454	704.2		3	180	153.5
1	1	1817	493.6				
	2	1675	305.9				
	3	1225	170				

已有疲劳试验研究表明,疲劳寿命 N_f 与累计耗散能 W_f 在双对数坐标上具有较缓和的直线关系,即

$$W_\mathrm{f} = A N_\mathrm{f}^B \tag{4.12}$$

式中,W_f 为累计耗散能;N_f 为疲劳寿命;A、B 为疲劳试验确定的材料参数。

将表 4.1 中不同应力水平下疲劳试验的累计耗散能和疲劳寿命绘于双对数坐标中，如图 4.3 所示。

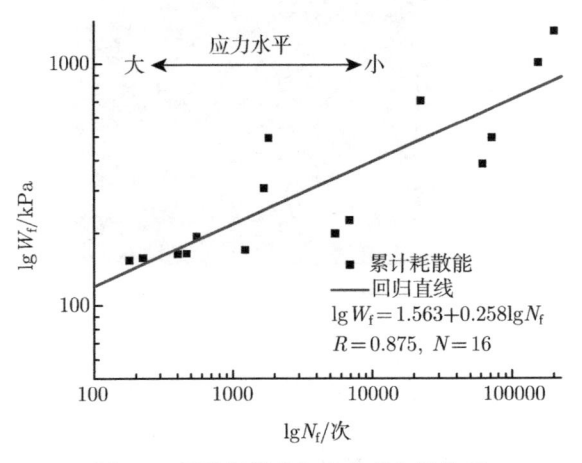

图 4.3　累计耗散能与疲劳寿命的关系

由图 4.3 可以看出，沥青混合料累计耗散能与疲劳寿命在双对数坐标中表现出较好的线性关系，对试验数据线性回归可得沥青混合料基于累计耗散能的疲劳方程如下：

$$\lg W_{\mathrm{f}} = 1.563 + 0.258 \lg N_{\mathrm{f}}$$
$$R = 0.875, \; N = 16$$

即

$$W_{\mathrm{f}} = 36.56 N_{\mathrm{f}}^{0.258} \tag{4.13}$$

已有研究基于耗散能对沥青混合料低温低频疲劳特性进行了分析，对不同老化程度沥青混合料建立了基于累计耗散能的疲劳方程，本节得到的结论与已有研究结果是一致的，累计耗散能随循环次数的增长而逐渐增大。已有研究的重点是模拟了沥青混合料的低温疲劳开裂和老化程度对疲劳的影响，而本次试验进行了几种应力水平下的疲劳试验，疲劳寿命与应力水平有关。当应力水平较大时，疲劳寿命 N_{f} 较小，这样累计耗散能 W_{f} 也较小，相反，当应力水平较小时，疲劳寿命 N_{f} 较大，疲劳破坏时能量大量逸失，累计耗散能 W_{f} 较大，沥青混合料累计耗散能 W_{f} 随疲劳寿命 N_{f} 的增加而增大。加卸载曲线之间面积的大小体现了耗散能的多少，等于总功减去其弹性变形能，该面积越大，沥青混合料对应的损伤则越多。疲劳破坏时累计耗散能并不是常量，若用耗散能定义的损伤变量来描述疲劳损伤演化规律和疲劳失效，说明临界疲劳损伤并不是定值。

4.2.2 应变随循环寿命比变化曲线

沥青混合料是典型的黏弹性材料，将加载段的每周期应变振幅 ε_i 分解为回弹应变 ε_{ei} 和黏塑性应变 ε_{vpi}，即 [4]

$$\varepsilon_i = \varepsilon_{ei} + \varepsilon_{vpi} \tag{4.14}$$

式中，ε_i 为每周期应变振幅；ε_{ei} 每周期回弹应变；ε_{vpi} 每周期黏塑性应变。

一个周期下应力、应变随时间的变化曲线如图 4.4 所示，图中给出了一个周期下加载段的应变振幅和卸载段的回弹应变。

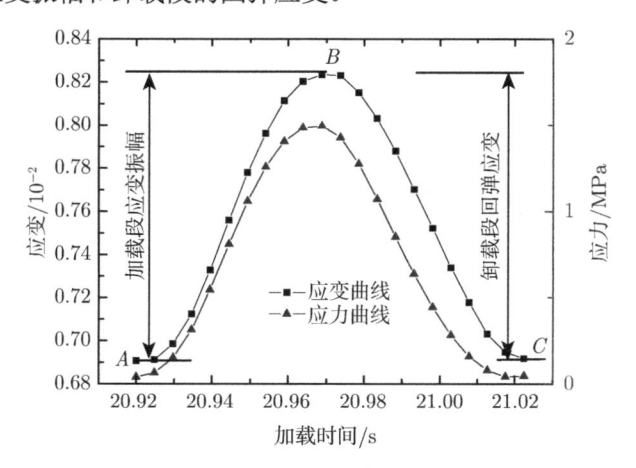

图 4.4 一个周期下应力、应变随时间的变化曲线

现以 0.5MPa 应力水平的 1#试件 (N_f=6874) 直接拉伸疲劳试验中的变形规律为例，第 6001~6010 周期和第 6601~6610 周期的变形情况汇总于表 4.2，表中第 2 列是随周期产生的位移峰值 U_{max} 即累计总变形，第 3 列是位移谷值 U_{min} 即卸载后产生的累计黏塑性变形，第 2 列峰值与第 3 列卸载后的位移谷值之差即每个周期产生的回弹变形。直接拉伸疲劳过程中沥青混合料切割试件长度 L 为 250mm，据此可以计算得到位移峰值对应的第 4 列累计总应变 ε_z (见式 (4.15))、位移谷值对应的第 5 列累计黏塑性应变 ε_c (见式 (4.16))。

$$\varepsilon_z = U_{max}/L \tag{4.15}$$

$$\varepsilon_c = U_{min}/L \tag{4.16}$$

式中，ε_z 为累计总应变；ε_c 为累计黏塑性应变；U_{max} 为位移峰值；U_{min} 为位移谷值；L 为试件长度。

第 6 列对应加载阶段的每周期应变振幅 ε_i，由同周期的累计总应变 ε_{zi} 减去前一周期的累计黏塑性应变 $\varepsilon_{c(i-1)}$ (见式 (4.17)) 得到；第 7 列对应卸载阶段的每周期

回弹应变 ε_{ei}, 由同一周期的累计总应变 ε_{zi} 减去累计黏塑性应变 ε_{ci} (见式 (4.18)) 得到; 第 8 列对应每周期下的黏塑性应变 ε_{vpi}, 由每周期加载段应变振幅 ε_i 减去回弹应变 ε_{ei} 得到 (见式 (4.19))。

$$\varepsilon_i = \varepsilon_{zi} - \varepsilon_{c(i-1)} \tag{4.17}$$

$$\varepsilon_{ei} = \varepsilon_{zi} - \varepsilon_{ci} \tag{4.18}$$

$$\varepsilon_{vpi} = \varepsilon_i - \varepsilon_{ei} \tag{4.19}$$

式中, ε_i 为每周期应变振幅; ε_{zi} 为同周期的累计总应变; $\varepsilon_{c(i-1)}$ 为前一周期的累计黏塑性应变; ε_{ci} 为同周期的累计黏塑性应变; ε_{ei} 为每周期的回弹应变; ε_{vpi} 为每周期的黏塑性应变。

表 4.2 0.5MPa-1#试件第 6001~6010 和第 6601~6610 周期的变形情况汇总

循环周期 N/次	位移峰值 $U_{\max}$/mm	位移谷值 $U_{\min}$/mm	累计总应变 $\varepsilon_z/10^{-6}$	累计黏塑性应变 $\varepsilon_c/10^{-6}$	每周期应变振幅 $\varepsilon_i/10^{-6}$	每周期回弹应变 $\varepsilon_{ei}/10^{-6}$	每周期黏塑性应变 $\varepsilon_{vpi}/10^{-6}$
6001	4.190	4.064	16760	16252	—	508	—
6002	4.193	4.063	16772	16252	520	520	0
6003	4.191	4.064	16764	16256	512	508	4
6004	4.193	4.065	16772	16260	516	512	4
6005	4.193	4.066	16772	16264	512	508	4
6006	4.195	4.067	16780	16268	516	512	4
6007	4.196	4.069	16784	16276	516	508	8
6008	4.196	4.068	16784	16272	512	512	0
6009	4.198	4.068	16792	16272	520	520	0
6010	4.198	4.070	16792	16280	520	512	8
6601	4.821	4.686	19284	18744	—	540	—
6602	4.822	4.687	19288	18748	544	540	4
6603	4.825	4.687	19300	18748	552	552	0
6604	4.826	4.690	19304	18760	556	544	12
6605	4.827	4.692	19308	18768	548	540	8
6606	4.829	4.694	19316	18776	548	540	8
6607	4.830	4.696	19320	18784	544	536	8
6608	4.831	4.694	19324	18776	548	548	0
6609	4.832	4.697	19328	18788	552	540	12
6610	4.836	4.699	19344	18796	556	548	8

图 4.5 为 0.5MPa 应力水平的 1#试件直接拉伸疲劳试验第 6001~6010 和第 6601~6610 周期的应变变化规律图。

由表 4.2 和图 4.5 可以看出, 首先在半正矢波的应力控制直接拉伸疲劳过程中拉应变变化规律也呈半正矢波变化; 第 6001~6010 周期与第 6601~6610 周期比较,

4.2 直接拉伸疲劳变形特性分析

后者比前者位移峰值和位移谷值均增加，说明随重复加载周期的增长总变形和蠕变变形都增加；且后一阶段比前者产生的回弹应变也增大，如第 6001 周期的回弹应变为 504 微应变 ($\mu\varepsilon$)，第 6601 周期的回弹应变增长为 540 微应变，即在 600 个周期后回弹应变增加了 36 微应变。最后两列计算结果说明，在重复荷载作用下每周期产生的黏塑性应变 $\varepsilon_{\mathrm{vpi}}$ 很小，直接拉伸疲劳过程中每次循环荷载产生的主要是回弹应变 $\varepsilon_{\mathrm{ei}}$。

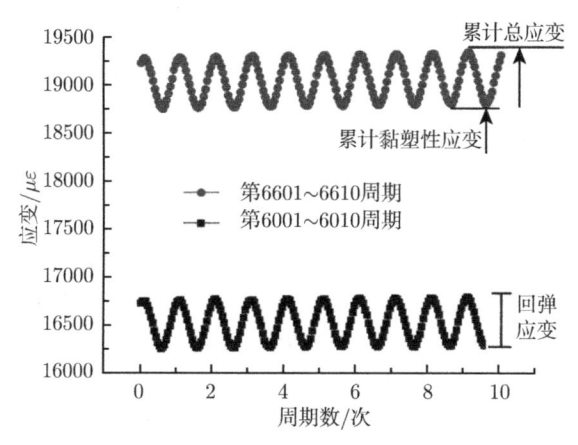

图 4.5　直接拉伸疲劳试验第 6001~6010 和第 6601~6610 周期的应变变化规律

为了便于比较不同应力水平下疲劳过程中变形特性的演化规律，将横坐标重复荷载作用次数作归一化处理，图 4.6 和图 4.7 分别示出了不同应力水平下回弹应变、黏塑性应变随寿命比 N/N_{f} 的变化规律。

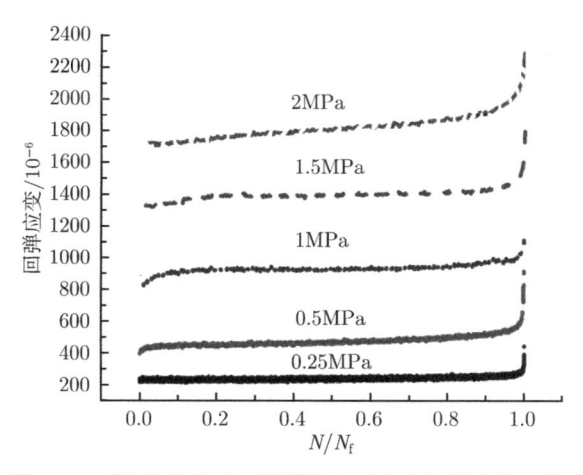

图 4.6　不同应力水平下回弹应变随寿命比的变化规律

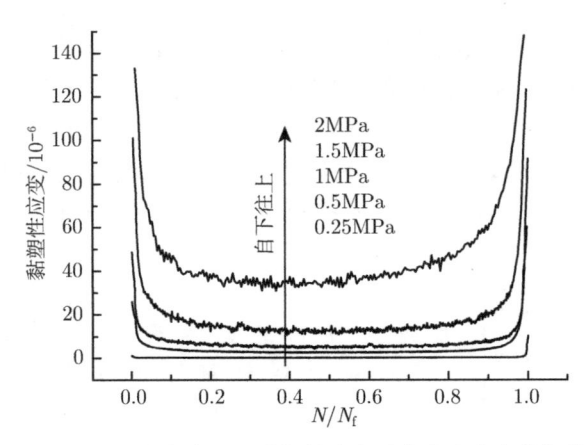

图 4.7　不同应力水平下黏塑性应变随寿命比的变化规律

由图 4.6 可以看出，自下往上从 0.25MPa 到 2MPa 应力水平越高对应的回弹应变越大；由图 4.7 可以看出，自下往上从 0.25MPa 到 2MPa 应力水平越高产生的每周期黏塑性应变也越大，每周期黏塑性应变平均值依次为 0.2 微应变、4.3 微应变、7.8 微应变、18.8 微应变和 47.2 微应变；单从某一应力水平下的变化规律来看，开始阶段每周期黏塑性应变较大，逐渐变小直至稳定，到疲劳寿命末期，每周期黏塑性应变又逐渐增大，直至疲劳破坏。应力水平大对应疲劳寿命较短，相应黏塑性应变的累计时间也比较短，在较大应力作用下容易趋于某一薄弱面产生应力集中而总变形还相对较小时便发生一次受拉强度破坏；反之，应力水平低时疲劳寿命长，相应黏塑性应变的累计时间也较长，试件变形得到充分发展，产生的总变形越大。

4.3　直接拉伸疲劳动模量衰变模型的建立

本章损伤变量定义是以模量衰变描述损伤过程，一般选择重复荷载作用过程中弹性模量的退化作为损伤演化的一个度量，在沥青混合料疲劳过程中选择卸载段的弹性模量，即动模量的衰减来定义疲劳损伤。本节主要分析直接拉伸疲劳过程中动模量衰变规律，动模量是轴向应力和可恢复轴向回弹应变的比值，可恢复回弹应变为重复荷载作用下每个周期卸载过程中产生的应变，即变形的波峰值与卸载后的波谷值的差值对应的回弹应变，如图 4.4 中 BC 段的应变值；动模量 E 的计算公式如下[5]：

$$E = \frac{\sigma}{\varepsilon_{ei}} \qquad (4.20)$$

式中，E 为动模量；σ 为疲劳试验所施加的应力水平；ε_{ei} 为每周期的回弹应变。

4.3 直接拉伸疲劳动模量衰变模型的建立

直接拉伸疲劳过程中每一周期荷载循环可以得到一个动模量值，疲劳试验数据一般比较庞大，专门利用 Matlab 软件编制了疲劳试验数据分析程序，可以方便快捷地提取到每个循环的荷载，位移的峰、谷值及对应的时间，进而计算得到每个周期的动模量，解决了以往高周期疲劳试验模量分析难的问题[6]。

4.3.1 动模量初始值的确定

目前广泛采用第 50 个荷载循环时的模量作为初始模量；然而不同应力下的疲劳寿命相差很大，从 200 次到 20 万次不等，因此按这种方法选取不尽合适。本节取疲劳寿命比 $N/N_f = 0.01$ 时的模量，考虑疲劳试验中模量数据的离散性，故取 $N/N_f = 0.01$ 附近 5 次荷载循环的平均值为动模量的初始值，将不同应力水平各平行试件的动模量初始值 E_0 汇总于表 4.3 中。

表 4.3 动模量初始值 E_0 汇总

σ/MPa	序号	N_f/次	E_0/MPa	E_0 平均值/MPa	E_0 变异系数 C_v
0.25	1	154449	1056	1080	0.02
	2	200337	1073		
	3	61705	1078		
	4	72032	1114		
0.5	1	6874	1163	1090	0.09
	2	5447	1021		
	3	22454	1085		
1	1	1817	1149	1112	0.04
	2	1675	1058		
	3	1225	1129		
1.5	1	552	1177	1199	0.02
	2	406	1200		
	3	469	1221		
2	1	223	1210	1224	0.02
	2	227	1208		
	3	180	1253		

由表 4.3 中动模量初始值变异系数可见，相同应力水平平行疲劳试验得到的初始值变异性不大；并且动模量初始值随应力水平增大而略有增大，初始值保持在 1000~1250MPa。

4.3.2 破坏时动模量的确定

因为在实际的试验测定中试件在没有完全断裂前模量不可能衰变到零，在疲劳寿命的末期总能找到模量衰变后的最小值，将不同应力水平下疲劳破坏时的动模量 E_{min} 值汇总于表 4.4，破坏时动模量 E_{min} 为试验中试件临近断裂前最后 5 次采集到的有效数据计算得到的动模量的平均值。将平行试件的疲劳寿命、动模量 $E_{\min}$ 及平均值、变异系数一并列于表 4.4 中。

表 4.4 不同应力水平下疲劳破坏时的动模量 $E_{\min}$ 值汇总

σ/MPa	序号	N_f/次	$E_{\min}$ 值/MPa	$E_{\min}$ 平均值/MPa	$E_{\min}$ 变异系数 C_v
0.25	1	154449	597	586	0.13
	2	200337	491		
	3	61705	670		
	4	72032	584		
0.5	1	6874	623	639	0.03
	2	5447	631		
	3	22454	663		
1	1	1817	842	881	0.07
	2	1675	852		
	3	1225	948		
1.5	1	552	1045	1043	0.01
	2	406	1051		
	3	469	1033		
2	1	223	1053	1077	0.02
	2	227	1074		
	3	180	1105		

疲劳破坏时动模量 $E_{\min}$ 值与应力水平有关，随应力水平增大而增大；说明应力水平较高的疲劳试验中试件还在较大的刚度(模量)时便发生疲劳破坏，也证明应力水平越大，疲劳最后一次破坏造成的刚度(模量)衰变也越大。反之，应力水平越小，疲劳最后一次破坏时造成的刚度(模量)衰变也越小。

4.3.3 动模量衰变模型的建立

图 4.8 给出了不同应力水平下动模量随寿命比的衰变规律，图中自上往下依次是应力水平 2MPa、1.5MPa、1MPa、0.5MPa 和 0.25MPa 的动模量衰变曲线。

动模量衰变大致可以分为两个阶段，第 1 阶段动模量衰变速度稳定，第 2 阶段在寿命比 90% 左右时衰变速度加快，进入急剧衰变阶段。由动模量衰变规律显见，疲劳过程中动模量的衰变并不满足线性规律，具有确定的非线性特性。为了便于比较，对模量衰变和循环寿命均进行归一化处理，应用如下与循环寿命比相关的幂函数进行动模量衰变的拟合：

$$\frac{E - E_{\min}}{E_0 - E_{\min}} = \left(1 - \frac{N}{N_f}\right)^m, \quad 0 < m < 1 \quad (4.21)$$

式中，E 为疲劳过程中的动模量；E_0 为动模量初始值；$E_{\min}$ 为疲劳破坏时动模量的最小值；N 为疲劳荷载循环次数；N_f 为疲劳寿命；m 为模量衰变规律的幂指数。

4.3 直接拉伸疲劳动模量衰变模型的建立

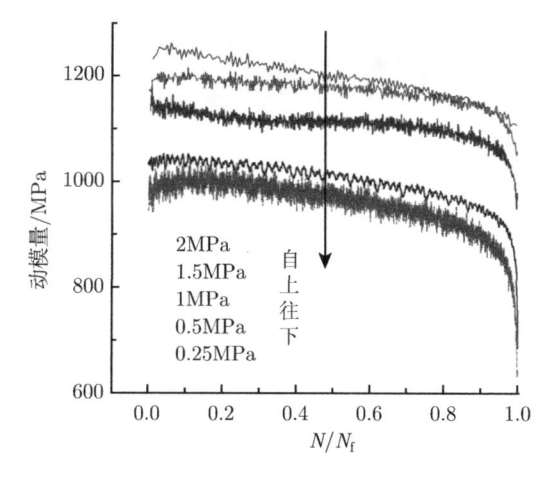

图 4.8 不同应力水平下动模量随寿命比的衰变规律

动模量初始值 E_0 表示沥青混合料疲劳的初始状态，即当 $N=0$ 时，有 $E(0)=E_0$；因为以模量衰减定义疲劳损伤时，动模量在实际试验测定时不能衰减到零，当 $N=N_f$ 时，有 $E(N_f)=E_{\min}$，$E_{\min}$ 表示为疲劳破坏时动模量的最小值，式 (4.21) 也可表示成如下动模量幂函数衰变模型：

$$E(N) = (E_0 - E_{\min})\left(1 - \frac{N}{N_f}\right)^m + E_{\min} \qquad (4.22)$$

在建立刚度衰变模型时，要能满足刚度的边界条件和刚度不断降低的规律。对动模量衰变模型的边界条件和衰变规律进行验证如下：

$$\begin{cases} E(0) = E_0 \\ E(N_f) = E_{\min} \\ \dfrac{\mathrm{d}E}{\mathrm{d}N} = (E_0 - E_{\min})m\left(1 - \dfrac{N}{N_f}\right)^{(m-1)}\left(-\dfrac{1}{N_f}\right) < 0 \\ \dfrac{\mathrm{d}^2 E}{\mathrm{d}N^2} = -(E_0 - E_{\min})\dfrac{m}{N_f}(m-1)\left(1 - \dfrac{N}{N_f}\right)^{(m-2)}\left(-\dfrac{1}{N_f}\right) < 0 \end{cases} \qquad (4.23)$$

经验证，动模量幂函数衰变模型 (4.23) 满足边界条件和随疲劳次数增大而减小的规律，且二阶导数小于零，说明该模型反映了动模量衰变的非线性特征。

采用式 (4.21) 对不同应力水平下动模量随寿命比的衰变曲线进行拟合，0.25MPa、0.5MPa、1MPa、1.5MPa 和 2MPa 五种不同应力水平拟合结果分别举例如图 4.9 所示，拟合动模量幂函数衰变模型参数 m 汇总于表 4.5 中。

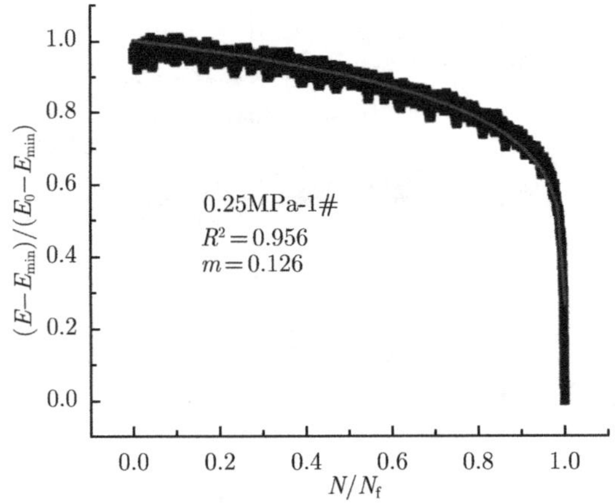
0.25MPa-1#
$R^2=0.956$
$m=0.126$
$(E-E_{min})/(E_0-E_{min})$
N/N_f
0.0
0.2
0.4
0.6
0.8
1.0

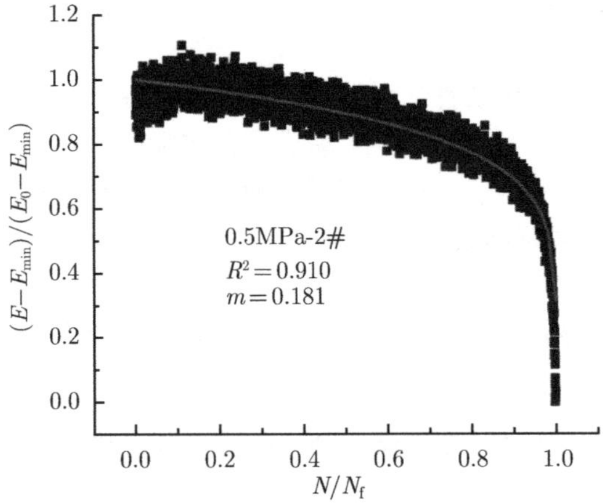
0.5MPa-2#
$R^2=0.910$
$m=0.181$
$(E-E_{min})/(E_0-E_{min})$
N/N_f
0.0
0.2
0.4
0.6
0.8
1.0
1.2

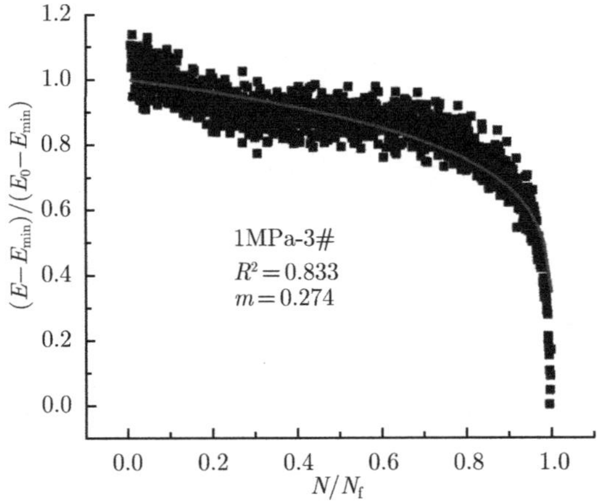
1MPa-3#
$R^2=0.833$
$m=0.274$
$(E-E_{min})/(E_0-E_{min})$
N/N_f
0.0
0.2
0.4
0.6
0.8
1.0
1.2

4.3 直接拉伸疲劳动模量衰变模型的建立

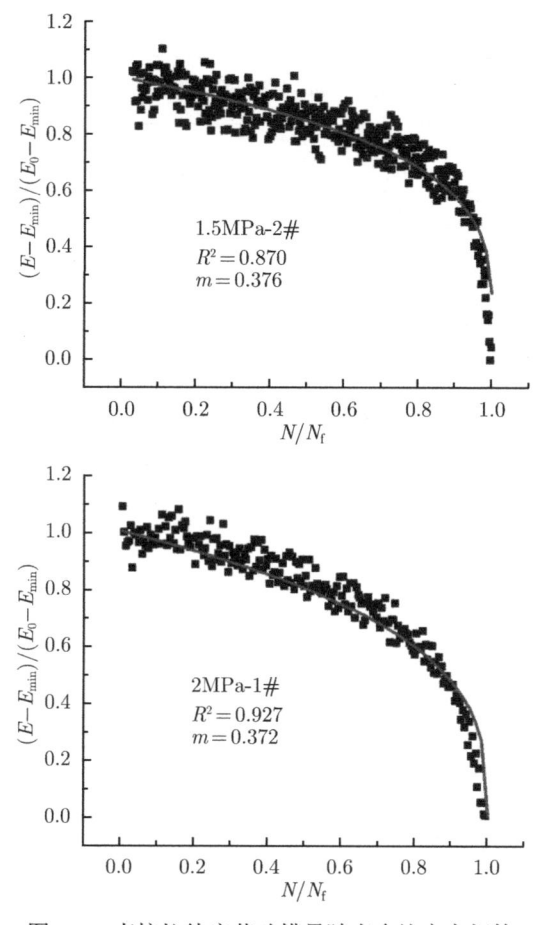

图 4.9 直接拉伸疲劳动模量随寿命比衰变规律

表 4.5 拟合动模量幂函数衰变模型参数 m 汇总表

σ/MPa	名义应力比 t_m	序号	N_f/次	m	m 平均值	m 标准偏差	m 变异系数	R^2
0.25	0.20	1	154449	0.126	0.121	0.015	0.124	0.956
		2	200337	0.104				0.706
		3	61705	0.115				0.737
		4	72032	0.139				0.835
0.5	0.41	1	6874	0.169	0.179	0.010	0.054	0.950
		2	5447	0.181				0.910
		3	22454	0.188				0.896
1	0.81	1	1867	0.239	0.260	0.018	0.071	0.736
		2	1675	0.266				0.752
		3	1225	0.274				0.833

续表

σ/MPa	名义应力比 t_m	序号	N_f/次	m	m 平均值	m 标准偏差	m 变异系数	R^2
1.5	1.22	1	552	0.369				0.758
		2	406	0.376	0.392	0.033	0.085	0.870
		3	469	0.430				0.942
2	1.63	1	223	0.372				0.927
		2	227	0.420	0.451	0.099	0.219	0.923
		3	180	0.562				0.959

由图 4.9 及表 4.5 可见，采用幂函数的衰变模型与试验数据拟合得很好，相关系数 R 也较高；动模量衰变参数 m 随应力水平增大而增大，随应力水平增大动模量也衰变得越快。通过将不同应力水平均除以准静载强度进行无量纲化处理，m 值与名义应力比 t_m 的关系绘于图 4.10 中。

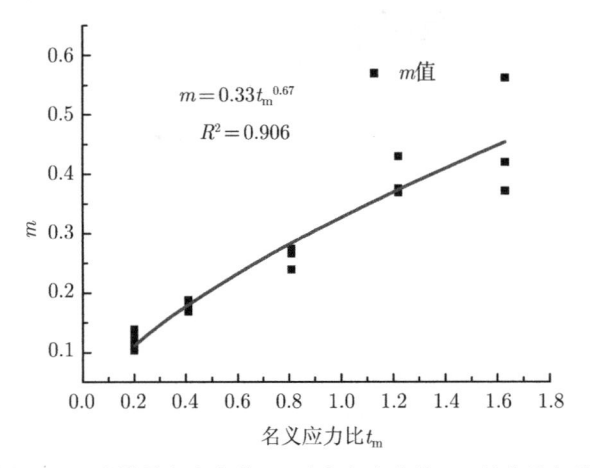

图 4.10 动模量衰变参数 m 随名义应力比 t_m 的变化规律

由图 4.10 可见，动模量衰变参数 m 随名义应力比增大而增大，将两者按幂函数增长规律拟合，获得如下回归方程：

$$m = 0.33 t_m^{0.67}, \quad R^2 = 0.906 \tag{4.24}$$

4.4 基于刚度衰变的疲劳损伤模型的建立

无论是以模量、剩余强度，还是以有效应力、应变幅值变化度量疲劳损伤，这些物理量在实际的实验测定中材料在没有完全断裂前均不可能衰变到零，在试件断裂前存在一累计疲劳损伤临界值，将该临界疲劳损伤表示为 D_c，本节首先基于模量定义的损伤变量计算临界疲劳损伤，并进而提出考虑临界疲劳损伤的修正模型。

4.4.1 临界疲劳损伤的计算

通过对疲劳破坏全过程的分析,整个疲劳破坏过程分为两个阶段,即第一阶段为循环荷载下的疲劳损伤累计过程,第二阶段为最后一次加载的强度破坏过程,即疲劳损伤累计阶段和强度破坏阶段;材料所受到的全部损伤中包含两部分,一部分是疲劳损伤 D_p,另一部分是最后强度破坏造成的损伤 D_q,如图 4.11 所示。当疲劳次数达到 $N_f - 1$ 次时,材料承载能力大为降低;从而当第 N_f 次荷载作用时,材料在应力控制的疲劳试验中,荷载应力幅值 σ 在大于或等于材料承载能力的情况下便发生一次受拉强度破坏。D_p 和 D_q 成因不同,D_p 是重复荷载作用下由疲劳作用造成的损伤累计,损伤增加速度较慢,而 D_q 是强度一次作用下造成的材料破坏,表现为损伤急剧增加,达到破坏时总损伤度极限值 1;D_p 和 D_q 损伤或缺陷的分布"形态"也不同,D_p 表现为在较大的范围内的较均匀分布,而 D_q 则表现为在某一局部的高密度分布 [7]。

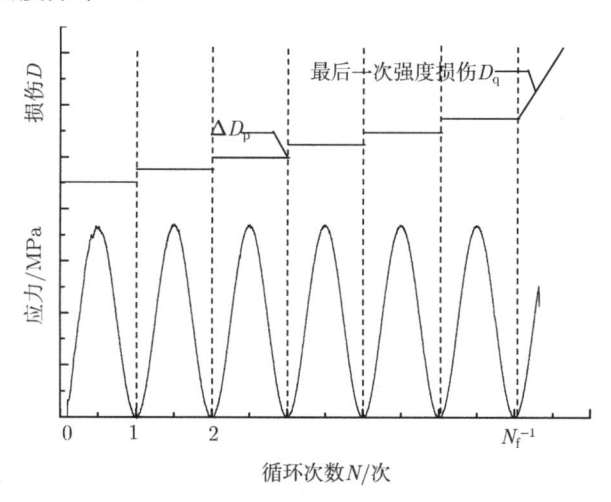

图 4.11 疲劳损伤全过程示意图

临界损伤是疲劳破坏与否的判据。无论荷载 (或损伤) 历程如何,当且仅当疲劳损伤达到一个固定的临界值时发生疲劳破坏。如常用的最简单的 Miner 线性损伤理论,即定义临界损伤为 1,当疲劳次数 N 等于疲劳寿命 N_f 时损伤也等于 1。但事实远非如此,在断裂力学中,用应力强度因子 $K(\sigma, a)$ 作为强度参量,这里包括两个参数:应力 σ 和裂纹长度 a,判据是当应力强度因子 K 达到其临界值 K_c 时失效。这意味着是否发生破坏由两个量 (σ 和 a) 共同决定,一个表示外因 (应力水平 σ),另一个表示内因 (裂纹长度 a,相当于损伤力学中的损伤状态)[8,9]。通过循环应力应变滞回曲线分析也发现累计耗散能并不是常量,而是与应力水平有关。

说明如果用耗散能定义损伤变量,得到的临界损伤也并不是固定值。

由于在不同条件下发生破坏时有不同的临界损伤,所以研究损伤临界值的规律及其影响因素,对于准确预测失效是很有意义的。用基于动模量定义的疲劳损伤变量,得到临界疲劳损伤计算公式为

$$D_{cf} = 1 - \frac{E_{min}}{E_0} \tag{4.25}$$

式中,D_{cf} 为基于动模量定义损伤变量的疲劳损伤临界值;E_0 为动模量初始值;E_{min} 为破坏时动模量值。

按照式 (4.26) 计算 0.25MPa、0.5MPa、1MPa、1.5MPa 和 2MPa 五种不同应力水平下的临界疲劳损伤,以动模量定义的临界损伤计算结果汇总于表 4.6 中。

表 4.6 不同应力水平动模量定义的临界疲劳损伤计算结果汇总

σ/MPa	名义应力比 t_m	$1-t_s$	序号	N_f/次	临界疲劳损伤 D_{cf}	D_{cf} 平均值	D_{cf} 变异系数
0.25	0.20	0.93	1	154449	0.435	0.458	0.151
			2	200337	0.542		
			3	61705	0.378		
			4	72032	0.476		
0.5	0.41	0.878	1	6874	0.464	0.412	0.111
			2	5447	0.382		
			3	22454	0.389		
1	0.81	0.787	1	1867	0.146	0.167	0.149
			2	1675	0.195		
			3	1225	0.160		
1.5	1.22	0.706	1	552	0.112	0.130	0.166
			2	406	0.124		
			3	469	0.154		
2	1.63	0.63	1	223	0.130	0.120	0.079
			2	227	0.111		
			3	180	0.118		

由第 2 章中真实应力比的概念,即在疲劳试验中应力水平与动载强度的比值,该动载强度在无损试件初始状态下得到,对应的真实应力比也即初始真实应力比。在重复荷载作用下,材料的承载能力不断下降,疲劳损伤的本质即体现为材料的强度的衰变,当强度衰变到与加载应力水平相等时,材料便发生强度破坏。按强度定义的损伤 $D = 1 - S/S_0$,当强度 S 衰变到等于应力水平 σ 时,即有临界损伤为

$$D_{cs} = 1 - \sigma/S_0 = 1 - t_s \tag{4.26}$$

式中,D_{cs} 为基于强度定义损伤变量的疲劳损伤临界值;t_s 为初始真实应力比;S_0

4.4 基于刚度衰变的疲劳损伤模型的建立

为初始动载强度；σ 为相应应力水平。

根据损伤变量的定义，基于强度的临界疲劳损伤计算结果即为 $1-t_s$，$1-t_s$ 在表 4.6 第 3 列中已给出，现将以动模量定义的临界疲劳损伤和以强度定义的临界疲劳损伤随真实应力比的变化规律均绘于图 4.12 中。

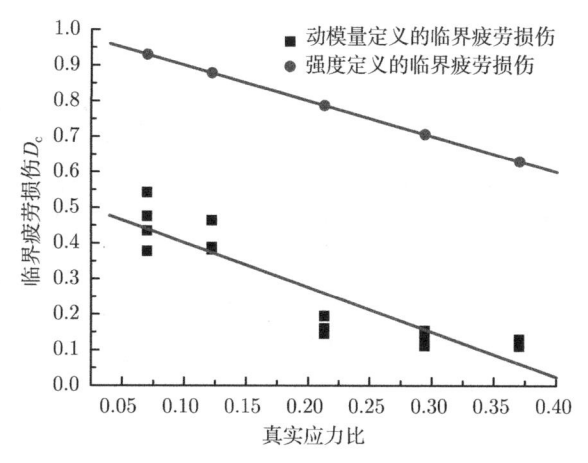

图 4.12 临界疲劳损伤随真实应力比的变化规律

考虑以动载强度定义的临界损伤与真实应力比满足线性关系，因此对以动模量定义计算得到的临界疲劳损伤与真实应力比也按线性关系回归，得到线性方程如下：

$$D_{cf} = 0.53 - 1.26t_s, \quad R = 0.911 \tag{4.27}$$

式中，D_{cf} 为基于动模量定义损伤变量的疲劳损伤临界值；t_s 为真实应力比。

临界疲劳损伤相当于最后一次疲劳之前的累计损伤值，临界损伤随真实应力比增大而减小，并较好地满足线性规律衰减。按照损伤力学的观点，材料在破坏时总损伤度极限值为 1；随着应力水平的增大，材料损伤更容易趋于在某一薄弱面上的集中分布，当材料内部的承载能力等于或小于此应力水平对应的外部荷载时，试件将在此外部荷载作用下一次被拉断，因而产生较大的一次强度损伤；并且由于应力水平的增大，疲劳寿命减小，产生的疲劳损伤较小，疲劳损伤得不到充分发展，即在应力水平较大条件下疲劳损伤临界值也相应较小。

但是，通过将基于强度定义和基于动模量定义计算的临界疲劳损伤值进行对比，发现动模量定义的临界损伤与强度定义的相差较大，动模量定义的临界损伤回归直线明显位于强度定义的临界损伤回归直线的下方，动模量定义的临界损伤明显要小于强度定义的临界损伤；由极值的大小也可以发现，强度定义的临界损伤极大值为 1，而动模量定义计算的临界损伤极大值仅为 0.53；以动模量定义的损伤变量描述材料损伤的合理性有待进一步的完善。

4.4.2 疲劳损伤修正模型的提出及验证

随着荷载循环次数的增加,损伤逐渐累计。目前最简单的疲劳损伤模型是 Miner 线性疲劳损伤模型,其疲劳损伤演化描述为

$$D = N/N_{\rm f} \tag{4.28}$$

如果损伤演化不仅依赖于 $N/N_{\rm f}$,而且与荷载的循环参数 (应力幅 $\Delta\sigma$,平均应力 $\bar{\sigma}$) 相关,即损伤与表示荷载的参数不是独立的变量,则应该采用损伤的非线性累计方法。疲劳损伤的非线性包括累计非线性和演化非线性两方面:通过两级荷载试验,显然有 $n_1/N_{\rm f1} + n_2/N_{\rm f2} \neq 1$,后续沥青混合料两级荷载疲劳试验已证明损伤累计非线性;在分析单级应力疲劳模量衰变规律时可发现其为非线性衰变过程,按前述用模量来定义损伤变量,即可显见损伤演化也为非线性;因此沥青混合料疲劳损伤演化并不满足线性规律,具有非线性特征。

在考虑应力幅值影响情况下,Chaboche 提出的一种常用的非线性疲劳损伤演化方程为 [10]

$$\frac{{\rm d}D}{{\rm d}N} = \left(\frac{\Delta\sigma}{2B(1-D)}\right)^{\beta}(1-D)^{-\gamma} \tag{4.29}$$

式中,B,β 和 γ 为与温度、应力幅值等相关的材料参数;B 还依赖于平均应力 $\bar{\sigma}$,$B = B(\bar{\sigma})$。对上式分离变量积分可导出损伤随循环次数变化的关系式:

$$(1-D)^{\beta+\gamma}{\rm d}D = \left(\frac{\Delta\sigma}{2B}\right)^{\beta}{\rm d}N, \quad 1-D = \left[1-(\beta+\gamma+1)\left(\frac{\Delta\sigma}{2B}\right)^{\beta}N\right]^{\frac{1}{\beta+\gamma+1}} \tag{4.30}$$

$$D(N) = 1 - \left(1 - \frac{N}{N_{\rm f}}\right)^{\frac{1}{\beta+\gamma+1}} \tag{4.31}$$

式中,疲劳寿命 $N_{\rm f}$ 的表达式为

$$N_{\rm f}(\Delta\sigma,\bar{\sigma}) = \frac{1}{\beta+\gamma+1}\left[\frac{\Delta\sigma}{2B(\bar{\sigma})}\right]^{-\beta} \tag{4.32}$$

式 (4.31) 中当 $N = N_{\rm f}$ 时,临界损伤 $D_{\rm c} = 1$;但是由临界疲劳损伤分析可知,无论是基于动模量定义损伤变量,还是基于强度定义损伤变量计算的临界疲劳损伤均不等于 1,不同应力水平下临界损伤均不同,临界损伤随应力水平增大而减小,临界损伤与真实应力比较好地呈线性减小的关系;因此有必要对以损伤力学为基础建立的非线性疲劳损伤模型进行修正,考虑临界疲劳损伤的影响。下面从以动模量为损伤变量的定义出发,结合动模量幂函数衰变模型,建立如下基于动模量衰变

4.4 基于刚度衰变的疲劳损伤模型的建立

的非线性疲劳损伤修正模型:

$$\begin{aligned} D_{\rm f}(N) &= 1 - \frac{E}{E_0} = 1 - \frac{(E_0 - E_{\min})(1 - N/N_{\rm f})^m + E_{\min}}{E_0} \\ &= \left(1 - \frac{E_{\min}}{E_0}\right)\left[1 - \left(1 - \frac{N}{N_{\rm f}}\right)^m\right] \\ &= D_{\rm cf}\left[1 - \left(1 - \frac{N}{N_{\rm f}}\right)^m\right] \end{aligned} \quad (4.33)$$

式中,$D_{\rm f}$ 为基于刚度 (动模量) 定义的疲劳损伤;$D_{\rm cf}$ 为临界疲劳损伤;m 为疲劳损伤模型拟合参数;N 为疲劳循环次数;$N_{\rm f}$ 为疲劳寿命。

疲劳损伤修正模型式 (4.33) 与 Chaboche 提出的疲劳损伤模型式 (4.31) 相比的先进性是修正模型可以考虑临界损伤,当 $N = N_{\rm f}$ 时,临界损伤为 $D_{\rm cf}$;该修正模型结合了动模量的幂函数衰变规律,并且修正模型中的参数 m 与动模量幂函数衰变模型的参数 m 是一致的。

下面通过不同应力水平下的疲劳试验获得的原始数据,验证本节提出的非线性疲劳损伤修正模型式 (4.33)。因为临界损伤随应力水平而变化,拟合前对非线性模型式 (4.33) 左边作归一化处理,以 4.4.1 节中计算得到的疲劳损伤临界值为标准,将疲劳过程中的损伤均除以该损伤临界值,即为 $D(N)/D_{\rm cf}$;对疲劳循环次数也作归一化处理,$N/N_{\rm f}$ 即为循环寿命比;分别为图 4.13 中的纵坐标和横坐标。作如此处理后可更清晰地了解疲劳损伤随寿命比的变化规律,并且可更方便、更容易地比较不同应力水平、不同寿命的疲劳损伤变化规律。将式 (4.33) 变化为

$$\frac{D(N)}{D_{\rm cf}} = 1 - \left(1 - \frac{N}{N_{\rm f}}\right)^m \quad (4.34)$$

$D_{\rm cf}$ 为破坏前对应的临界疲劳损伤,没有包含疲劳过程中最后一次强度破坏造成的强度损伤。采用式 (4.34) 对不同应力水平下基于动模量的衰变疲劳损伤 $D(N)/D_{\rm cf}$ 随寿命比的演化曲线进行验证,0.25MPa、0.5MPa、1MPa、1.5MPa 和 2MPa 五种不同应力水平验证结果分别举例见图 4.13,图中由密集的疲劳试验数据点形成了一定宽度较粗的数据带,数据带中有一根较细的实线,该实线由非线性疲劳修正模型式 (4.35) 所绘得,其中模型参数 m 与拟合动模量衰变规律时确定的参数一致。

由图 4.13 可看出,通过验证提出的非线性疲劳损伤修正模型与疲劳试验原始数据吻合得很好;疲劳损伤演化随寿命比变化明显具有非线性特性,揭示了沥青混合料非线性疲劳损伤演化规律。为了比较不同应力水平下的直接拉伸疲劳损伤率演化规律,用动模量衰变拟合得到的表 4.5 中 m 的平均值,将不同应力水平下直接拉伸疲劳损伤率随寿命比的演化规律汇总于图 4.14 中。

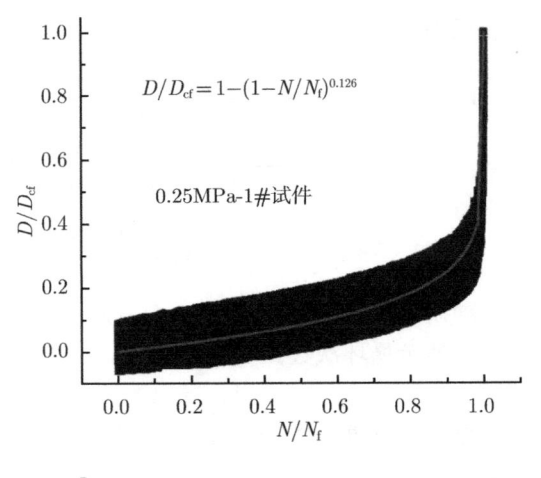

$D/D_{cf} = 1-(1-N/N_f)^{0.126}$

0.25MPa-1#试件

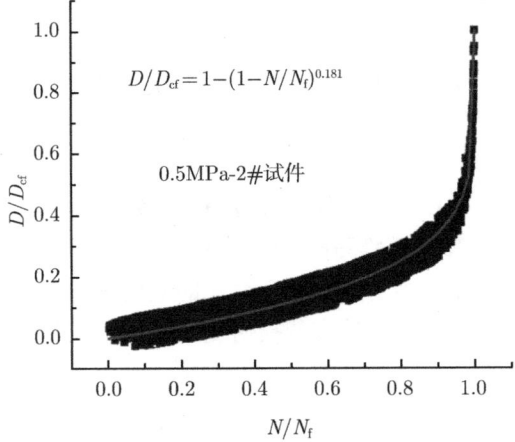

$D/D_{cf} = 1-(1-N/N_f)^{0.181}$

0.5MPa-2#试件

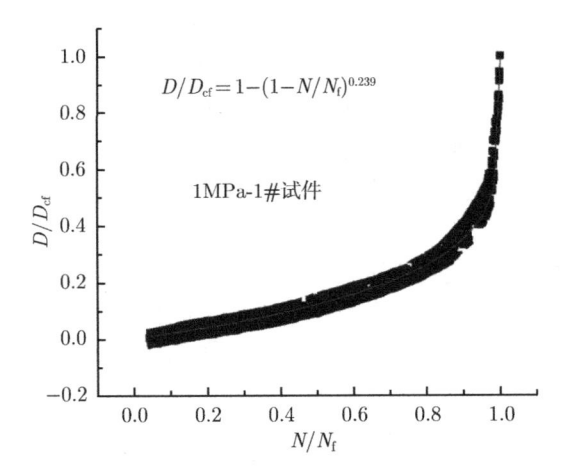

$D/D_{cf} = 1-(1-N/N_f)^{0.239}$

1MPa-1#试件

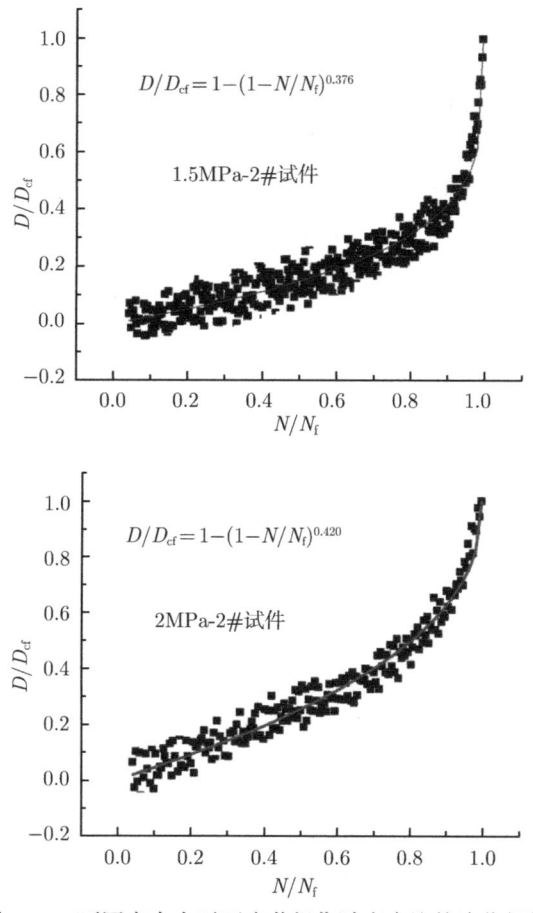

图 4.13 不同应力水平下疲劳损伤随寿命比的演化规律

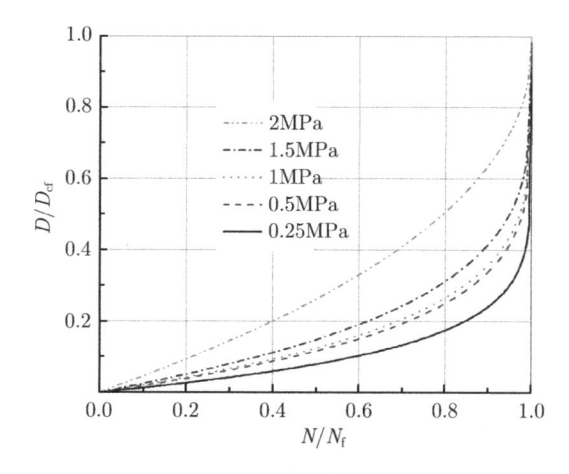

图 4.14 不同应力水平下直接拉伸疲劳损伤率随寿命比的演化规律汇总

由图 4.14 可以看出：不同应力水平疲劳损伤率的演化规律表现为损伤率的增加随寿命比开始阶段增长比较缓慢，随着寿命比的增大，损伤率增长的速度越来越快，特别是寿命比的后期增速急剧增加。图中自下往上分别为 0.25MPa、0.5MPa、1MPa、1.5MPa 和 2MPa 的损伤率演化曲线，随应力水平增大损伤率也增长得越快；不同应力水平相同寿命比作用后，应力水平越大所造成的损伤率越大，这个损伤率是指破坏前的疲劳损伤的比率，即当前损伤与临界疲劳损伤 D_c 的比值，不包括最后一次强度破坏造成的强度损伤。

由前面获得的动模量衰变幂指数 m 和临界疲劳损伤 D_c 的回归公式，将式 (4.24) 和式 (4.27) 代入修正模型式 (4.33) 得到如下非线性疲劳损伤演化方程：

$$\begin{aligned} D_f(N) &= D_{cf}\left[1-\left(1-\frac{N}{N_f}\right)^m\right] \\ &= (0.53-1.26t_s)\left[1-\left(1-\frac{N}{N_f}\right)^{0.33\cdot t_m^{0.67}}\right] \end{aligned} \quad (4.35)$$

式中，t_s 为真实应力比；t_m 为名义应力比；其余参数意义与式 (4.33) 相同。

由真实应力比 t_s 和名义应力比 t_m 的定义，二者均可以用应力水平 σ 来表示。联立式 (4.2)~ 式 (4.4)，可以求得真实应力比的应力表达式 (见式 (4.36)) 和名义应力比的应力表达式 (见式 (4.37))。

$$t_s = \frac{\sigma}{S_{dz}} = \frac{\sigma}{2.583v^{0.2}} = \frac{\sigma}{2.583(2f\cdot\sigma)^{0.2}} = 0.213\sigma^{0.8} \quad (4.36)$$

式中，t_s 为真实应力比；S_{dz} 为动载强度；σ 为应力水平；v 为疲劳加载速率；f 为疲劳加载频率，本次疲劳试验为 10Hz。

$$t_m = \frac{\sigma}{S_j} = \frac{\sigma}{1.228} = 0.814\sigma \quad (4.37)$$

式中，t_m 为名义应力比；σ 为应力水平；S_j 为静载强度。

将以上两式代入式 (4.35) 中得到关于应力水平的非线性疲劳损伤演化方程：

$$\begin{aligned} D_f(N) &= (0.53-1.26t_s)\left[1-\left(1-\frac{N}{N_f}\right)^{0.33\cdot t_m^{0.67}}\right] \\ &= (0.53-0.27\sigma^{0.8})\left[1-\left(1-\frac{N}{N_f}\right)^{0.29\cdot\sigma^{0.67}}\right] \end{aligned} \quad (4.38)$$

按式 (4.38) 用 Origin7.5 软件绘图工具将不同应力水平疲劳损伤随寿命比的演化规律绘于图 4.15 中，并给出 (0.9~1) 寿命比的局部放大图 4.16。

4.4 基于刚度衰变的疲劳损伤模型的建立

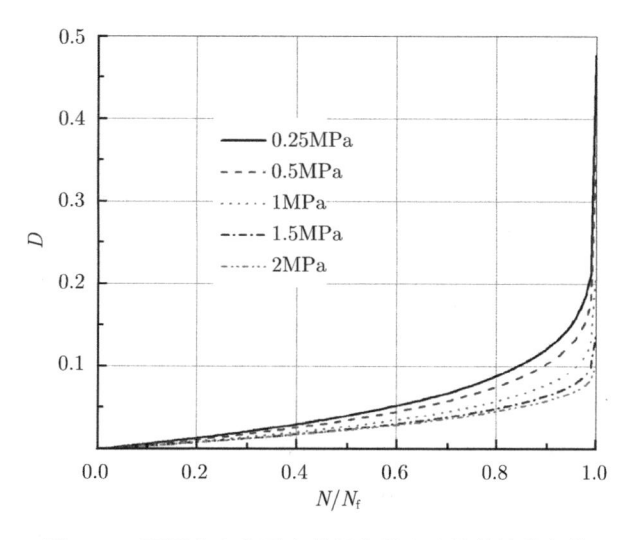

图 4.15 不同应力水平疲劳损伤随寿命比的演化规律

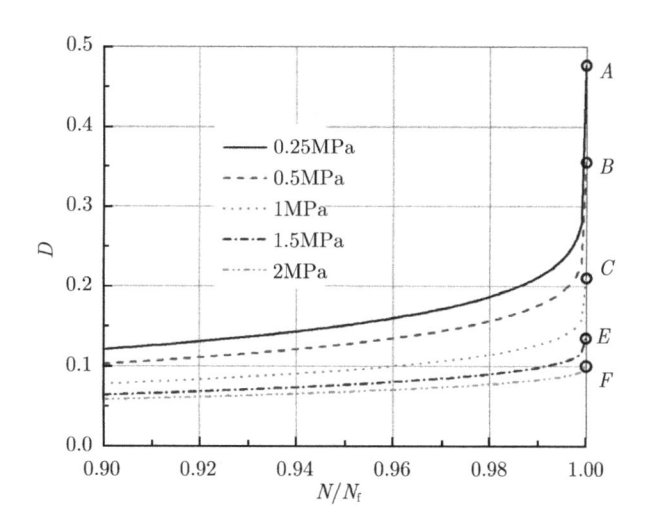

图 4.16 不同应力水平疲劳损伤随寿命比的演化规律局部放大图

由图 4.15 和图 4.16 可以看出：不同应力水平下疲劳损伤演化规律为在寿命比开始阶段损伤缓慢增长，随着寿命比的增大损伤增长的速度逐渐加快，特别是寿命比的后期增速急剧增加。比较图 4.15 和图 4.14 发现，纵坐标为损伤 D 的图 4.15 中自下往上分别为 2MPa、1.5MPa、1MPa、0.5MPa 和 0.25MPa 的疲劳损伤演化曲线，应力水平越大损伤演化曲线越靠下，与图 4.14 中纵坐标为损伤率 D/D_{cf} 演化曲线的应力水平排列顺序刚好相反，其原因是两图中的纵坐标不同，图 4.14 中

的纵坐标为损伤率 D/D_{cf}，而图 4.15 的纵坐标为疲劳损伤 D，并且不同应力水平下的临界疲劳损伤不同；由局部放大图 4.16 也说明，A、B、C、E 和 F 点分别为 0.25MPa、0.5MPa、1MPa、1.5MPa 和 2MPa 临界疲劳损伤，局部放大图上的交点再次说明应力水平越大临界疲劳损伤越小，应力水平越大最后一次疲劳造成的强度损伤越大，也正是临界损伤的影响使得两个图中的曲线随应力水平的排列顺序正好相反。

4.5 疲劳损伤非线性累计的试验验证

目前沥青混合料估计疲劳损伤时广泛采用 Miner 线性理论，Miner 理论不仅认为疲劳损伤演化过程为线性的，而且在多级加载情况下，疲劳损伤累计也是线性的，它认为任意交换荷载次序对疲劳寿命或损伤累计没有影响；然而实际上加载次序对疲劳寿命的影响很大，对此其他材料 (如金属、水泥混凝土等) 已进行了大量的二级或多级加载的疲劳试验证实这一观点。在沥青混合料的疲劳损伤特性已有研究中，还很少见有这方面的试验报道。为了分析荷载次序对沥青混合料疲劳寿命或损伤的影响，设计了两级荷载条件下疲劳试验，并对试验结果进行分析。前面损伤分析时试验数据显见损伤演化具有确定的非线性，下面通过两级荷载试验验证累计的非线性。

4.5.1 两级荷载疲劳试验设计

选用 1MPa 和 0.25MPa 两级荷载进行疲劳试验，加载频率均为 10Hz，温度为 20°C，仍采用小梁直接拉伸疲劳，原材料和配合比设计均与第 2 章中的疲劳试验相同。首先分别进行两种单级等幅应力下的疲劳试验，分别获得 0.25MPa 下的平均疲劳寿命为 N_{f1}=122131 次，1MPa 下的平均疲劳寿命为 N_{f2}=1719 次；接着进行两级荷载作用下疲劳试验。按低到高的加载顺序先施加第一级低荷载 0.25MPa 重复作用 N_1=24426 次 (20%N_{f1})；然后作用第二级荷载 1MPa 直至试件破坏，可得到第二级剩余荷载作用次数 N_2。在按高到低的加载顺序先施加第一级高荷载 1MPa 重复作用 N_2 次，N_2 取按低到高加载顺序时第二级荷载下的剩余寿命的平均值，N_2=820 次 (47.7%N_{f2}) 为低到高加载时剩余寿命 N_2 的平均值；然后作用第二级低荷载 0.25MPa 直至试件破坏，可得到第二级剩余荷载作用次数 N_1。根据应用广泛的"损伤等效状态"假定存在，那么可以认为第一级荷载 0.25MPa 重复作用 N_1 次与荷载 1MPa 重复作用 $(N_{f2} - N_2)$ 次能达到相同的损伤量。根据得到的循环比 $(N_1/N_{f1}+N_2/N_{f2})$ 与 1 的关系，如果两者之和等于 1 则认为疲劳损伤累计属于线性，不等于 1 则认为疲劳损伤累计属于非线性。按照以上两级荷载下的试验方案将疲劳寿命结果汇总于表 4.7 中。

4.5 疲劳损伤非线性累计的试验验证

表 4.7　两级荷载疲劳寿命结果

加载顺序	N_{f1}	N_{f2}	N_1	N_2	$N_1/N_{f1}+N_2/N_{f2}$
低到高 0.25~1MPa	122131	1719	24426(20% N_{f1})	907(53% N_{f2})	0.73
				866(50% N_{f2})	0.70
				687(40% N_{f2})	0.60
高到低 1~0.25MPa	122131	1719	89345(73.2% N_{f1})	820 (47.7% N_{f2})	1.21
			78449(64.2% N_{f1})		1.12
			84042(68.8% N_{f1})		1.17

注：以 1 为下标的 N_1、N_{f1} 对应 0.25MPa 下的疲劳次数；以 2 为下标的 N_2、N_{f2} 对应 1MPa 下的疲劳次数。

4.5.2　两级荷载疲劳试验结果分析

从两级荷载疲劳试验结果可知，无论是从低到高还是从高到低的加载顺序，循环比 $N_1/N_{f1}+N_2/N_{f2}$ 均不等于 1，因此说明沥青混合料疲劳损伤累计属于非线性，其损伤累计受到加载次序的影响。试验结果表明：从低应力水平 0.25MPa 到高应力水平 1MPa 加载时，$N_1/N_{f1}+N_2/N_{f2}<1$；而从高应力水平 1MPa 到低应力水平 0.25MPa 加载时，$N_1/N_{f1}+N_2/N_{f2}>1$；以下绘出不同加载顺序的加载路径和疲劳损伤演化图，见图 4.17 和图 4.18，可以直观地解释上述的试验结果。

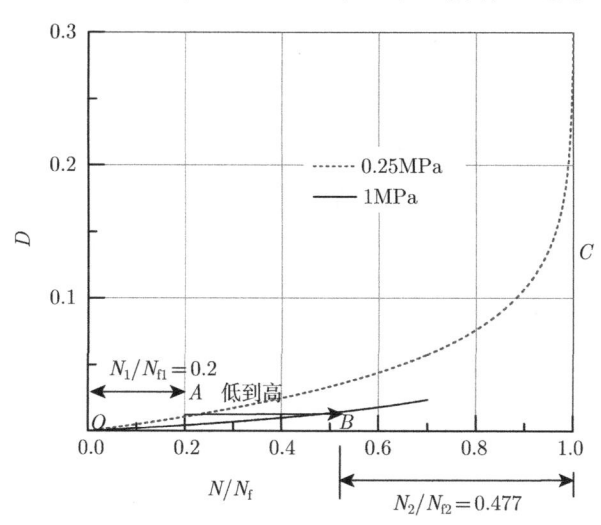

图 4.17　从低到高的加载路径和疲劳损伤演化

图 4.17 给出了从低应力水平 0.25MPa 到高应力水平 1MPa 的加载路径 $OABC$，AB 段为 "损伤等效状态" 的表达，图中可以显见 $N_1/N_{f1}+N_2/N_{f2}<1$；图 4.18 给出了从高应力水平 1MPa 到低应力水平 0.25MPa 的加载路径 $OBAE$，图中可以

显见 $N_1/N_{f1} + N_2/N_{f2} > 1$。由此不仅验证了沥青混合料疲劳损伤累计的非线性，而且也验证了由关于应力水平的非线性疲劳损伤方程 (4.39) 绘出的损伤曲线 (图 4.15) 的演化规律的正确性，两级荷载下的损伤演化规律或疲劳寿命的相互关系同试验数据相吻合。

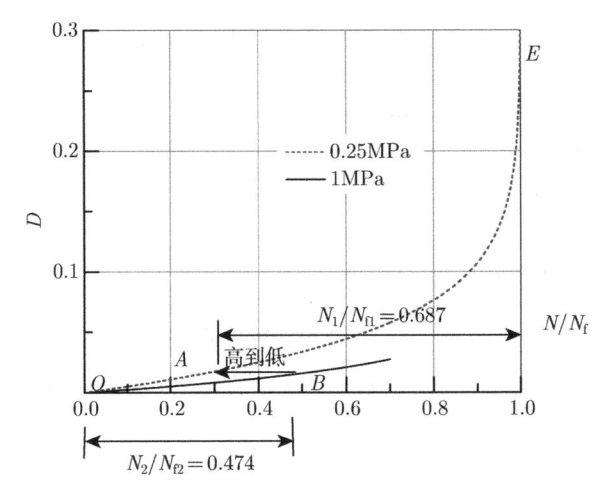

图 4.18 从高到低的加载路径和疲劳损伤演化

将本次试验结果与大量的金属材料两级荷载试验结果对比，发现结果完全相反。金属一般的规律是从高到低的加载顺序时，有 $N_1/N_{f1} + N_2/N_{f2} < 1$；而从低到高的加载顺序时，有 $N_1/N_{f1} + N_2/N_{f2} > 1$，这就是金属材料疲劳中常说的"锻炼"效应。分析沥青混合料两级加载试验结果相反的原因是：在不同应力水平的沥青混合料疲劳试验中其临界损伤完全不同，在低应力水平时临界疲劳损伤较大，即在低应力水平疲劳过程所累计的疲劳损伤值要大于高应力水平所累计的，在损伤随寿命比演化图中表现为低应力水平在疲劳过程中的损伤曲线始终在高应力水平的上方；因此取相同寿命比条件下，低应力水平所累计的疲劳损伤要大于高应力水平的；反之，要达到相同的疲劳累计损伤，低应力水平所需要的寿命比要比高应力水平的小。所以从低到高加载时，在达到相同的"等效损伤状态"前疲劳寿命关系有 $N_1/N_{f1} < 1 - N_2/N_{f2}$，即 $N_1/N_{f1} + N_2/N_{f2} < 1$；反之，从高到低加载时，在达到相同的"等效损伤状态"前疲劳寿命关系有 $1 - N_1/N_{f1} < N_2/N_{f2}$，即 $N_1/N_{f1} + N_2/N_{f2} > 1$。

而金属材料在两级加载试验中把不同应力水平下有相同的临界损伤作为前提，因为在相同临界损伤的前提下，肯定有高应力水平的损伤演化比低应力水平的要快，即在损伤随寿命比演化图中表现为高应力水平的损伤曲线始终在低应力水平的上方；同样取相同寿命比条件下，高应力水平所累计的疲劳损伤要大于低应力水平的；反之，要达到相同的疲劳累计损伤，高应力水平所需要的寿命比要比低应力水平的小。所以从高到低加载时，在达到相同的"等效损伤状态"前疲劳寿命关系有 $N_2/N_{f2} < 1 - N_1/N_{f1}$，即 $N_1/N_{f1} + N_2/N_{f2} < 1$；反之，从低到高加载时，在达到相同的"等效损伤状态"前疲劳寿命关系有 $N_1/N_{f1} > 1 - N_2/N_{f2}$，即 $N_1/N_{f1} + N_2/N_{f2} > 1$。金属材料典型的不同应力水平下的损伤曲线见图 4.19[11]。高低应力水平损伤演化曲线在图中的上下顺序与沥青混合料的刚好相反。

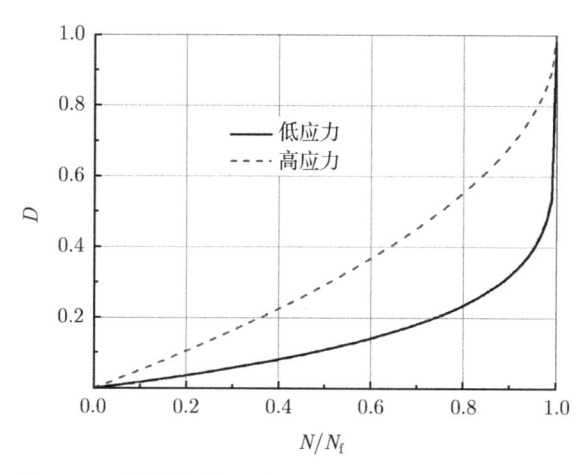

图 4.19 金属材料典型的不同应力水平下的损伤曲线

参 考 文 献

[1] 余寿文，冯西桥. 损伤力学 [M]. 北京：清华大学出版社，1997

[2] 杨光松. 损伤力学与复合材料损伤 [M]. 北京：国防工业出版社，1995

[3] Birgisson B, Roque R. Evaluation of the gradation effect on the dynamic modulu [J]. Transportation Research Board, 2005, (1):193-199

[4] Lee K H, Kim H O, Jang M S. Predictive equation of dynamic modulus for hot mix asphalt with granite aggregates [J]. 大韩土木学会论文集，2006

[5] Dongre R, Myers L, D' Angelo J, et al. Field evaluation of Witczak and Hirsch models for predicting dynamic modulus of hot-mix asphalt [J]. AAPT, 2005, 74: 381-442

[6] Kim J, Sholar G, Kim S. Determination of accurate creep compliance and relaxation modulus at a single temperature for viscoelastic solids [J]. Journal of Materials in Civil Engineering, ASCE, 2008, 20(2): 147-156

[7] Bhasin A, Branco V T F C, Masad E, et al. Quantitative comparison of energy methods to characterize fatigue in asphalt materials [J]. ASCE, 2009, 117(6): 1024-1035

[8] 范天佑. 断裂理论基础 [M]. 北京：科学出版社，2002
[9] 丁遂栋，孙利民. 断裂力学 [M]. 北京：机械工业出版社，1997
[10] 余寿文，冯西桥. 损伤力学 [M]. 北京：清华大学出版社，1997
[11] 沈金安. 沥青及沥青混合料路用性能 [M]. 北京：人民交通出版社，2001

第5章 基于强度衰变的沥青混合料疲劳损伤模型

沥青路面疲劳的本质是重复荷载作用下混合料内部产生了损伤而导致其性能不断退化的过程，剩余强度随损伤累计而衰减，当剩余强度降低到小于或等于疲劳应力水平时发生疲劳破坏[1]。因此沥青混合料可定义剩余强度为损伤变量，其优点在于剩余强度的衰减与疲劳损伤的原始定义相符合，并且强度模型的破坏准则非常简明，便于破坏失效的判断，测量十分简便，精度也较高；但是剩余强度试验由于其不能连续测量，一个试件只能得到一个数据，不同疲劳次数后的剩余强度试验需要大量的试件，耗时耗力。关于剩余强度定义的损伤变量描述的沥青混合料疲劳损伤，在国内外文献中还鲜有报道。

本章首先设计不同应力水平下疲劳剩余强度试验，根据试验结果揭示剩余强度衰变规律，建立基于剩余强度衰变的非线性疲劳损伤模型，通过不同疲劳次数后的直接拉伸剩余强度试验结果确定模型参数，对分别基于刚度和剩余强度衰变定义的损伤变量进行比较，分析二者的差异，建立两种变量描述损伤的联系。

5.1 疲劳剩余强度试验设计和试验结果

疲劳剩余强度试验需要测定试件初始强度、疲劳寿命和不同疲劳次数后剩余强度。本次试验的原材料和配合比同第2章中疲劳特性分析的沥青混合料保持一致，为了确定剩余强度试验时的不同疲劳次数，一般遵循以下两个原则：一是疲劳次数不能过大，过大往往会使试件在没有达到预定的次数就发生疲劳破坏，大大降低试验的成功率；二是确定不同剩余强度时的疲劳次数要有一定的差距，使试验结果能充分反映剩余强度的衰变规律。剩余强度试验疲劳寿命标准值的选取是影响试验结果的关键之一，本节取表2.10中的疲劳寿命平均值为疲劳寿命标准值，重复加载疲劳寿命平均值的20%、50%、65%和80%疲劳次数，卸载3s后，在与疲劳试验一致的加载速率下测定试件的动载强度，即不同疲劳次数的剩余强度结果。原计划每种应力水平下设计了测定疲劳寿命95%后的剩余强度，但是由于在1MPa的疲劳寿命95%比例下剩余强度试验很难成功，1MPa以下的疲劳寿命离散性更大，试验成功的难度更大，并且即使得到剩余强度也是筛选掉"较弱"试件后得到的，相对来说无形中提高了剩余强度，因此在0.5MPa、0.25MPa下没有进行疲劳寿命95%后的剩余强度试验。不同应力水平下设计疲劳次数见表5.1。

表 5.1 剩余强度试验中不同疲劳次数的设计

寿命比	疲劳次数		
	1MPa	0.5MPa	0.25MPa
$\bar{N}_f$	1719	11414	122131
$20\%\bar{N}_f$	344	2283	24426
$50\%\bar{N}_f$	860	5707	61066
$65\%\bar{N}_f$	1117	7419	79385
$80\%\bar{N}_f$	1375	9131	97705
$95\%\bar{N}_f$	1633	—	—

疲劳剩余强度试验仍然采用直接拉伸疲劳，加载频率为 10Hz，试验温度为 20℃。首先测试了三种不同应力水平下的初始动载强度，1MPa、0.5MPa 和 0.25MPa 下的加载速率分别为 20MPa/s、10MPa/s 和 5MPa/s；然后在重复作用相应疲劳次数后测定试件的剩余强度，剩余强度测试时的加载速率与初始强度时的加载速率保持一致。为保证试验数据的可靠性，每一水平组合的平行试验次数 ≥3 次。对平行试验结果按数据的离散程度进行弃差处理。弃差标准为一组平行试验测定值中某个数据与平均值之差大于标准差的 k 倍时，则舍弃该值，并以其余测定值重新计算平均值。当试件数目 n 为 3 根、4 根、5 根、6 根时，k 值分别为 1.15、1.46、1.67、1.82[2]。1MPa、0.5MPa、0.25MPa 三种应力水平下的疲劳剩余强度试验结果分别汇总于表 5.2~表 5.4 中。

表 5.2 1MPa 下的疲劳剩余强度试验结果汇总

序号	面积A/mm²	N/次	$N/\bar{N}_f$	破坏荷载F_{max}/N	剩余强度S_r/MPa	S_r 平均值/MPa	标准差	变异系数
1	2776.0	0	0.0%	13330	4.802	4.577	0.226	4.95%
2	2830.5			12196	4.309			
3	2869.8			13550	4.722			
4	2765.3			12376	4.475			
5	2711.3	344	20.0%	12192	4.497	4.793	0.368	7.68%
6	2818.8			14970	5.311			
7	2816.4			12865	4.568			
8	2803.5			13446	4.796			
9	2719.9	860	50.0%	13965	5.134*	4.558	0.036	0.79%
10	2708.5			12386	4.573			
11	2717.4			12274	4.517			
12	2661.0			12198	4.584			

5.1 疲劳剩余强度试验设计和试验结果

续表

序号	面积A/mm²	N/次	$N/\bar{N}_f$	破坏荷载F_{max}/N	剩余强度S_r/MPa	S_r平均值/MPa	标准差	变异系数
13	2663.0			11659	4.378			
14	2747.4	1117	65.0%	11356	4.133	4.338	0.194	4.47%
15	2736.6			11639	4.253			
16	2713.5			12446	4.587			
17	2815.6			8324	2.956			
18	2818.8	1375	80.0%	9666	3.429	3.629	0.607	16.73%
19	2692.2			11862	4.406			
20	2745.9			10231	3.726			
21	2724.5	1633	95.0%	10044	3.687	3.456	0.461	14.28%
22	2732.7			8817	3.226			

注：标记 * 的数据按处理方法舍弃，没有纳入统计分析。

表 5.3　0.5MPa 下的疲劳剩余强度试验结果汇总

序号	面积A/mm²	N/次	$N/\bar{N}_f$	破坏荷载F_{max}/N	剩余强度S_r/MPa	S_r平均值/MPa	标准差	变异系数
1	2680.1			10683	3.986			
2	2684.2	0	0.0%	10699	3.986	4.071	0.112	2.74%
3	2651.8			11195	4.222			
4	2636.8			10778	4.088			
5	2621.1			10348	3.948			
6	2677.7	2283	20.0%	10060	3.757	3.993	0.262	6.56%
7	2670.3			11415	4.275			
9	2731.6			10563	3.867			
10	2657.4	5707	50.0%	10560	3.974	3.749	0.216	5.76%
11	2631.7			9177	3.487			
12	2709.0			9931	3.666			
13	2616.3			8783	3.357			
14	2610.9	7419	65.0%	9381	3.593	3.572	0.205	5.73%
15	2671.7			10059	3.765			
17	2669.3			7925	2.969			
18	2642.0	9131	80.0%	9281	3.513	3.278	0.259	7.89%
19	2676.9			9286	3.469			
20	2659.9			8411	3.162			

表 5.4　0.25MPa 下的疲劳剩余强度试验结果汇总

序号	面积A/mm²	N/次	$N/\bar{N}_f$	破坏荷载F_{max}/N	剩余强度S_r/MPa	S_r 平均值/MPa	标准差	变异系数
1	2686.9			9546	3.553			
2	2651.9	0	0.0%	8754	3.301	3.415	0.128	3.74%
3	2716.0			9210	3.391			
4	2667.1			9063	3.398			
5	2711.6	24426	20.0%	8528	3.145	3.411	0.272	7.98%
6	2646.7			9764	3.689			
7	2675.3			7525	2.813			
8	2714.3	61066	50.0%	9752	3.593	3.191	0.391	12.24%
9	2688.1			8516	3.168			
10	2696.0			8447	3.133			
11	2670.0	79385	65.0%	8491	3.180	2.980	0.307	10.31%
12	2688.4			7060	2.626			
13	2712.2			8446	3.114			
14	2621.3	97705	80.0%	7041	2.686	2.726	0.370	13.58%
15	2690.9			6396	2.377			

沥青混合料不同疲劳次数后强度的衰变是十分复杂的，从表 5.2~表 5.4 中试验结果可见，对应疲劳寿命强度的变异性较大，平行试件的变异系数主要分布于 5%~15%；变异性大的原因：一方面，不同试件的初始强度本身差异大；另一方面，不同试件的疲劳寿命差异大，确定对应疲劳寿命的依据仅为 4 个平行试件疲劳寿命的平均值。沥青混合料试验规程中圆柱体抗压强度试验规定试件平行试验的容许误差为 10%，而 ASTM 及 AASHTO 中规定重复性精密度为，两组试件 (每组 3 个) 平均值误差不得大于 407kPa，试验结果中最大值与最小值之差不得大于 841kPa，复现性精密度分别为 372kPa 及 1055kPa。对于马歇尔试件劈裂强度试验的精密度与允许误差，第 18 届世界道路会议报告提到其变异系数为 5%~10%(重复性) 及 10%~20%(复现性)。由于直接拉伸强度试验没有纳入沥青混合料试验规程中，尚缺乏这方面的经验和资料，本章主要分析相应疲劳寿命后强度的衰变规律，对试验结果进行弃差处理后的数据均纳入衰变规律的统计分析。

5.2　疲劳剩余强度衰变模型的建立

不同疲劳次数后的剩余强度的加载速率与疲劳试验加载速率保持一致，即测得的疲劳剩余强度为动载强度，考虑了沥青混合料强度的速度特性。不同材料有不

5.2 疲劳剩余强度衰变模型的建立

同的强度退化规律,本节将在剩余强度试验数据的基础上,建立描述沥青混合料的剩余强度退化模型。

基于剩余强度衰减是分析材料疲劳损伤特性的重要手段之一,选取合适的衰变模型来准确描述剩余强度的变化规律是关键。

Brutman 等提出了一个剩余强度的线性衰变模型[2]:

$$S_r(N) = S_0 - (S_0 - \sigma_{max})\left(\frac{N}{N_f}\right) \tag{5.1}$$

式中,$S_r(N)$ 为疲劳剩余强度;S_0 为初始强度;σ_{max} 为疲劳荷载的最大应力;N 为疲劳荷载循环次数;N_f 为疲劳寿命。

Chacewicz 等提出了一种广义的剩余强度模型[3]:

$$S_r(N) = S_0 - (S_0 - \sigma_{max})f\left(\frac{N}{N_f}\right) \tag{5.2}$$

其中,函数 $0 < f(N/N_f) < 1$,其表达式可根据试验数据确定;其余各参数意义与式 (5.1) 相同。

顾怡等研究复合层合板的剩余强度衰变规律时,在 Charewicz 模型的基础上给出了函数 $f(N/N_f)$ 的表达式:

$$f(x) = \frac{\sin\beta x \cos(\beta - \alpha)}{\sin\beta \cos(\beta x - \alpha)}, \quad x = \frac{N}{N_f} \tag{5.3}$$

式中,α、β 是两个待定常数,可通过试验拟合确定,其中 $\pi - \beta < \alpha < \pi/2$。

谢里阳等在分析金属材料的剩余强度衰变中认为按如下对数规律退化:

$$S_r(N) = A + B\ln(1 - N/N_f) \tag{5.4}$$

式中,A、B 是两个待定参数;其余各参数意义与式 (5.1) 相同。

当 $N=0$ 时表示材料的初始状态,故有 $S_r(0) = S_0$,S_0 即为初始强度,依此边界条件可得 $A = S_0$;当 $N = N_f - 1$ 时表示剩余强度已达到临界破坏状态,并认为剩余强度与当前作用应力最大值 σ_{max} 相等时发生疲劳破坏,即 $S_r(N_f - 1) = \sigma_{max}$,由此可得 $B = (S_0 - \sigma_{max})/\ln N_f$,将 A、B 代入式 (5.4) 中可得剩余强度对数退化模型:

$$S_r(N) = S_0 + (S_0 - \sigma_{max})\frac{\ln(1 - N/N_f)}{\ln N_f} \tag{5.5}$$

式中,各参数意义与式 (5.1) 相同,为满足对数函数的要求,其中 $N \leqslant N_f - 1$。

上述国内外学者在研究不同材料的剩余强度衰变规律时提出了自己的数学模型,表达式各有不同,在建立剩余强度衰变模型时,一般需符合以下两个条件:

(1) 要能满足剩余强度的边界条件和不断降低的规律, 即需满足下式:

$$\begin{cases} S_\mathrm{r}(0) = S_0 \\ S_\mathrm{r}(N_\mathrm{f}) = \sigma_\mathrm{max} \\ \dfrac{\mathrm{d}S_\mathrm{r}(N)}{\mathrm{d}N} < 0 \\ \dfrac{\mathrm{d}^2 S_\mathrm{r}(N)}{\mathrm{d}N^2} \leqslant 0 \end{cases} \qquad (5.6)$$

式中, S_r、S_0 分别为剩余强度和初始强度; σ_max 为疲劳荷载的最大应力, 即临界剩余强度等于最大应力时试件破坏。

剩余强度衰变模型应能反映随疲劳次数增加而减小, 即满足式 (5.6) 中第 3 式, 剩余强度与疲劳次数的一阶导数小于 0; 式 (5.6) 中第 4 式剩余强度与疲劳次数的二阶导数小于 0, 表示剩余强度的衰变速率随疲劳次数逐渐增大, 即说明该数学模型能反映疲劳损伤演化的非线性。

(2) 临界破坏时要能反映剩余强度突然下降的特点, 即通常所说的 "突然死亡" 的特点。

为了便于与刚度 (动模量) 衰变规律比较, 与第 4 章中式 (4.21) 类似地建立如下沥青混合料剩余强度幂函数衰变模型:

$$\frac{S_\mathrm{r} - S_\mathrm{rc}}{S_0 - S_\mathrm{rc}} = \frac{S_\mathrm{r} - \sigma_\mathrm{max}}{S_0 - \sigma_\mathrm{max}} = \left(1 - \frac{N}{N_\mathrm{f}}\right)^u, \quad 0 < u < 1 \qquad (5.7)$$

式中, S_rc 为失效时的临界剩余强度, 一般认为当剩余强度 S_rc 等于所加荷载 σ_max 时失效发生, 即 $S_\mathrm{rc} = \sigma_\mathrm{max}$; u 为模型拟合待定参数; 其余各参数的意义与式 (5.6) 中的相同。

当 $N = 0$ 时表示材料的初始状态, 故有 $S_\mathrm{r}(0) = S_0$, S_0 即为沥青混合料动载强度初始值; 当 $N = N_\mathrm{f}$ 时, 有 $S_\mathrm{r}(N_\mathrm{f}) = \sigma_\mathrm{max}$, σ_max 表示疲劳破坏时的剩余强度, 式 (5.7) 也可表示成如下剩余强度幂函数衰变模型:

$$S_\mathrm{r}(N) = (S_0 - \sigma_\mathrm{max}) \left(1 - \frac{N}{N_\mathrm{f}}\right)^u + \sigma_\mathrm{max} \qquad (5.8)$$

在建立刚度衰变模型时, 已验证了该衰变模型的边界条件和衰变规律, 该模型能满足边界条件并反映衰变的非线性特征。该模型的特点是能符合剩余强度模型的基本条件且模型参数简单、容易确定。

采用式 (5.8) 拟合剩余强度和寿命比的关系, 1MPa 下的拟合曲线见图 5.1, 剩余强度随寿命比的幂函数回归结果见式 (5.9)。

5.2 疲劳剩余强度衰变模型的建立

$$S_{\mathrm{r}}(N) = (S_0 - 1)\left(1 - \frac{N}{N_{\mathrm{f}}}\right)^{0.1548} + 1 \tag{5.9}$$

$S_0 = 4.788, \quad R^2 = 0.856$

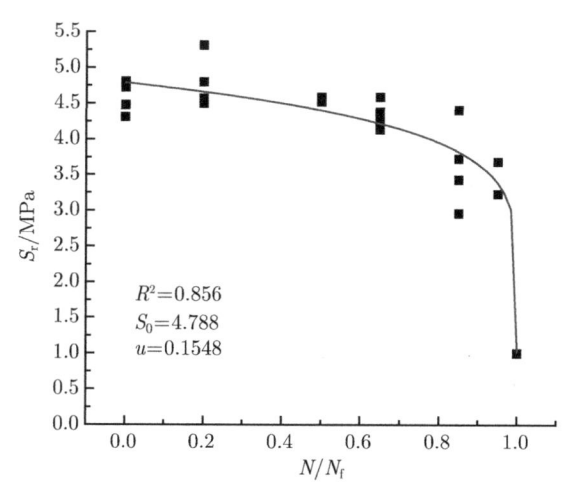

图 5.1 1MPa 下剩余强度随寿命比的衰变规律

0.5MPa 下的拟合曲线见图 5.2,剩余强度随寿命比幂函数回归结果见式 (5.10)。

$$S_{\mathrm{r}}(N) = (S_0 - 0.5)\left(1 - \frac{N}{N_{\mathrm{f}}}\right)^{0.1556} + 0.5 \tag{5.10}$$

$S_0 = 4.097, \quad R^2 = 0.949$

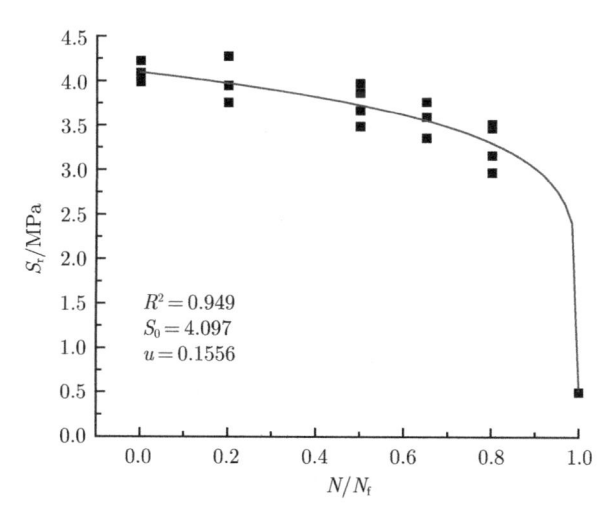

图 5.2 0.5MPa 下剩余强度随寿命比的衰变规律

0.25MPa 下的拟合曲线见图5.3,剩余强度随寿命比幂函数回归结果见式(5.11)。

$$S_\mathrm{r}(N) = (S_0 - 0.25)\left(1 - \frac{N}{N_\mathrm{f}}\right)^{0.1575} + 0.25 \tag{5.11}$$

$$S_0 = 3.476, \quad R^2 = 0.901$$

式 (5.9)~(5.11) 中的初始强度 S_0 由曲线拟合获得。

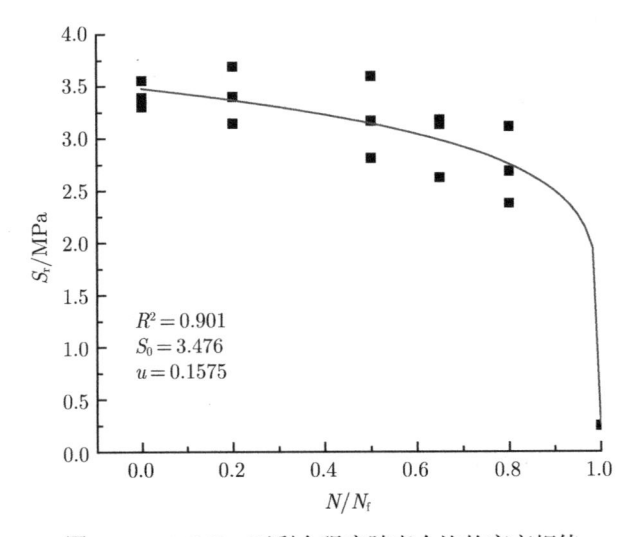

图 5.3 0.25MPa 下剩余强度随寿命比的衰变规律

由图 5.1~图 5.3 可见,剩余强度的幂函数衰变模型能够较好地反映材料在疲劳初期强度衰减较慢,而在接近失效临界时强度迅速减小,直至最终快速断裂的特性。

5.3 基于剩余强度衰变的损伤模型的建立及验证

5.3.1 以剩余强度定义的损伤变量

由不同疲劳次数后的剩余强度试验发现随疲劳次数增加强度逐渐衰减,这与疲劳过程中重复荷载作用下性能劣化规律相符,因此选用剩余强度这一宏观物理力学特性的指标描述损伤程度,用剩余强度的变化定义损伤变量是合适的,宏观地表征沥青混合料内部结构由于损伤而发生的变化。根据剩余强度的退化规律,本节将损伤变量定义为强度的退化量 $S_0 - S_\mathrm{r}(N)$ 与初始强度 S_0 的比值:

$$D_\mathrm{s}(N) = \frac{S_0 - S_\mathrm{r}(N)}{S_0} = 1 - \frac{S_\mathrm{r}(N)}{S_0} \tag{5.12}$$

5.3 基于剩余强度衰变的损伤模型的建立及验证

式中，$D_s(N)$ 为用剩余强度定义的损伤，假设试件的初始损伤为零，初始强度 S_0 由剩余强度衰变规律拟合得到，1MPa、0.5MPa 和 0.25MPa 的初始强度 S_0 分别为 4.788MPa、4.097MPa 和 3.476MPa。

当剩余强度 $S_r(N)$ 降低到等于应力水平 $\sigma_{\max}$ 时即发生疲劳断裂，根据式 (5.12) 计算不同疲劳次数后，以剩余强度定义的损伤汇总于表 5.5~表 5.7 中。

由表 5.5~表 5.7 中损伤数据可发现有个别试件算出的损伤为负值，即经过一定疲劳次数其剩余强度反而比初始强度要大，其原因是相同材料的试件存在差异，可能由于试件本身的强度较大，另外初始强度的确定也只是根据幂函数衰变规律拟合得到的，因此个别试件出现剩余强度要比初始强度大的现象。

表 5.5　1MPa 下不同疲劳次数后的损伤

序号	N/次	$N/\bar{N}_f$	剩余强度 S_r/MPa	损伤 D_s	D_s 平均值	D_s 标准差
1	0	0.0%	4.788	0	—	—
2			4.497	0.061		
3	344	20.0%	5.311	−0.109	−0.001	0.077
4			4.568	0.046		
5			4.796	−0.002		
6			4.573	0.045		
7	860	50.0%	4.517	0.057	0.048	0.008
8			4.584	0.043		
9			4.378	0.086		
10	1117	65.0%	4.133	0.137	0.094	0.041
11			4.253	0.112		
12			4.587	0.042		
13			2.956	0.383		
14	1375	80.0%	3.429	0.284	0.242	0.127
15			4.406	0.080		
16			3.726	0.222		
17	1633	95.0%	3.226	0.326	0.278	0.068
18			3.687	0.230		
19	1719	100%	1.000	0.791	—	—

表 5.6 0.5MPa 下不同疲劳次数后的损伤

序号	N/次	$N/\bar{N}_f$	剩余强度 S_r/MPa	损伤 D_s	D_s 平均值	D_s 标准差
1	0	0.0%	4.097	0	—	—
2			3.948	0.036		
3	2283	20.0%	3.757	0.083	0.025	0.064
4			4.275	−0.043		
5			3.867	0.056		
6	5707	50.0%	3.974	0.030	0.085	0.053
7			3.487	0.149		
8			3.666	0.105		
9			3.357	0.181		
10	7419	65.0%	3.593	0.123	0.128	0.050
11			3.765	0.081		
12			2.969	0.275		
13	9131	80.0%	3.513	0.143	0.200	0.063
14			3.469	0.153		
15			3.162	0.228		
16	11414	100%	0.500	0.878	—	—

表 5.7 0.25MPa 下不同疲劳次数后的损伤

序号	N/次	$N/\bar{N}_f$	剩余强度 S_r/MPa	损伤 D_s	D_s 平均值	D_s 标准差
1	0	0.0%	3.476	0	—	—
2			3.398	0.022		
3	24426	20.0%	3.145	0.095	0.019	0.078
4			3.689	−0.061		
5			2.813	0.191		
6	61066	50.0%	3.593	−0.034	0.082	0.112
7			3.168	0.089		
8			3.133	0.099		
9	79385	65.0%	3.180	0.085	0.143	0.088
10			2.626	0.245		
11			3.114	0.104		
12	97705	80.0%	2.686	0.227	0.216	0.106
13			2.377	0.316		
14	122131	100%	0.250	0.928	—	—

5.3.2 基于剩余强度的损伤失效的判断

按照以剩余强度定义的损伤,不同应力水平的临界损伤在表 5.5~表 5.7 中的最后一行已给出,1MPa、0.5MPa 和 0.25MPa 下以剩余强度计算的临界损伤 D_{cs} 分别为 0.791、0.878 和 0.928,1MPa、0.5MPa 和 0.25MPa 下对应的真实应力比分别为 0.213、0.122 和 0.070,将剩余强度定义的临界损伤随真实应力比的变化规律绘于图 5.4 中。

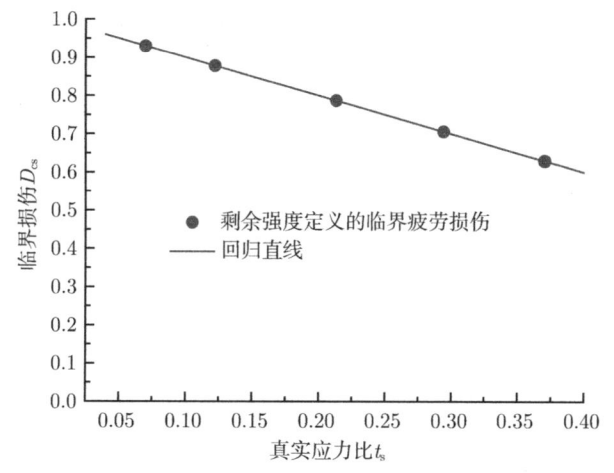

图 5.4 剩余强度定义的临界损伤随真实应力比的变化规律

由图 5.4 可见,以剩余强度计算的临界损伤 D_{cs} 与真实应力比的相关性很好,可近似表示为 $D_{cs} = 1 - t_s$。

根据谢里阳提出的"疲劳失效的二元判据"和本节建立的剩余强度幂函数的退化式 (5.8),从应力的角度建立如下疲劳失效的判据[4]:

$$\sigma > (S_0 - \sigma_{\max})\left(1 - \frac{N}{N_f}\right)^u + \sigma_{\max} \qquad (5.13)$$

式中,σ 为当前作用应力;其余各参数意义与式 (5.8) 相同。

疲劳破坏是由损伤和当前作用应力这两个量共同决定的,不等式的右边是与 N/N_f 有关的函数,表现为剩余强度衰减。谢里阳提出原判据式的右边剩余强度采用对数退化规律,判据式 (5.13) 的右边采用的是剩余强度幂函数退化规律。"疲劳失效的二元判据"表明:一方面,作用应力水平一定时,破坏与否取决于损伤程度或剩余强度的衰减量;另一方面,在一定的损伤状态下,破坏与否由当前作用应力水平决定。

根据该疲劳失效判据,可以很合理地解释以剩余强度定义的临界损伤随应力水平增大而减小的变化规律。作用应力水平较大时,在较大的剩余强度下就会发生疲劳失效；反之，当作用应力水平较小时，则要在剩余强度较小时才发生疲劳失效。根据金属材料已有疲劳试验断口分析也可知，最终断裂是由于剩余承载截面不能承担当时作用的拉伸荷载而发生的瞬态断裂，并呈现随循环应力水平越高瞬断区越大的变化规律，这也在一定程度上证明了疲劳是否失效的判据是剩余强度是否大于作用应力。

5.3.3 基于剩余强度衰变损伤模型的建立

与基于刚度衰变建立的疲劳损伤修正模型类似，基于剩余强度衰变的损伤模型也需考虑临界损伤的影响，下面基于剩余强度为损伤变量的定义出发，结合剩余强度幂函数衰变模型，建立如下基于剩余强度衰变的非线性损伤模型[5]：

$$\begin{aligned} D_s(N) &= 1 - \frac{S_r}{S_0} = 1 - \frac{(S_0 - \sigma_{\max})(1 - N/N_f)^u + \sigma_{\max}}{S_0} \\ &= \left(1 - \frac{\sigma_{\max}}{S_0}\right)\left[1 - \left(1 - \frac{N}{N_f}\right)^u\right] \\ &= D_{cs}\left[1 - \left(1 - \frac{N}{N_f}\right)^u\right] \end{aligned} \quad (5.14)$$

式中，$D_s(N)$ 为基于剩余强度定义的疲劳损伤；D_{cs} 为以剩余强度计算的临界疲劳损伤；损伤模型中参数 u 与剩余强度幂函数衰变模型的参数 u 是一致的；其余各参数意义与式 (5.7) 相同。

根据表 5.5~表 5.7 中的损伤结果，对基于剩余强度衰变的非线性损伤模型 (5.14) 进行验证，不同应力水平下的非线性疲劳损伤演化规律分别见图 5.5~图 5.7。

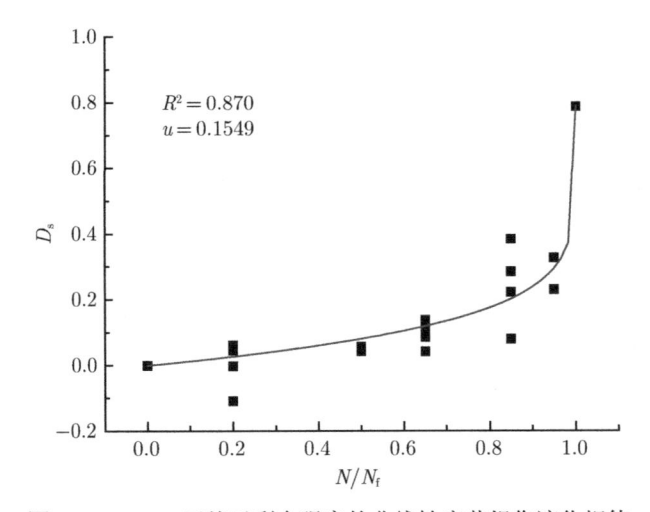

图 5.5 1MPa 下基于剩余强度的非线性疲劳损伤演化规律

5.3 基于剩余强度衰变的损伤模型的建立及验证

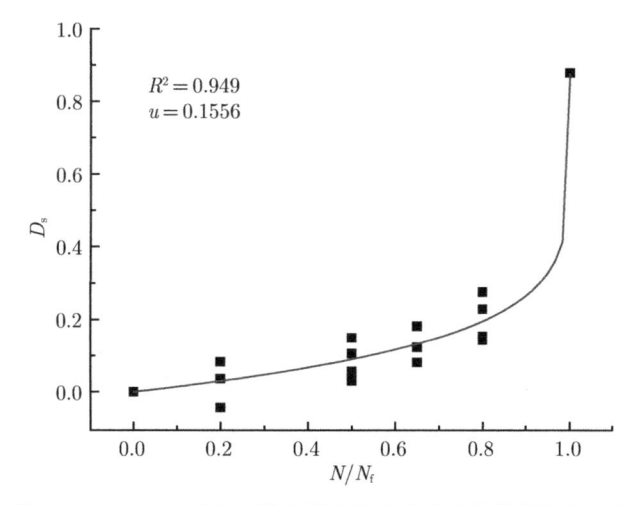

图 5.6　0.5MPa 下基于剩余强度的非线性疲劳损伤演化规律

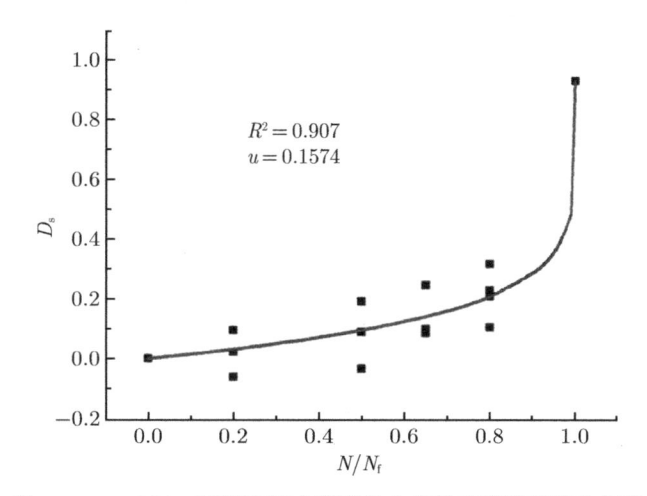

图 5.7　0.25MPa 下基于剩余强度的非线性疲劳损伤演化规律

图 5.5~图 5.7 中沥青混合料的损伤随寿命比的演化规律的拟合方程分别见式 (5.15)~式 (5.17)：

1MPa：
$$D_s = D_{cs}\left[1-\left(1-\frac{N}{N_f}\right)^{0.1549}\right] \tag{5.15}$$
$$D_{cs} = 0.791, \quad R^2 = 0.870$$

0.5MPa：
$$D_s = D_{cs}\left[1-\left(1-\frac{N}{N_f}\right)^{0.1556}\right] \tag{5.16}$$
$$D_{cs} = 0.878, \quad R^2 = 0.949$$

0.25MPa：
$$D_{\mathrm{s}} = D_{\mathrm{cs}}\left[1-\left(1-\frac{N}{N_{\mathrm{f}}}\right)^{0.1574}\right] \quad (5.17)$$
$$D_{\mathrm{cs}} = 0.928, \quad R^2 = 0.907$$

以上各式中的各参数意义与式 (5.14) 的相同。

从回归结果来看，不同应力水平回归参数 u 与基于剩余强度衰变规律确定的参数是一致的，不同应力水平的回归参数 u 值非常接近，由于剩余强度试验数据的离散性，为了简化，回归参数 u 取 3 种应力水平下的平均值为 0.156；且根据剩余强度的临界损伤与真实应力比的关系，基于疲劳剩余强度的损伤方程为[6]

$$D_{\mathrm{s}}(N) = (1-t_{\mathrm{s}})\left[1-\left(1-\frac{N}{N_{\mathrm{f}}}\right)^{0.156}\right] \quad (5.18)$$

式中，t_{s} 为真实应力比，其余各参数意义与式 (5.14) 相同。

比较不同应力水平下基于剩余强度的疲劳损伤演化规律，依据式 (5.18) 将不同应力水平下基于剩余强度的损伤随寿命比的演化曲线绘于图 5.8。

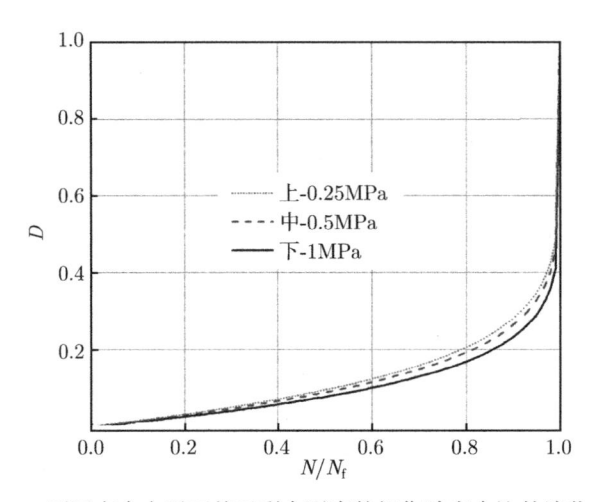

图 5.8 不同应力水平下基于剩余强度的损伤随寿命比的演化曲线

由图 5.8 可以看出：基于剩余强度的损伤演化规律表现为损伤在寿命比开始阶段呈较慢增长，随着寿命比的增大损伤增长的速度越来越快，特别是寿命比的后期损伤急剧增加。图中自下往上依次为 1MPa、0.5MPa 和 0.25MPa 的损伤演化曲线，应力水平越大损伤演化曲线越靠下，与基于刚度得到的疲劳损伤演化规律相同。按临界破坏条件，当 $S_{\mathrm{r}} = \sigma_{\max}$ 时试件发生断裂，所以在较大应力水平的重复荷载作用时，沥青混合料在剩余强度较大时便发生断裂，最后一次强度破坏造成的损伤比应力水平较小的造成的损伤要大；应力水平越大时破坏前的累计损伤越小，即临界损伤越小；因此在图中应力水平越大对应的损伤曲线越靠下。

5.4 刚度和剩余强度定义的损伤变量比较

对同种研究对象细粒式沥青混合料 AC-13C，分别基于刚度和剩余强度定义的损伤变量分析了其疲劳损伤演化规律，并且建立了形式相同的基于刚度和剩余强度的损伤演化方程，分别见式 (4.38) 和式 (5.18)。现将两种损伤变量得到的非线性损伤演化曲线绘于图 5.9 中进行对比。

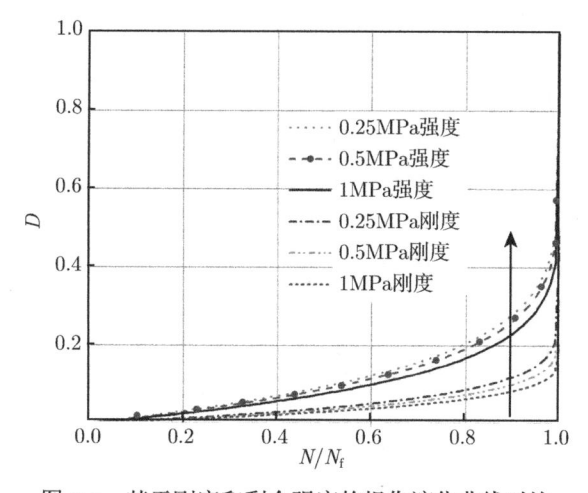

图 5.9　基于刚度和剩余强度的损伤演化曲线对比

图 5.9 中给出了 0.25MPa、0.5MPa、1MPa 三种应力水平的基于刚度和剩余强度衰变的损伤演化曲线对比，由图中可见：首先，从两者曲线的位置上比较，基于剩余强度的疲劳损伤曲线均明显高于基于刚度的损伤曲线，说明基于剩余强度定义的损伤要比基于刚度的大；其次，从两者曲线的演化趋势上比较，基于剩余强度的损伤从开始阶段便不断增加，而基于刚度的损伤发展在初、中期一直增加很缓慢，只有在接近破坏阶段才有急剧增加，说明用剩余强度定义的损伤要比刚度定义损伤在演化上更加敏感。两者定义的损伤曲线相同的地方是各自不同应力水平间的曲线位置顺序是一致的，均为应力水平小的曲线高于应力水平大的曲线。

通过基于刚度和剩余强度的疲劳损伤曲线的对比，发现两者存在差异，下面就这两种定义在描述沥青混合料损伤特性时表现不同的原因解释如下：

损伤变量可用有效弹性模量 E 和初始弹性模量 E_0 表示为[7]

$$D = 1 - \frac{E}{E_0} \tag{5.19}$$

式中，E_0 为初始动模量；E 为荷载作用 N 次后试件的动模量；D 为重复荷载作用过程中的损伤。

选取疲劳重复荷载作用下卸载段的弹性模量即沥青混合料动模量为刚度指标，式 (5.19) 实际上是目前最常用的利用模量退化来测量损伤的方法的基本依据。但是，由于刚度 (动模量) 定义的损伤变量是应用本构关系应力等价原理，即 Lemaitre 应变等效原理推导而来，假设损伤对于受损物体的影响只需通过有效应力来修正，然而该假设在理论上还不完善；基于刚度 (动模量) 定义的损伤变量，其弱点是不能全面反映疲劳损伤机理，在用刚度分析疲劳损伤的过程中只有在寿命的后期或试件破坏稍前时，才能较好地测得损伤，亦即弹性模量才会有明显的变化，而在寿命的初、中期损伤变量很小，这与疲劳损伤特点有些不相符；另一方面，以刚度 (动模量) 为依据的损伤变量，没有考虑损伤过程中引起应力集中的影响，因而基于刚度衰变的定义难以表示损伤对材料组织敏感特性的影响。

基于刚度衰变的疲劳损伤特性分析，其实质是由疲劳过程中的变形特性变化来反映的，从刚度定义出发，刚度即材料或结构一种抵抗变形的能力，而变形特性是由材料或结构各部位的平均值所决定的，属于一种对内部结构缺陷或损伤分布反应钝感的材料特性，体现的是材料内部各个部分性质的总平均值，在一定缺陷或损伤密度和尺寸范围内一般是与各种形式的破坏或失效条件无关的量。在缺陷或损伤密度和尺寸不大时，即可对应到本节中沥青混合料疲劳过程的初、中期，单位体积的异常部位和正常部位对整体性能所起的作用是同等程度的，因而某一部位材料性能的强弱变化会被平均效应所掩盖，对总体性能的影响不大。通过考察各种不同型号的钢材变形特性而得到验证，不同工艺、不同型号的钢材，由于内部缺陷及组织结构的不同，其强度会有很大的差别，但其弹性模量等变形特性系数则基本是一样的[7]。但是必须特别指出的是，当缺陷或损伤的密度或尺寸变得较大时，即可对应到沥青混合料疲劳过程的后期，缺陷或损伤对弹性模量等这类变形特性系数是会有一定影响的，故在疲劳寿命的后期用模量分析疲劳特性时，由于材料内部富含损伤，其模量会有明显的降低过程。

根据剩余强度的退化规律，本节将损伤变量定义为强度的退化量 $S_0 - S_{\rm r}(n)$ 与初始强度 S_0 的比值[4]

$$D_{\rm s}(N) = 1 - \frac{S_{\rm r}(N)}{S_0} \tag{5.20}$$

式中，$D_{\rm s}(N)$ 为用剩余强度定义的损伤，假设试件的初始损伤为零，初始强度 S_0 由剩余强度衰变规律拟合得到。

在外载和环境的作用下，由细观结构的缺陷 (如微裂缝、微孔洞) 引起的材料或结构的劣化过程，称为损伤。基于剩余强度衰变定义的损伤变量与损伤的原始定义吻合，即材料或结构性能的退化。基于剩余强度衰变的损伤特性分析，其实质是由疲劳过程中的强度特性变化来反映的,从强度定义出发,强度即材料或结构抵抗破坏的一种能力;而强度特性往往是由材料内部缺陷或损伤所决定的,属于一种对内部结构缺陷或损伤分布反应敏感的材料特性,体现了材料内部体积含量很小的或最弱部分的决定性作用,称为关键缺陷或核,是破坏的发生源,关键缺陷或损伤决定了材料的整体性能,它不具有各部分平均值的性质,此时单位体积的异常部位和正常部位对整体性能所起的作用是大不一样的,异常部位的作用占支配地位[5]。强度特性这类对内部结构组织敏感量与材料异常部位的形状、大小以及出现在各处的概率有关。由于材料的异常组织结构(如各种缺陷或损伤等)的分布具有随机性,因此由其决定的强度特性实际上只是一个统计学意义上的概念。正如实际中的材料,强度特性总会有一定的分散性。现实中仍认为均质材料各部分的强度特性是相同的,这实际上已经引入了缺陷分布假定,即决定强度特性的强弱或最小的微结构出现在各处(指在一定尺度以上的区域)的概率是相同的。对于材料的静强度特性(如本书加载速率为 5mm/min 条件下测得的小梁直接拉伸强度,即可看作准静载强度),该种条件下的缺陷分布的概率分布被认为是比较均匀的,而把这种静载强度作为材料的固有特性。但对于沥青混合料的疲劳强度、动载强度等特性,由于受到不同加载应力或应变等级、不同加载速率等因素的影响,在承载过程中的缺陷或损伤演化和累计破坏了这种关键缺陷概率分布上的均匀性,因此,相同材料在不同加载条件下的疲劳强度、动载强度是不同的。这也体现了疲劳强度、动载强度是一种对内部组织结构敏感的特征。

由于试件中损伤的累计,试件的强度会变小,因此,所能承受的瞬间最大荷载也会减小。考虑材料内部的损伤演化后,材料强度在使用过程中是变化的。剩余强度显然不是一个材料常数,而是与当前损伤程度有关的一个材料特性。利用损伤力学将剩余强度与损伤程度联系起来,即只要把握了材料的损伤程度,就可知道材料的剩余强度。

由于损伤对材料特性的影响是通过微结构的变化实现的,因此一般情况下,基于刚度特性定义的损伤在疲劳过程中大部分寿命比对损伤是不敏感的,而基于剩余强度定义的损伤在疲劳全过程中对损伤均为敏感量。经对比分析可见,在定义损伤变量和应用损伤测量方法时,选用组织敏感量剩余强度比组织不敏感量刚度(模量)作为评价参数更具有优越性。

5.5 刚度和剩余强度定义的损伤变量的统一

通过以上刚度和剩余强度定义的损伤变量的比较发现,用刚度作为疲劳损伤的度量由有效应力等价原理推导得到,在理论上还不完善,另一方面是刚度(模量)对疲劳损伤不十分敏感,破坏准则也不太容易确定。但是刚度(模量)可在疲劳试验过程中连续测量,它随着材料内部损伤的不断累计而单调下降,能够描述沥青混合料在疲劳过程中的损伤状态。剩余强度定义的疲劳损伤有着天然的物理准则,与损伤的原始定义吻合,由材料内部缺陷或损伤所决定,属于一种对内部结构缺陷或损伤分布反应敏感的材料特性;但剩余强度具有破坏性,不具有连续性,一个试件仅能得到一个试验数据点,不同试件的剩余强度之间可比性差[8]。

已有基于剩余强度和刚度衰变的损伤模型往往是被独立提出的,这导致在对沥青混合料疲劳损伤进行描述时,要么需要大量的试验,要么对疲劳损伤度量不准确。对同一种细粒式沥青混合料 AC-13 在相同条件下进行了疲劳及剩余强度试验,假设剩余强度和刚度因基于同样的损伤而存在确定的关系。结合剩余强度和刚度在描述损伤时的优点,以剩余强度定义的损伤变量 D_s 为标准,对以刚度(动模量)定义的损伤变量 D_f 进行修正,统一基于剩余强度和刚度的损伤变量定义方法。

对基于刚度(动模量)定义的损伤变量 D_f 和基于剩余强度定义的损伤变量 D_s 建立如下幂函数的关系:

$$D_s = \left(1 - \frac{S_r}{S_0}\right) = \left(1 - \frac{E}{E_0}\right)^\omega \tag{5.21}$$

式中,ω 为剩余强度和刚度定义的损伤的关联系数;D_s 为剩余强度定义的损伤;D_f 为刚度(动模量)定义的损伤。

将第 3 章中建立的基于刚度(动模量)衰变的非线性疲劳损伤演化方程代入式 (5.21) 中,与应力水平相关的基于刚度的疲劳损伤表达式为

$$D_f(N) = 1 - \frac{E}{E_0} = (0.53 - 0.27\sigma^{0.8})\left[1 - \left(1 - \frac{N}{N_f}\right)^{0.29 \cdot \sigma^{0.67}}\right]$$

通过拟合不同疲劳次数后剩余强度定义的损伤,确定关联系数 ω,应力水平 1MPa、0.5MPa 和 0.25MPa 下的拟合曲线分别见图 5.10~图 5.12,图中实线是基于刚度和剩余强度关联的损伤拟合曲线,虚线是前面 5.3 节中单独以剩余强度定义损伤的拟合曲线。图 5.10~图 5.12 中实线的拟合方程分别为

$$\text{应力水平 1MPa 时:} \quad D_s = \left(1 - \frac{E}{E_0}\right)^{0.685}, \quad R^2 = 0.756 \tag{5.22}$$

$$\text{应力水平 0.5MPa 时:} \quad D_s = \left(1 - \frac{E}{E_0}\right)^{0.642}, \quad R^2 = 0.720 \tag{5.23}$$

$$\text{应力水平 0.25MPa 时:} \quad D_s = \left(1 - \frac{E}{E_0}\right)^{0.610}, \quad R^2 = 0.704 \tag{5.24}$$

5.5 刚度和剩余强度定义的损伤变量的统一

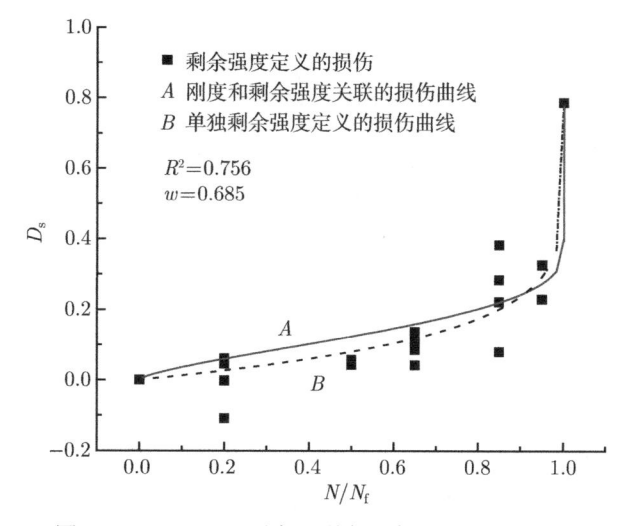

图 5.10　1MPa 下刚度和剩余强度关联的损伤曲线

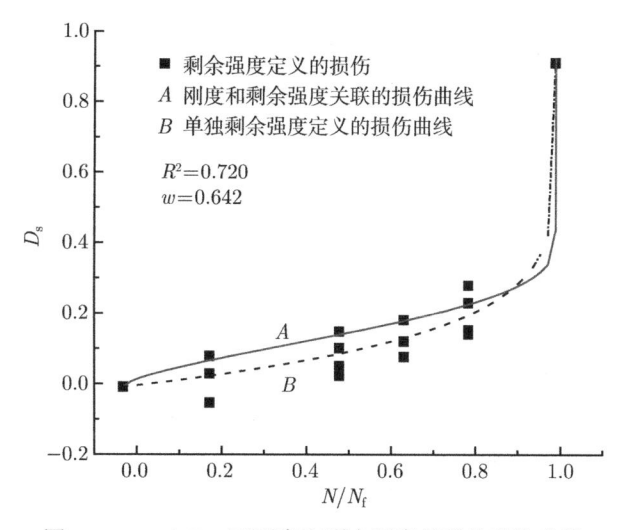

图 5.11　0.5MPa 下刚度和剩余强度关联的损伤曲线

图 5.10~图 5.12 的拟合结果表明：基于刚度和剩余强度关联的损伤拟合曲线与单独以剩余强度定义的损伤数据吻合得很好，并且与单独以剩余强度定义的损伤曲线也很接近，能较好地预测沥青混合料的损伤演化规律；在不同的应力水平下，单独基于刚度或剩余强度定义的损伤演化规律存在差异，但是剩余强度和刚度定义的损伤的关联系数 ω 的拟合值却很接近，考虑到试验数据的分散性，可以认为关联系数 ω 是一材料常数，本节取 3 种应力水平下获得的 ω 的平均值为 0.646。因此，以剩余强度定义的损伤变量为标准，提出对以刚度 (动模量) 定义的损伤变

量的修正式：

$$D = \left(1 - \frac{E}{E_0}\right)^{0.646} \tag{5.25}$$

式中，E_0 为初始动模量；E 为荷载作用 N 次后试件的动模量；D 为重复荷载作用过程中基于刚度和剩余强度关联的损伤。

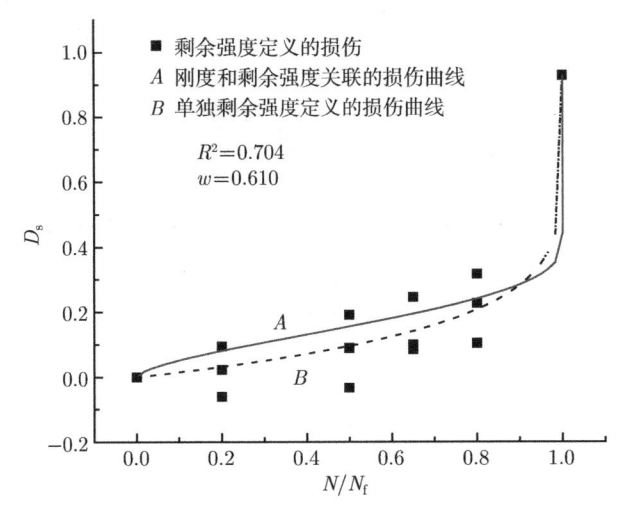

图 5.12　0.25MPa 下刚度和剩余强度关联的损伤曲线

修正式中与基于刚度 (动模量) 的损伤模型中的参数取值相同，应用简便。基于刚度和剩余强度关联的损伤，一方面与单独基于刚度定义的损伤相比，结合了以剩余强度定义的损伤，与损伤的原始定义相符，准确性得到提高；另一方面与单独基于剩余强度定义的损伤相比，结合了刚度 (动模量) 定义的损伤，可连续测量，大大降低了费用和试验工作量，省时省力。

5.6　本章小结

本章通过不同应力水平下的疲劳剩余强度试验，揭示了剩余强度随寿命比的幂函数退化规律；以剩余强度定义的损伤变量，建立了基于剩余强度衰减的非线性疲劳损伤方程；依据基于剩余强度的疲劳损伤失效判据，分析了疲劳损伤演化规律与应力水平、临界损伤的关系；分析了基于刚度和剩余强度衰变定义的损伤变量的差异，建立了基于剩余强度和刚度定义的损伤变量 D_s 和 D_f 的相关函数关系。获得如下主要结论：

(1) 根据不同疲劳次数后疲劳剩余强度试验，建立了剩余强度幂函数退化模型 $S_r(N) = (S_0 - \sigma_{\max})(1 - N/N_f)^u + \sigma_{\max}$，揭示了不同应力水平下剩余强度的衰变规律。

(2) 以剩余强度定义的损伤变量，建立了与应力水平有关的、基于剩余强度的沥青混合料疲劳损伤演化方程：

$$D_s(N) = \left(1 - 0.213 \cdot \sigma^{0.8}\right)\left[1 - (1 - N/N_f)^{0.156}\right]$$

基于剩余强度的损伤演化规律表现为，损伤在寿命比开始阶段呈较慢增长，随着寿命比的增大损伤增长的速度越来越快，特别是寿命比的后期损伤急剧增加。自下往上依次为 1MPa、0.5MPa 和 0.25MPa 的损伤演化曲线，应力水平越大损伤演化曲线越靠下，与基于刚度得到的疲劳损伤演化曲线的上下关系相同。

(3) 引入疲劳损伤失效的"二元判据"：$\sigma > (S_0 - \sigma_{max})(1 - N/N_f)^u + \sigma_{max}$，合理解释了剩余强度试验中的疲劳损伤失效，作用应力水平较大时，在较大剩余强度下便发生破坏；而当作用应力水平较小时，相应则在剩余强度较小时才发生破坏。

(4) 相同材料同等寿命比的条件下，基于剩余强度的损伤要比基于刚度的损伤大；基于刚度(模量)定义的损伤变量，由有效应力等价原理推导得到，在理论上还不完善，刚度即变形特性是由材料或结构各部位的平均值所决定的，属于一种对内部结构缺陷或损伤分布反应钝感的材料特性；刚度对疲劳损伤不十分敏感，破坏准则也不太容易确定。而基于剩余强度来度量疲劳损伤有着天然的物理准则，与损伤的原始定义吻合，由材料内部缺陷或损伤所决定，属于一种对内部结构缺陷或损伤分布反应敏感的材料特性，因此选用组织敏感量剩余强度比组织不敏感量刚度作为疲劳损伤评价参数更具有优越性。

(5) 统一了基于剩余强度和刚度的损伤变量定义方法，基于刚度和剩余强度关联的损伤曲线能较好地预测沥青混合料的损伤演化规律；关联系数 ω 可认为是一材料常数，提出了对以刚度(动模量)定义的损伤变量的修正式：

$$D = \left(1 - \frac{E}{E_0}\right)^{0.646}$$

基于刚度和剩余强度关联的损伤，一方面与单独基于刚度定义的损伤相比准确性得到提高；另一方面与单独基于剩余强度定义的损伤相比大大降低了费用和试验工作量，省时省力。

参 考 文 献

[1] 孟宪宏, 宋玉普. 混凝土抗拉疲劳剩余强度损伤模型 [J]. 大连理工大学学报, 2007, 47(4): 563-566
[2] 孟宪宏. 混凝土疲劳剩余强度试验及理论研究 [D]. 大连：大连理工大学, 2006
[3] 虞将苗. 沥青混合料疲劳性能研究 [D]. 广州：华南理工大学, 2006

[4] 苏志霄. 基于剩余强度退化规律的疲劳损伤非线性演化模型 [J]. 机械强度, 2000, 22(3): 238-240
[5] Charewicz A M, Daniel I M. Damage mechanisms and accumulation in graphite/epoxy laminates [J] // Hahn H T. Composite Materials: Fatigue and Fracture. ASTM STP 907, 1986: 274-297
[6] Broutman L J, Sahu S. A new theory to predict cumulative fatigue damage in fibre-glass re inforced plastics [J] // Composite Materials: Testing and Design(2nd Conference). ASTM STP497, 1972: 170-188
[7] 顾怡. 复合材料拉伸剩余强度及其分布 [J]. 南京航空航天大学学报, 1999, 31(2): 164-173
[8] 谢里阳, 于凡. 疲劳损伤临界值分析 [J]. 应用力学学报, 1994, 11(3): 57-64

第6章 考虑拉压差异性的沥青混合料疲劳损伤模型

从大量路面结构层力学性能测试中得到，沥青结构层中同时存在着拉应力区与压应力区，然而各国沥青路面设计的理论基础均认为沥青路面各结构层是各向同性的，即材料在受拉和受压时表现出相同的弹性性质。实际上，沥青路面面层、基层材料并非是各向同性的均质材料，层底的抗拉强度与抗拉模量均小于其层顶的抗压强度与抗压模量[1,2]。因此使用单一模量来表征处于复杂应力状态下的路面力学响应是不合适的，建立基于双模量理论的路面结构力学分析方法将是提高沥青路面设计科学性与精准性的重要途径。

本章通过开展拉压不同模量下沥青混合料的四点弯曲疲劳试验，分析沥青混合料拉压模量的差异性；探寻四点弯曲疲劳过程中拉、压模量衰变规律及疲劳损伤特性；探寻疲劳过程中拉、压模量的初始值、临界破坏值、破坏转折点以及模量衰变速率等影响因素；揭示沥青混合料弯拉疲劳试验过程中拉、压、弯模量的衰变规律，本研究对解决路面材料参数的测定问题具有重要意义，同时对沥青路面设计理论及计算方法提供理论与试验基础。

6.1 沥青混合料四点弯曲疲劳试验拉、压模量衰变规律

6.1.1 拉、压模量初始值随应力水平变化规律

本章拉、压模量初始值的取值方法与弯拉模量取值方法相同，本节确定以试验疲劳加载循环比 0.01 时，选取计算所得数据附近 10 次的平均值作为拉、压模量的初始模量。将岩沥青 (BRA) 改性沥青混合料与 SBS 改性沥青混合料拉、压模量的初始值分别汇总于表 6.1~表 6.4 中。

表 6.1 岩沥青压缩模量初始值

应力比 t	序号	E_0/MPa	E_0 平均值/MPa	E_0 变异系数 C_v
0.2	1	29183		
	2	29715	29384	0.0075
	3	29253		
0.3	1	30962		
	2	30806	30798	0.004
	3	30625		

续表

应力比 t	序号	E_0/MPa	E_0 平均值/MPa	E_0 变异系数 C_v
0.4	1	32104		
	2	31599	31862	0.0086
	3	31883		
0.6	1	32242		
	2	32682	32697	0.016
	3	33167		

表 6.2　SBS 压缩模量初始值

应力比 t	序号	E_0/MPa	E_0 平均值/MPa	E_0 变异系数 C_v
0.2	1	30209		
	2	30686	30282	0.0089
	3	29950		
0.3	1	32016		
	2	31404	32138	0.0060
	3	32994		
0.4	1	33256		
	2	33564	32973	0.0195
	3	32098		
0.6	1	33056		
	2	33487	33381	0.113
	3	33601		

表 6.3　岩沥青拉伸模量初始值

应力比 t	序号	E_0/MPa	E_0 平均值/MPa	E_0 变异系数 C_v
0.2	1	17040		
	2	16270	17291	0.049
	3	18564		
0.3	1	19054		
	2	19068	18861	0.014
	3	18460		
0.4	1	19521		
	2	20986	19892	0.014
	3	19170		
0.6	1	21114		
	2	20813	20654	0.020
	3	20035		

6.1 沥青混合料四点弯曲疲劳试验拉、压模量衰变规律

表 6.4 SBS 拉伸模量初始值

应力比 t	序号	E_0/MPa	E_0 平均值/MPa	E_0 变异系数 C_v
0.2	1	17836	18042	0.0076
	2	18202		
	3	18088		
0.3	1	19489	19436	0.0088
	2	19628		
	3	19192		
0.4	1	20379	20403	0.0157
	2	19862		
	3	20967		
0.6	1	20153	20837	0.0098
	2	20468		
	3	21889		

表 6.1~表 6.4 分别列出了岩沥青与 SBS 改性沥青混合料拉、压模量的初始值，随着应力的增大模量值也表现出了增大的趋势；两种沥青混合料拉、压模量值基本处于同一范围：压缩模量的初始值基本介于 29000~34000MPa；拉伸模量初始值基本介于 16000~22000MPa，岩沥青与 SBS 拉、压模量初始值如图 6.1 所示。

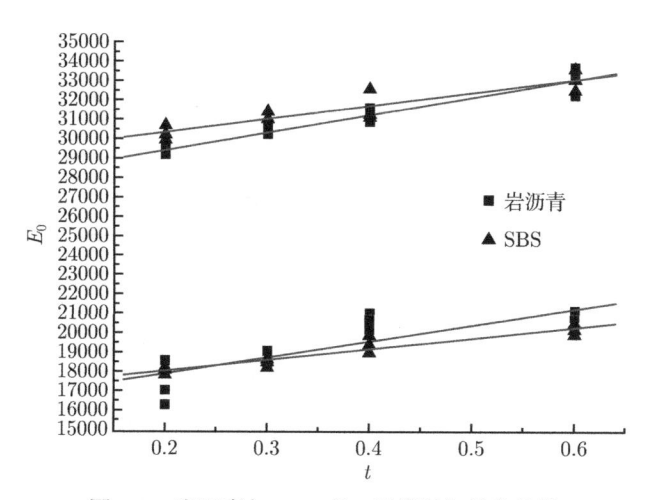

图 6.1 岩沥青与 SBS 拉、压模量初始值比较

对模量初始值进行线性回归分别得到岩沥青改性沥青混合料压缩、拉伸模量的线性回归方程：

$$E_{0P} = 27612 + 9054t, \quad R^2 = 0.97 \tag{6.1}$$

$$E_{0\text{T}} = 16263 + 8235x, \quad R^2 = 0.82 \tag{6.2}$$

SBS 改性沥青混合料压缩、拉伸模量的线性回归方程:

$$E_{0\text{P}} = 28989 + 6767t, \quad R^2 = 0.91 \tag{6.3}$$

$$E_{0\text{T}} = 16942 + 5523x, \quad R^2 = 0.94 \tag{6.4}$$

由图 6.1 可知,沥青混合料拉、压模量有着明显差异,且随着应力水平的增大模量值也相应增大。SBS 沥青混合料与岩沥青拉、压模量初始值相差不大。

将表 6.5~表 6.8 中岩沥青与 SBS 拉、压模量的疲劳方程参数进行拟合,岩沥青混合料拉伸模量拟合参数与应力比拟合结果如图 6.2、式 (6.5)、式 (6.6) 所示。

表 6.5 岩沥青拉伸模量拟合参数

应力比 t	m	n	R^2
0.2	0.06321	0.04584	0.70563
0.3	0.08163	0.05775	0.74893
0.4	0.10124	0.08133	0.80138
0.6	0.20021	0.18074	0.85323

表 6.6 岩沥青压缩模量拟合参数

应力比 t	m	n	R^2
0.2	0.04857	0.01806	0.6352
0.3	0.10124	0.0233	0.7562
0.4	0.20669	0.04584	0.91618
0.6	0.24856	0.11354	0.8811

表 6.7 SBS 压缩模量拟合参数

应力比 t	m	n	R^2
0.2	0.08051	0.05365	0.71884
0.3	0.09159	0.05621	0.86065
0.4	0.13699	0.12402	0.76354
0.6	0.20235	0.18095	0.84521

表 6.8 SBS 拉伸模量拟合参数

应力比 t	m	n	R^2
0.2	0.00604	0.05869	0.65222
0.3	0.02681	0.06341	0.7314
0.4	0.02786	0.11335	0.82816
0.6	0.13557	0.15635	0.71966

6.1 沥青混合料四点弯曲疲劳试验拉、压模量衰变规律

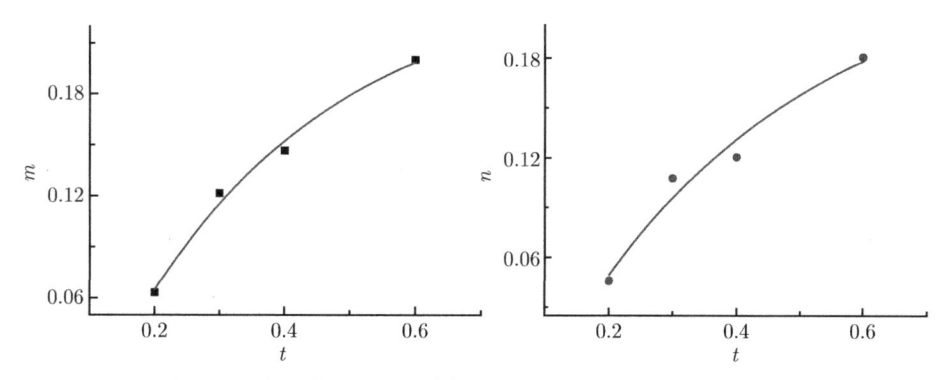

图 6.2 岩沥青混合料拉伸模量拟合参数与应力比拟合曲线

拟合方程分别为

$$m(t) = 0.25162 - 0.35072\mathrm{e}^{-3.15564t}, \quad R^2 = 0.97 \tag{6.5}$$

$$n(t) = 0.24229 - 0.33444\mathrm{e}^{-2.75423t}, \quad R^2 = 0.97 \tag{6.6}$$

岩沥青混合料压缩模量拟合参数与应力比拟合结果如图 6.3、式 (6.7)、式 (6.8) 所示。

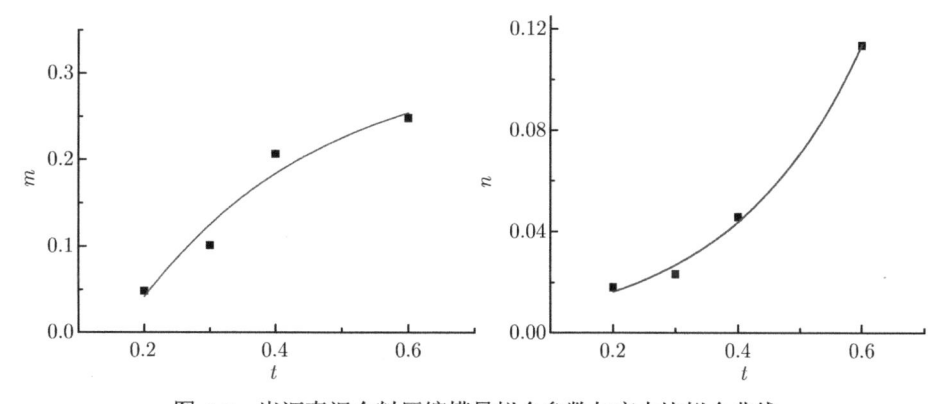

图 6.3 岩沥青混合料压缩模量拟合参数与应力比拟合曲线

拟合方程分别为

$$m(t) = 0.32357 - 0.56935\mathrm{e}^{-3.72149t}, \quad R^2 = 0.97 \tag{6.7}$$

$$n(t) = -0.00172 + 0.0071\mathrm{e}^{4.64706t}, \quad R^2 = 0.99 \tag{6.8}$$

SBS 沥青混合料压缩模量拟合参数与应力比拟合结果如图 6.4、式 (6.9)、式 (6.10) 所示。

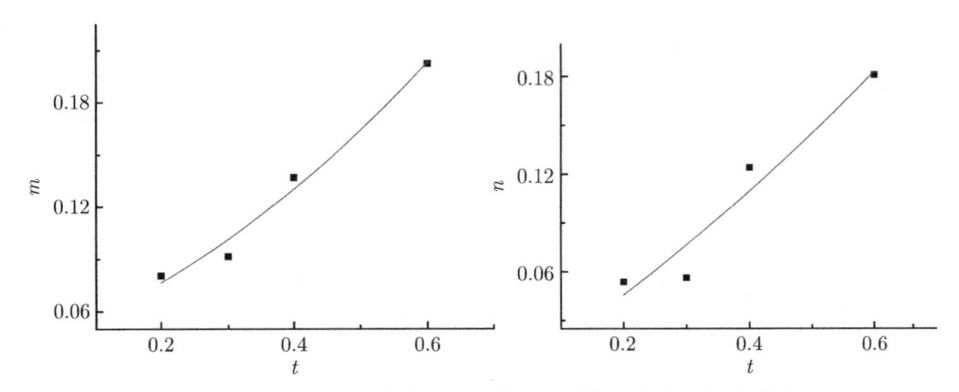

图 6.4 SBS 沥青混合料压缩模量拟合参数与应力比拟合曲线

拟合方程分别为

$$m(t) = -0.07627 + 0.1129e^{1.51096t}, \quad R^2 = 0.95 \tag{6.9}$$

$$n(t) = -0.37116 + 0.36149e^{0.71247t}, \quad R^2 = 0.82 \tag{6.10}$$

SBS 沥青混合料拉伸模量拟合参数与应力比拟合结果如图 6.5、式 (6.11)、式 (6.12) 所示。

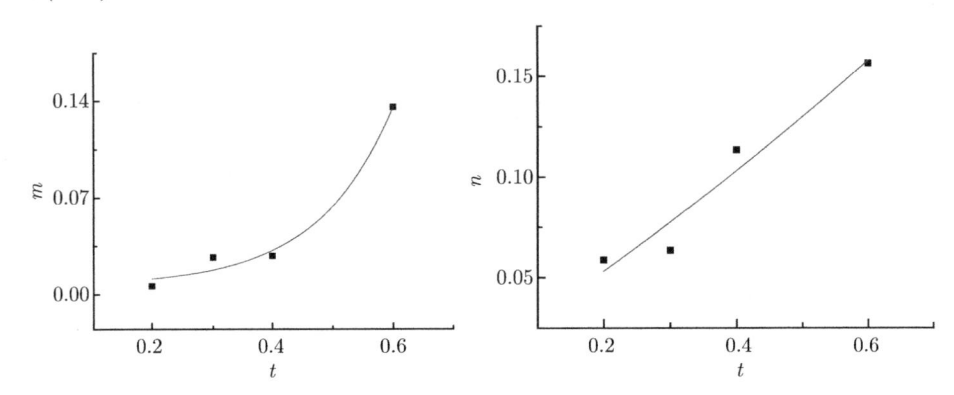

图 6.5 SBS 沥青混合料拉伸模量拟合参数与应力比拟合曲线

拟合方程分别为

$$m(t) = 0.00636 + 0.00993e^{8.1115t}, \quad R^2 = 0.96 \tag{6.11}$$

$$n(t) = -0.44239 + 0.4503e^{0.47931t}, \quad R^2 = 0.85 \tag{6.12}$$

图 6.2~图 6.5 分别给出了岩沥青与 SBS 改性沥青混合料拉、压模量拟合参数 m、n 与应力比的拟合曲线，参数 m、n 均随着应力比的增大而增大，这与前面所推得疲劳损伤模型参数与温度、应力幅值等相关这一结论相吻合，间接证明了所使用疲劳损伤模型的合理性。

6.1.2 拉、压模量临界值随应力水平变化规律

模量衰变的临界值通常出现在疲劳寿命的末期。试件破坏时拉、压临界模量 $E_{\min}$ 选取疲劳试验中试件破坏前最后 10 个循环周期采集到数据的平均值。为方便比较，临界值只列出试验均值，见表 6.9、表 6.10。

表 6.9　岩沥青拉、压模量临界值

应力比 t	拉伸模量临界值 $E_{\min}$ 平均值/MPa	压缩模量临界值 $E_{\min}$ 平均值/MPa
0.2	9510	18806
0.3	11316	21862
0.4	13569	24956
0.6	14251	27415

表 6.10　SBS 拉、压模量临界值

应力比 t	拉伸模量临界值 $E_{\min}$ 平均值/MPa	压缩模量临界值 $E_{\min}$ 平均值/MPa
0.2	9743	19985
0.3	10693	22108
0.4	12611	24678
0.6	14321	26769

表 6.9、表 6.10 分别列出了岩沥青与 SBS 改性沥青混合料拉、压模量的临界值，随着应力的增大模量值也表现出了增大的趋势；两种沥青混合料拉、压模量临界值基本处于同一范围：拉伸模量的临界值基本介于 9500~15000MPa；压缩模量临界值基本介于 18000~28000MPa，岩沥青和 SBS 拉、压模量临界值线性拟合如图 6.6 所示。

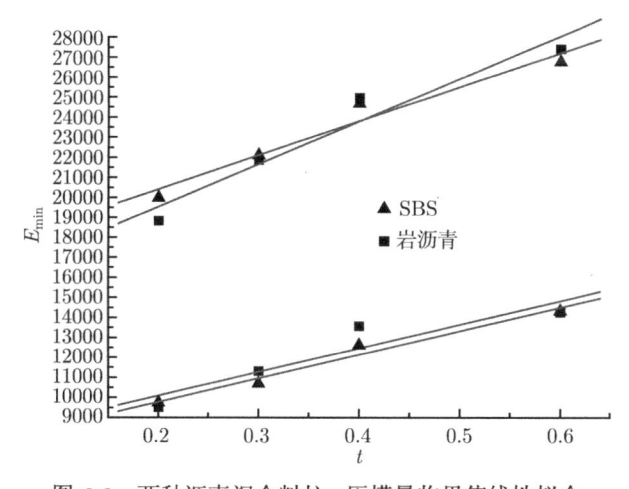

图 6.6　两种沥青混合料拉、压模量临界值线性拟合

对模量临界值进行线性回归分别得到岩沥青改性沥青压缩、拉伸模量线性回归方程：

$$E_{0P} = 15281 + 21279t, \quad R^2 = 0.97 \tag{6.13}$$

$$E_{0T} = 7735 + 11802t, \quad R^2 = 0.93 \tag{6.14}$$

SBS 改性沥青压缩、拉伸模量线性回归方程：

$$E_{0P} = 17022 + 16965t, \quad R^2 = 0.98 \tag{6.15}$$

$$E_{0T} = 7425 + 11777t, \quad R^2 = 0.98 \tag{6.16}$$

沥青混合料拉、压模量临界值与初始值较为相似，沥青混合料拉、压模量临界值有着明显差异，随着应力水平的增大模量值也相应增大。

6.1.3 临界疲劳损伤随应力水平变化规律

损伤是疲劳破坏与否的判据。在疲劳试验过程中，材料在每个时刻所测得的疲劳损伤都是不一样的，研究材料损伤演化规律的影响因素及其发展规律，对于准确推测试件的疲劳寿命是很有意义的。以动模量的衰减定义的疲劳损伤变量，所得到临界疲劳损伤计算公式为[3,4]

$$D = 1 - E_{\min}/E_0 \tag{6.17}$$

式中，D 为定义模量衰减为损伤变量的疲劳损伤临界值；E_0 为模量初始值；$E_{\min}$ 为模量临界均值。

岩沥青和 SBS 拉、压模量临界疲劳损伤值见表 6.11 和表 6.12。

表 6.11 岩沥青拉、压模量临界疲劳损伤值汇总

应力比 t	拉伸模量初始均值 E_0/MPa	拉伸模量临界均值 $E_{\min}$/MPa	临界疲劳损伤 D	压缩模量初始均值 E_0/MPa	压缩模量临界均值 $E_{\min}$/MPa	临界疲劳损伤 D
0.2	17291	9510	0.45	29384	18806	0.36
0.3	18860	11316	0.40	30364	21862	0.28
0.4	20559	13569	0.34	31195	24956	0.20
0.6	20654	14251	0.31	33030	27415	0.17

表 6.12 SBS 拉、压模量临界疲劳损伤值汇总

应力比 t	拉伸模量初始均值 E_0/MPa	拉伸模量临界均值 $E_{\min}$/MPa	临界疲劳损伤 D	压缩模量初始均值 E_0/MPa	压缩模量临界均值 $E_{\min}$/MPa	临界疲劳损伤 D
0.2	18042	9743	0.46	30281	19985	0.34
0.3	18436	10693	0.42	31138	22108	0.29
0.4	19402	12611	0.35	31639	24678	0.22
0.6	20170	14321	0.29	33048	26769	0.19

将岩沥青与 SBS 改性沥青混合料拉、压模量临界疲劳损伤进行线性拟合汇总于图 6.7。

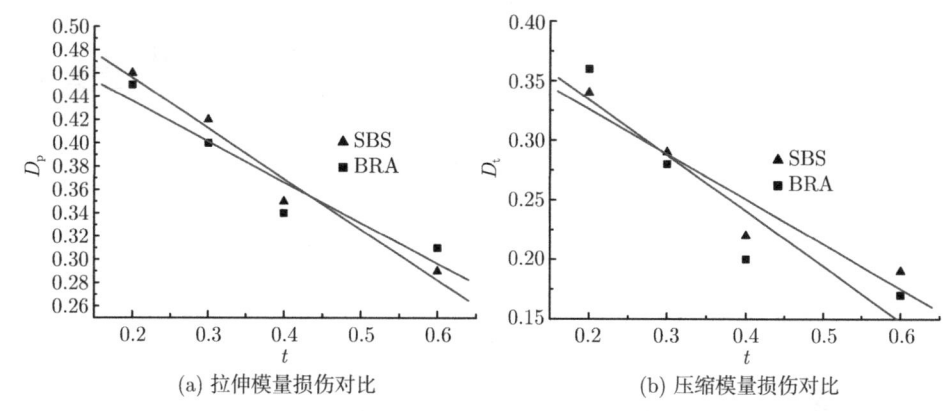

(a) 拉伸模量损伤对比

(b) 压缩模量损伤对比

图 6.7 岩沥青与 SBS 改性沥青混合料拉、压模量临界疲劳损伤线性回归

对拉伸模量疲劳损伤值 D_t 进行线性回归分别得到岩沥青与 SBS 沥青混合料线性回归方程：

$$D_{tBRA} = 0.505 - 0.35t, \quad R^2 = 0.95 \qquad (6.18)$$

$$D_{tSBS} = 0.543 - 0.434t, \quad R^2 = 0.98 \qquad (6.19)$$

对压缩模量疲劳损伤值 D_p 进行线性回归分别得到岩沥青与 SBS 沥青混合料线性回归方程：

$$D_{pBRA} = 0.427 - 0.465t, \quad R^2 = 0.93 \qquad (6.20)$$

$$D_{pSBS} = 0.401 - 0.377t, \quad R^2 = 0.95 \qquad (6.21)$$

由图 6.7、式 (6.18)~式 (6.21) 得到的岩沥青与 SBS 改性沥青混合料临界疲劳损伤差别不大，说明两者在疲劳试验过程中试件所受到的疲劳损伤较为接近，直接反映出了岩沥青与 SBS 改性沥青混合料抗疲劳性能相当。

疲劳破坏时的拉、压模量值与应力水平有关，随应力水平的增大而增大；证明疲劳试验中应力水平越大，试件最后一次破坏所造成的模量衰变也越大；随着应力水平的增大疲劳试验对试件所造成的疲劳损伤呈现出减小的趋势，说明随着应力水平的减小，疲劳试验对试件所造成的疲劳累计损伤量越大，即对试件的疲劳作用次数越多、时间越久，疲劳试验对试件所造成的疲劳损伤值越大。

6.1.4 基于拉、压模量衰变规律的沥青混合料疲劳损伤特性

在本小节中，重点分析岩沥青与 SBS 改性沥青混合料拉、压模量的衰变规律，拉、压模量衰变速率与转折点等影响因素。列出部分 BRA 与 SBS 改性沥青混合料拉、压模量衰变曲线，如图 6.8 所示。

(a) BRA-0.6 压缩模量衰变曲线 (b) BRA-0.4 拉伸模量衰变曲线

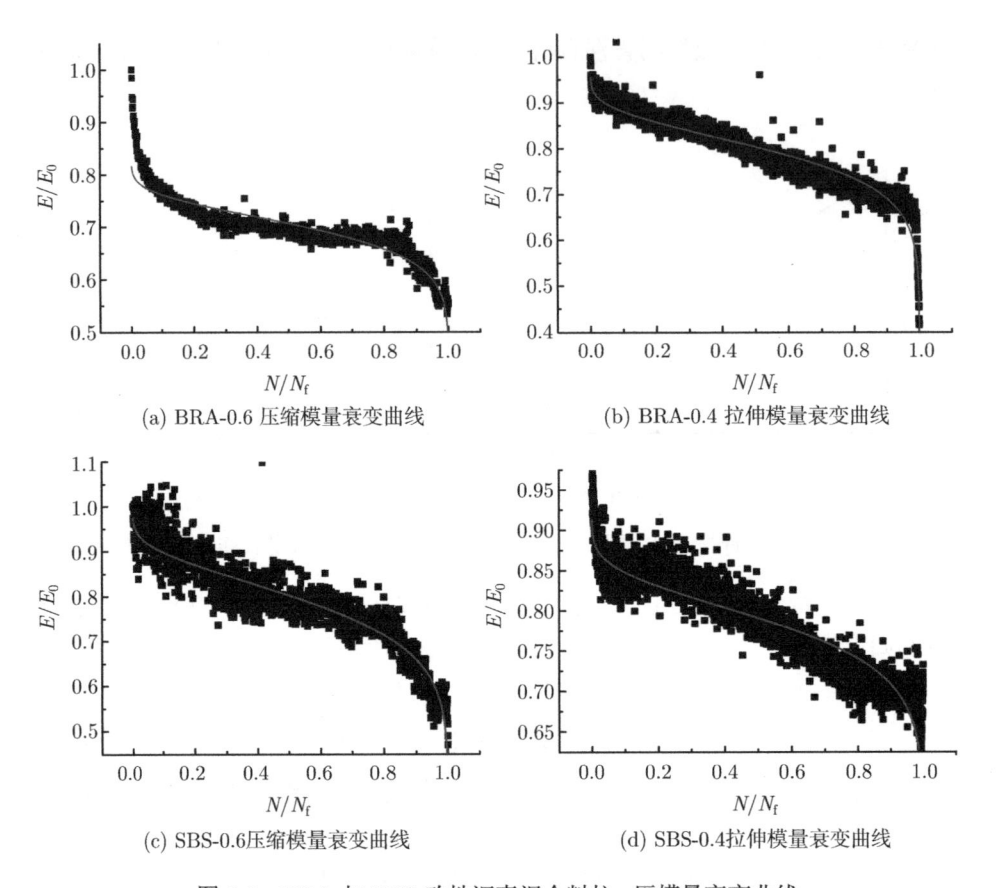

(c) SBS-0.6 压缩模量衰变曲线 (d) SBS-0.4 拉伸模量衰变曲线

图 6.8 BRA 与 SBS 改性沥青混合料拉、压模量衰变曲线

从图 6.8 中可以直观看出，BRA 与 SBS 拉伸模量、压缩模量、弯拉模量衰变规律较为相似，均经历了迁移阶段、稳定阶段和破坏阶段三个过程。

下面进行 SBS 沥青混合料拉、压、弯模量的疲劳损伤演化规律研究，分析疲劳的非线性损伤规律，所采用的拟合疲劳损伤方程如式 (6.22) 所示 [5,6]：

$$D(N) = 1 - \left[1 - \left(\frac{N}{N_f}\right)^{\frac{1}{1-\alpha}}\right]^{\frac{1}{1+\gamma}} \tag{6.22}$$

由图 6.9 可知，SBS 拉、压、弯模量的疲劳损伤演化规律与模量的衰变过程较为相似，即在寿命比开始阶段损伤增长较快，随着疲劳循环比的逐渐增大，材料内部的损伤增长速度逐渐趋于平稳，在疲劳寿命比的后期，材料的损伤急剧增大直至破坏。同时亦揭示了沥青混合料疲劳试验的非线性损伤规律，这与部分研究者的结论不谋而合，从而证明了疲劳损伤模型的合理性。疲劳损伤方程拟合参数与模量衰变方程拟合参数一致，这里不再重复列出。

(a) 弯拉模量-0.6

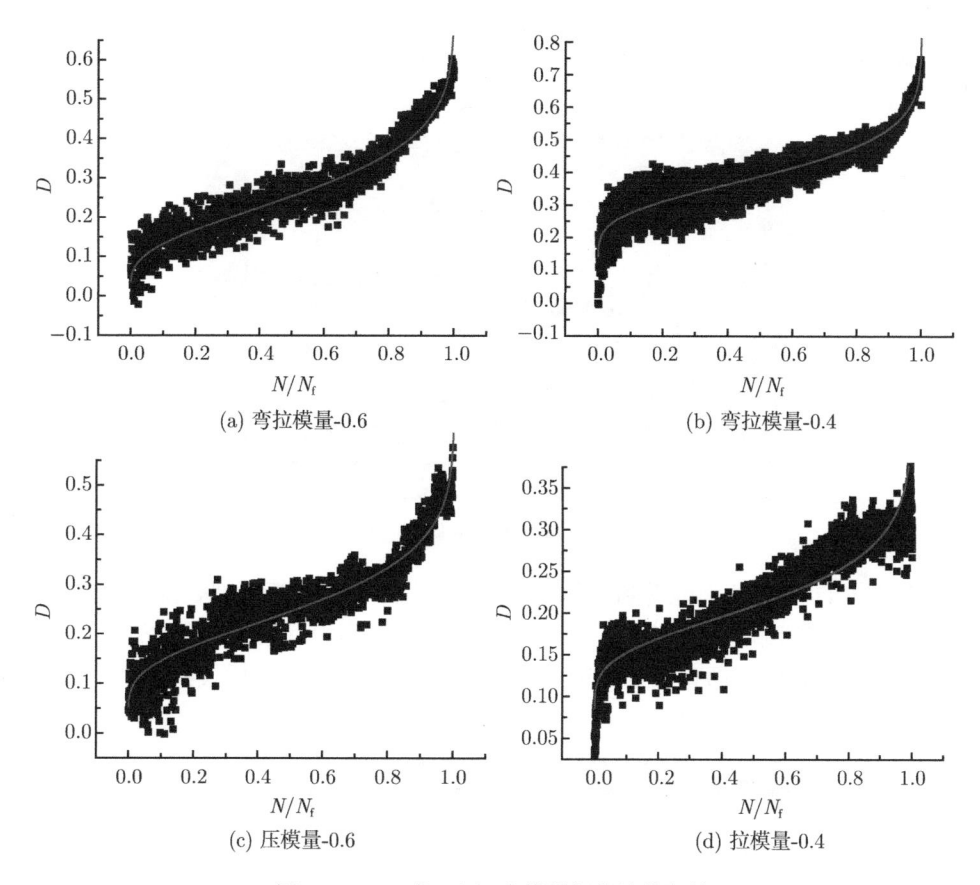

(b) 弯拉模量-0.4

(c) 压模量-0.6

(d) 拉模量-0.4

图 6.9 SBS 拉、压、弯模量损伤演化规律

6.2 疲劳试验过程中沥青混合料拉、压、弯模量差异性分析

在沥青路面的实际受力过程中，决定沥青混合料抗变形性能的主要因素有沥青砂浆作用下颗粒之间的黏结力、骨料之间的嵌挤作用、粗细集料之间的内摩阻力等[7,8]。

在弯曲试验中，试件下表面处于拉伸条件下，这时决定沥青混合料疲劳性能的主要因素是黏结力 (包括沥青胶浆的黏结、集料与沥青之间的黏结作用) 和内摩阻力作用，而骨料之间的嵌挤作用影响相对较弱黏结力与沥青胶浆的强度直接相关。与试件底面受拉条件相反，试件上表面处于抗压状态，集料的骨架结构、组成形式和摩阻系数决定了颗粒间的内摩阻力，这时抗疲劳性能主要取决于骨料之间的嵌挤作用。可以清晰地从图 6.10 中看到沥青混合料四点弯曲疲劳试验过程中，试件下表面受拉最先开裂，接着试件发生破坏，进而整个试件发生断裂。这是由于沥青胶浆的黏结作用产生的抗拉强度远小于主要由骨料之间的嵌挤作用产生的抗压强度。

图 6.10　四点弯曲试件断裂位置

从图 6.11 可以清晰地看到试件受拉伸作用的下表面附近断裂处没有发生骨料的破坏，说明其抵抗疲劳破坏的主要是沥青胶浆的黏结力。而上表面则发生了骨料的破坏，充分证明了沥青混合料试件上下部结构抗疲劳的主要因素不同所导致的疲劳破坏结果不同的结论。

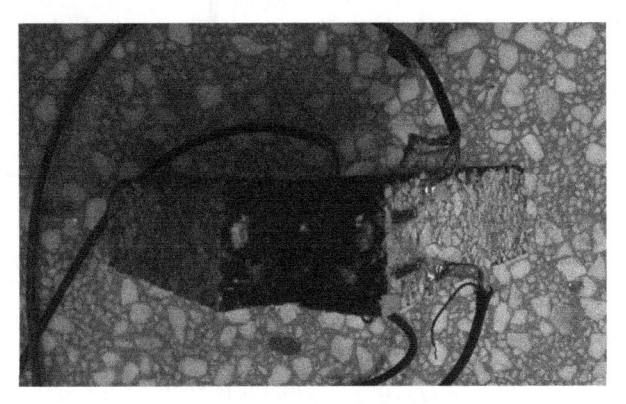

图 6.11　疲劳试件断裂面

综上，当材料处于不同的受力模式时，决定材料抗变形性能的外部因素不一致，这是材料的拉伸、压缩和弯拉刚度参数存在差异性的主要原因，也是一般情况下压缩模量要大于拉伸模量的根本原因。

6.3　沥青混合料拉、压、弯模量衰变特性对比分析

本节在以上试验结果的基础上，着重比较了沥青混合料拉、压、弯模量衰变拟

6.3 沥青混合料拉、压、弯模量衰变特性对比分析

合曲线在模量处于稳定阶段时切线的斜率以及临界破坏转折点的位置。选取应力比为 0.4 的岩沥青改性沥青混合料所测得拉、压、弯模量试验结果进行分析，得出了拉、压、弯三种动态模量的衰变规律。图 6.12 为 BRA-0.4 拉、压、弯模量衰变曲线。

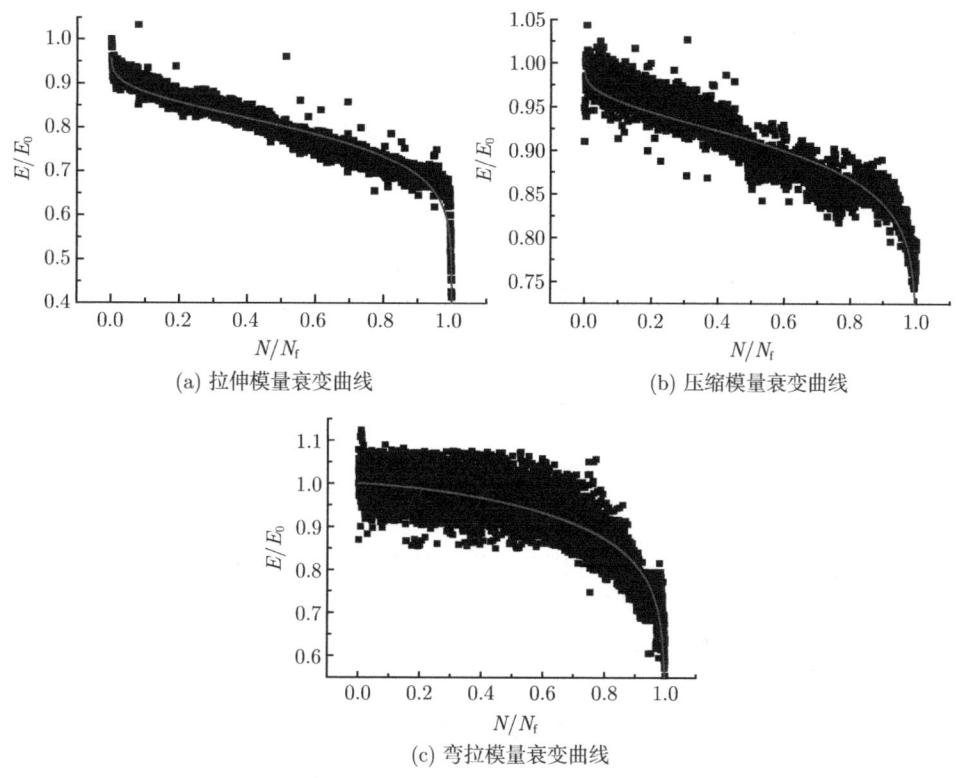

(a) 拉伸模量衰变曲线

(b) 压缩模量衰变曲线

(c) 弯拉模量衰变曲线

图 6.12　BRA-0.4 拉、压、弯模量衰变曲线

为了求得沥青混合料拉、压、弯模量衰变曲线的斜率及临界转折点位置，将模量衰变方程分别进行简化，然后分别进行一阶、二阶求导得出模量衰变曲线的斜率及临界转折点位置，分别如式 (6.23)~式 (6.26) 所示。

$$\frac{E}{E_0} = \left[1 - \left(\frac{N}{N_f}\right)^{\frac{1}{1-\alpha}}\right]^{\frac{1}{1+\gamma}} \tag{6.23}$$

$$y = (1 - x^m)^n \tag{6.24}$$

$$y' = -mnx^{m-1}(1-x^m)^{n-1} \tag{6.25}$$

$$y'' = m^2 n x^{2m-2}(n-1)(1-x^m)^{n-2} - mnx^{m-2}(m-1)(1-x^m)^{n-1} \tag{6.26}$$

通过将表 6.13 中的数据代入式 (6.24) 中得到了拉、压、弯三条模量衰变曲线的拐点位置分别处于疲劳循环比 0.38、0.34、0.32 处。如图 6.12 所示，三种模量衰变方程拟合曲线稳定区间基本处于疲劳循环比范围 0.2~0.8 内，因此分别选取三条模量衰变曲线所对应拐点位置作相应的一条切线。将拐点横坐标代入式 (6.19) 得到切线斜率与对应切点的纵坐标值，进而得到拉、压、弯三条模量衰变曲线在拐点位置时的切线方程及切点坐标，将结果列入表 6.14。

表 6.13　岩沥青-0.4 拉、压、弯模量拟合参数

受力模式	m	n	R^2
拉伸	0.10124	0.08133	0.80138
压缩	0.20669	0.04584	0.91618
弯拉	0.38619	0.10368	0.7793

表 6.14　拉、压、弯衰变曲线在拐点位置时的切线方程及切点坐标

受力模式	切线方程	切点坐标
拉伸	$y = -0.1796x + 0.9$	(0.38, 0.83)
压缩	$y = -0.1125x + 0.986$	(0.34, 0.95)
弯拉	$y = -0.164x + 1.03$	(0.32, 0.97)

在疲劳循环比 0.2~0.8，三种模量的衰变基本处于稳定阶段，从得到的切线斜率绝对值大小来看，拉伸模量斜率最大，其次是弯拉模量，压缩模量斜率最小，拉伸模量斜率值比压缩模量斜率高出 59.6%。由拉伸模量切点纵坐标大于压缩模量切点纵坐标可得，在相同的循环比条件下，以拉伸表征的模量衰变幅度大于以压缩代表的模量衰变幅度，说明此时在拉伸区域产生的损伤大于压缩区域产生的损伤。由于试件内部各点的应力状态不同，因此试件内部各点的模量衰变速率呈现不同的特征，传统的用弯拉模量的衰变表征衰变规律的设计方法则无法体现弯拉试件内部各点由应力状态的差异性而导致的模量衰变的差异性。由于拉伸模量过快的衰变速率导致中性面以下受拉区域损伤累计加剧，最先发生开裂，为试件的破坏源。

由拉、压、弯模量衰变曲线可知，在疲劳循环比 0.8~1 模量急剧衰减的阶段中，随着循环比的不断增大，曲线所对应各点切线斜率急剧变化。本节选取三条模量衰变曲线所对应拐点位置的切线方程及 $x = 1$ 对应的直线，取两条直线的角平分线与衰变曲线的交点定义为临界转折点，取点方式如图 6.13 所示。同时给出不同模量衰变曲线所得角平分线与临界转折点坐标，见表 6.15。

将拉、压、弯三种模量衰变曲线汇总于图 6.14。

从表 6.15 与图 6.14 中得到以下结论：

(1) 在疲劳循环比 0.8~1 范围内，曲线斜率的绝对值急剧增大直至试件发生破

6.3 沥青混合料拉、压、弯模量衰变特性对比分析

坏,同时该阶段在整个疲劳寿命过程中所占比例非常小,此时比较斜率的大小已经没有任何实质意义,故本节选取三条模量衰变曲线所对应疲劳循环比时的切线及 $x=1$ 时所对应的直线,取两条直线的角平分线与模量衰变曲线的交点,定义为破坏转折点。

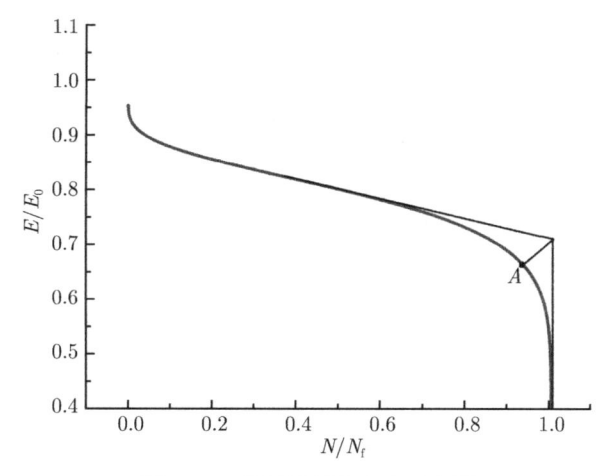

图 6.13 临界转折点取点示意图

表 6.15 不同模量衰变曲线所得角平分线方程与临界转折点坐标

受力模式	角平分线方程	临界转折点坐标
拉伸	$y=1.22x-0.5$	(0.949, 0.657)
压缩	$y=1.12x-0.26$	(0.954, 0.808)
弯拉	$y=1.195x-0.325$	(0.932, 0.789)

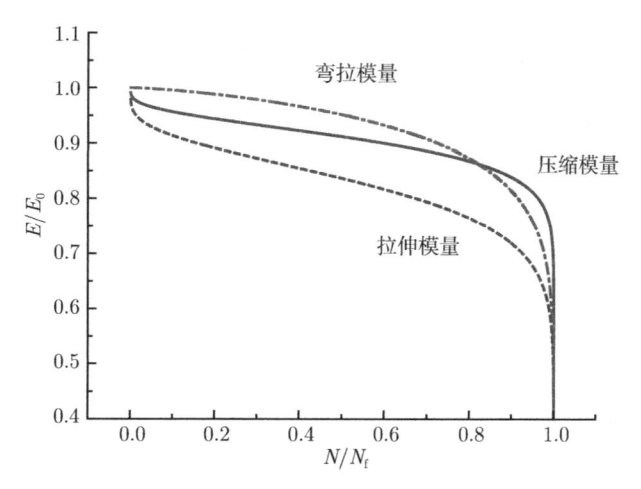

图 6.14 拉、压、弯三种模量衰变曲线图

(2) 从本节定义的破坏转折点横坐标值来看：压缩模量曲线所对应破坏转折点的横坐标值大于拉伸模量，说明压缩模量衰变曲线发生极限破坏的位置相对更为靠后，发生极限破坏的时间同样位于拉伸模量之后，即试件发生开裂破坏并非由压缩模量的衰减所致，而是由拉伸模量衰减过快所致。

(3) 在临界破坏点处，拉伸模量衰变曲线所对的纵坐标 y 值小于压缩模量所对的纵坐标，说明临界破坏时拉伸模量的衰减比大于压缩模量的衰减比。此时拉伸模量曲线的衰减比比压缩模量的衰减比高 79.0%，在定义模量衰减为损伤变量时，即拉伸产生的损伤大于压缩产生的损伤，试件首先在受拉区开裂。

以上结论充分说明了模量衰变曲线稳定期间拉伸模量衰变速率的过快及衰减末期压缩模量破坏转折点的滞后性，同时也间接反映出了拉伸模量衰变速率的快慢是决定沥青混合料疲劳性能能否优越的关键因素。

在疲劳试件最后的破坏阶段，可清楚看到拉伸模量比的值衰减最为明显，根据疲劳损伤方程 $D(N) = 1 - \left[1 - \left(\dfrac{N}{N_\mathrm{f}}\right)^{\frac{1}{1-\alpha}}\right]^{\frac{1}{1+\gamma}}$ 可知其疲劳损伤值最大，其次为弯拉模量，压缩模量损伤值最小。沥青混合料疲劳试验中试件中性面以下受拉区域不断发生损伤累计，而损伤的逐步累计致使受拉区域材料的力学性能不断下降直至最先发生破坏开裂，进而导致弯拉模量与压缩模量的急剧衰减，成为了试件发生破坏的根本原因。因此怎样考虑及重视拉伸模量及其演变规律在道路结构设计中的作用成为了提高我国沥青路面设计的科学性与精准性的关键所在。

6.4 基于沥青路面各点实际应力状态确定结构设计参数的新思想

《公路沥青路面设计规范》中规定在沥青路面结构层设计中无论是以路表弯沉值或是以层底拉应力为设计指标时，都要进行沥青混合料抗压回弹模量的测试[9]。而在路面实际的受力过程中，路面结构层同时存在着拉应力区与压应力区，拉、压应力同时存在的区域称之为中性面。在中性面中同时存在着拉、压、弯三种不同的模量，通过上述试验数据得到的结论可知：拉伸模量在沥青路面中性层中起着决定性作用，即拉伸模量的衰变速率决定着中性层的疲劳性能能否满足路面行车荷载的需求；而在沥青路面中性层以下受拉区域部分拉伸模量则占据着更为重要的位置。

因此《公路沥青路面设计规范》中单一考虑压缩模量数值及其衰变规律的设计理念与路面结构实际的受力状况不符，也是沥青路面发生早期病害、在使用过程中实际寿命远低于路面设计寿命的原因之一。本章所研究的模量与路面设计采用的模量是不同的,但研究的出发点是在于说明路面材料拉、压模量的差异性。基于上述分析,本章在前人研究的基础上,进而提出了考虑沥青路面各点所处位置的实际拉、压应力状态,进而选取相应的模量及其演变规律进行测试与分析的设计理念,弥补了现行沥青路面设计规范的不足。

6.5 本章小结

(1) 岩沥青与 SBS 拉、压模量初始值和破坏值,二者数值相差不大,变异性较小;得到四点弯曲疲劳试验中压缩模量初始值约为弯拉模量初始值的 3 倍,拉伸模量初始值约为弯拉模量初始值的 2 倍;探寻了四点弯曲疲劳过程中拉、压模量衰变规律及疲劳损伤特性,与弯拉模量衰变规律较为相似,三者均经历了迁移阶段、稳定阶段和破坏阶段三个过程。

(2) 岩沥青与 SBS 改性沥青混合料得到的临界损伤值较为接近,说明两种材料作为改性剂对沥青路面抗疲劳性能的提升较为接近,使用岩沥青作为改性剂可以有效地提高沥青路面的抗疲劳性能。

(3) 通过疲劳试验试件开裂位置与试件断裂面分析,沥青混合料拉、压模量的差异性是由试件上下部结构抗疲劳的主要因素不同所致。

(4) 从拉、压、弯模量衰变速率大小来看,拉伸模量衰变速率最大,其次是弯拉模量,压缩模量衰变速率最小,拉伸模量衰变速率值比压缩模量衰变速率值高出 59.6%。拉伸模量过快的衰变速率导致中性面以下受拉区域损伤累计加剧,最先发生开裂,为试件的破坏源。

(5) 压缩模量曲线所对应破坏转折点的横坐标 x 值大于拉伸模量,说明压缩模量衰变曲线发生极限破坏的位置相对更为靠后,发生极限破坏的时间同样位于拉伸模量之后;拉伸模量衰变曲线所对的纵坐标 y 值小于压缩模量所对的纵坐标,说明临界破坏时拉伸模量的衰减比大于压缩模量的衰减比。此时拉伸模量曲线的衰减比比压缩模量的衰减比高 79.0%,即试件发生开裂破坏并非由压缩模量的衰减所致,而是由拉伸模量衰减过快所致。

(6) 提出了考虑沥青路面各点所处位置的实际拉、压应力状态,进而选取相应的模量及其演变规律进行测试与分析的设计理念,弥补了现行沥青路面设计规范的不足。

参 考 文 献

[1] 李瑞霞,郝培文,王春,等. 布敦岩沥青改性机理 [J]. 公路交通科技,2011,28(12):16-20
[2] Liu G, Nielsen E, Komacka J, et al. Rheological and chemical evaluation on the age-

ing properties of SBS polymer modified bitumen: From the laboratory to the field [J].Construction & Building Materials, 2014, 51(51):244-248
[3] 朱桃. 布敦岩沥青 (BRA) 改性沥青结合料使用性能研究 [D]. 长沙: 湖南大学，2014
[4] 黄文通，徐国元. 布敦岩沥青混合料路用性能的试验研究 [J]. 华南理工大学学报 (自然科学版)，2012，40(2): 87-92
[5] 马峰，傅珍，栾媛媛. 国产天然沥青对基质沥青路用性能的影响 [J]. 广西大学学报: 自然科学版，2015，40(1): 171-177
[6] 沈金安. 国外沥青路面设计方法汇总 [M]. 北京：人民交通出版社，2004
[7] 邓学钧. 路基路面工程 [M]. 北京：人民交通出版社，2008
[8] 公路沥青路面设计规范 (JTG D50-2006) [S]. 北京：人民交通出版社，2006
[9] 姚祖康. 沥青路面结构设计 [M]. 北京：人民交通出版社，2011

第7章 不同应力状态下沥青混合料疲劳损伤模型的归一化

本章根据得到的不同加载速率下强度屈服面模型,结合疲劳试验确定不同应力状态下疲劳起始点和疲劳应力路径,开发一种基于屈服准则思想的疲劳特性分析新方法,能够消除应力状态、试件尺寸及成型方式对疲劳试验的影响,从而达到不同应力状态下疲劳特性的归一化。

疲劳开裂是沥青路面结构最常见的破坏形式,为了保证沥青路面具有良好的耐久性和使用性,世界各国沥青路面设计方法均以路面材料的抗疲劳特性作为确定设计寿命的依据[1],因此各国开展了多种耗资少、周期短的室内疲劳试验方法来研究沥青路面的抗疲劳特性。欧美多采用悬臂梯形试件或梁式试件,在其端部施加半正弦波荷载进行疲劳试验,受力模式为两点弯曲、三点弯曲和四点弯曲[2];日本多采用圆柱试件进行间接拉伸疲劳试验[3];中国多采用直接拉伸或间接拉伸疲劳试验,并通过分析模量的衰变规律,揭示材料的疲劳性能[4]。结果发现不同的沥青混合料疲劳试验方法得到的试验结果是不同的,疲劳试验结果对其试件的几何形状与尺寸、疲劳加载方式具有较高的敏感性,且现有疲劳模型存在一定的局限性,因此,究竟沥青混合料的抗疲劳性能如何也就无从下结论,这无疑对沥青路面设计发展造成了很大的阻碍。

关于疲劳模型,国内外学者开展了诸多研究,Lundström 等和 Kim 等[2,5]在疲劳循环试验下,应用黏弹性连续损伤力学模型评估疲劳特性,得到不同的测试方法及设备的疲劳试验结果不同,原因可能是不同试验方法的损伤机制不同。Benedetto 等[6]研究了11种不同的试验方法来评估沥青混合料的疲劳特性,包括单轴拉伸和单轴压缩,弯曲和间接拉伸试验。结果表明,使用经典疲劳方法获得的疲劳测试结果受测试类型和加载模式的显著影响,很难从不同试验模式中比较疲劳试验结果。上述现象无疑阻碍了沥青道路耐久性的发展,主要原因是疲劳特性分析方法的不合理,现阶段被广泛使用的 $S\text{-}N$ 疲劳方程具有局限性,无法对不同受力模式下的疲劳特性对比进行解释。因此,长沙理工大学的吕松涛等[7,8]基于直接拉伸疲劳试验,建立了基于真实应力比的疲劳方程,弥补了采用传统 $S\text{-}N$ 疲劳方程进行疲劳设计时的不足。

为了消除应力状态、试件形状及尺寸对疲劳特性分析评价的影响,Li 等[9-11]开发了一系列的测试方法来研究沥青混合料的疲劳性能,研究了尺寸效应对疲劳寿命的影响,得到不同尺寸的拉压疲劳试验对疲劳行为的影响并不显著,同时对三种不同尺寸的梁进行四点弯曲疲劳试验,得到试件的尺寸显著影响测量的弯曲刚度、疲劳寿命和疲劳极限。同时,他们还利用 Desai 强度屈服面模型对不同应力状态下的沥青混合料疲劳特性进行归一,对比分析了应力控制和应变控制两种模式下的疲劳试验结果,得到应力、应变两种控制模式下的疲劳特性均可以归一,但是认为不同加载速率下的抗拉强度是不变的,这与实际情况不相符合。因此,只有对疲劳特性分析方法进行发展和完善,才能达到不同应力状态下沥青混合料疲劳特性的归一化,进而提高沥青路面设计的科学性与精准性。

基于此,本章从材料疲劳破坏的本质出发,考虑了加载速率对疲劳试验的影响,开发了一种基于屈服准则思想的疲劳特性分析新方法对不同应力状态下沥青混合料疲劳结果进行分析,达到了对不同应力状态下沥青混合料疲劳特性进行归一化的目的,实现了不同疲劳试验方法试验结果的统一,同时为实现从材料疲劳到结构疲劳的科学转化提供了理论、方法与技术依据。

7.1 基于屈服准则强度屈服面的建立

7.1.1 Desai 强度屈服面模型

美国亚利桑那大学的 Desai 等 [12] 提出了一种屈服面的响应函数,可描述土工材料和沥青混合料在静水应力下的塑性响应,属强度理论的八面体剪应力系列 (J_2 理论)。该屈服面能够应用于应力不变量空间和应变不变量空间。在应力不变量空间条件下,屈服面的表达形式为

$$\varphi(\sigma_{ij}) = \frac{J_2}{P_a^2} - \frac{\left[-\alpha\left(\frac{I_1-R}{P_a}\right)^n + \gamma\left(\frac{I_1-R}{P_a}\right)^2\right]}{\sqrt{[1-\beta\cos(3\theta)]}} = 0 \tag{7.1}$$

式中,I_1 为第一应力张量不变量;J_2 分别为第二偏应力不变量,J_3 为第三偏应力不变量,$\cos(3\theta) = \frac{3\sqrt{3}}{2} \times \frac{J_3}{(J_2)^{\frac{3}{2}}}$;$P_a$ 为大气压;$\alpha, \beta, \gamma, n, R$ 为模型参数。

在 $(I_1, \sqrt{J_2}, \theta)$ 空间,式 (7.1) 表示的屈服面为一封闭曲面,在单向应力状态下,模型参数 α, β 在峰值应力处为 0,因此屈服面在 $(I_1, \sqrt{J_2})$ 空间将退化为一条直线,表达形式如下:

$$\frac{J_2}{P_a^2} = \gamma\left(\frac{I_1-R}{P_a}\right)^2 \tag{7.2}$$

即

$$J_2 = \gamma(I_1-R)^2 \Rightarrow \sqrt{J_2} = \sqrt{\gamma}|I_1-R| \tag{7.3}$$

7.1 基于屈服准则强度屈服面的建立

在 $(I_1, \sqrt{J_2})$ 空间，式 (7.3) 表示的屈服面很显然为一条直线，上式左边所示的表达式是 Mises 屈服条件的准则量，其物理意义为剪应力强度 $T = \sqrt{J_2}$。

7.1.2 不同加载速率下不同应力状态的沥青混合料强度试验及结果

根据疲劳试验的加载频率 f(周期为 T) 及应力水平 S 可以求出对应的加载速率：

$$v = \frac{S}{T/2} = 2fS \tag{7.4}$$

通过式 (7.4) 的计算，可以得到直接拉伸和间接拉伸疲劳试验时四个应力水平对应的加载速率分别为 5MPa/s、10MPa/s、20MPa/s、30MPa/s，而单轴压缩疲劳试验应力水平对应的加载速率为 40MPa/s、50MPa/s、60MPa/s、70MPa/s。对不同应力状态下沥青混合料进行如上不同加载速率下的强度试验，试验结果见表 7.1。

表 7.1 不同加载速率下沥青混合料的各种强度平均值

加载速率 v/(MPa/s)	直接拉伸强度 R_D/MPa	单轴压缩强度 R_C/MPa	间接拉伸强度 R_T/MPa
5	2.95	14.01	3.258
10	3.487	16.33	3.704
20	4.158	19.035	4.41
30	4.552	20.82	4.837
40	4.821	22.187	5.185
50	5.012	23.309	5.487
60	5.13	24.267	5.658
70	5.197	25.109	5.784

将不同应力状态下强度与加载速率变化关系在 $R = \alpha \times v^\beta$ 幂函数下进行拟合对比，如图 7.1 所示。

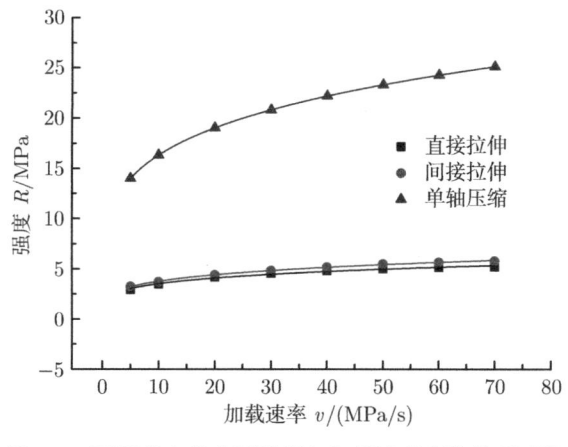

图 7.1 不同应力状态下强度与加载速率变化关系对比

得到的强度与加载速率关系拟合曲线参数如表 7.2 所示,不同应力状态的强度与加载速率关系曲线都是随加载速率增大而增大,且强度随加载速率增加的速率趋缓。

表 7.2　不同应力状态下强度与加载速率关系拟合曲线参数

拟合参数	α	β	R^2
直接拉伸	2.15852	0.21307	0.952
间接拉伸	2.24289	0.22571	0.957
单轴压缩	9.81584	0.22107	0.992

7.1.3　不同加载速率下强度屈服面的建立

本节研究了不同应力状态在不同加载速率下的强度值,根据 Desai 沥青混合料屈服面响应模型,可以得到直接拉伸、间接拉伸和单轴压缩三种不同应力状态下的屈服面模型坐标。将三种应力状态下的屈服面结合起来得到不同加载速率下的沥青混合料强度屈服面。

根据表 7.3 推算出的不同应力状态下屈服面模型坐标可以得到不同加载速率下三种应力状态的实际屈服面坐标,从而得到不同加载速率下的强度屈服面,如图 7.2 所示。

表 7.3　不同应力状态下的屈服面模型坐标

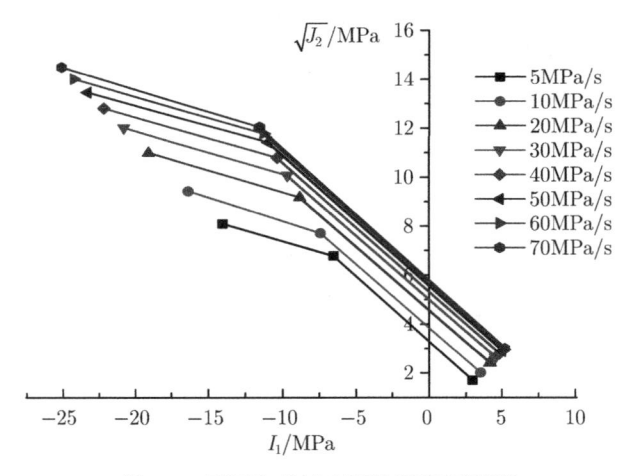

应力状态	强度	σ_1	σ_2	σ_3	I_1	$\sqrt{J_2}$	罗德角 (θ)
直接拉伸	R_D	R_D	0	0	R_D	$\sqrt{3}R_D/3$	$0°$
间接拉伸	R_T	R_T	0	$-3R_T$	$-2R_T$	$\sqrt{39}R_T/3$	$\theta = \arccos\dfrac{5}{\sqrt{52}} = 46°$
单轴压缩	R_C	0	0	$-R_C$	$-R_C$	$\sqrt{3}R_C/3$	$60°$

图 7.2　不同加载速率下的强度屈服面

相同加载速率下，直接拉伸的剪应力强度 $T=\sqrt{J_2}$ 最小，单轴压缩的剪应力强度最大。随着加载速率的增大，不同应力状态的剪应力强度均增大，且增大幅度随着加载速率的增大而减小，所以基于屈服准则思想的强度屈服面随着加载速率的增大而向外增大扩散，且扩散速率随着加载速率的增大而减小。

7.2 基于屈服准则思想不同应力状态下沥青混合料疲劳特性的归一化

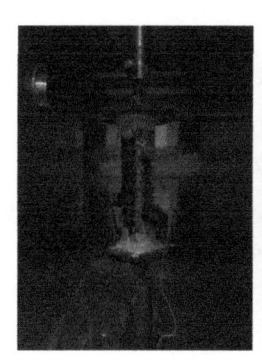

7.2.1 不同应力状态下沥青混合料疲劳试验

疲劳试验方案和控制标准有① 加载方式：应力控制；② 加载频率和波形：10Hz 连续半正弦；③ 应力水平：根据强度试验结果确定直接拉伸和间接拉伸均选用 0.25MPa、0.5MPa、1MPa 和 1.5MPa 四种应力水平进行疲劳试验，单轴压缩则选用 2MPa、2.5MPa、3MPa 和 3.5MPa 四种应力水平；④ 试验温度：(15±1)°C。不同应力状态下沥青混合料疲劳试件及试验分别如图 7.3 和图 7.4 所示。

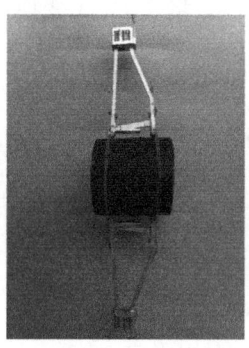

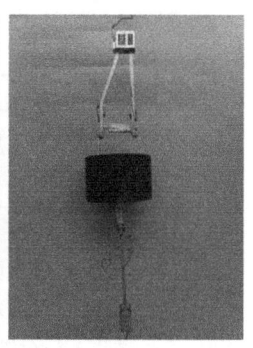

图 7.3 不同应力状态下沥青混合料疲劳试件

图 7.4 不同应力状态下沥青混合料疲劳试验

7.2.2 不同应力状态下沥青混合料疲劳试验结果及基于 S-N 疲劳方程的结果分析

1. 基于现象学法的疲劳方程

Chaboche[13] 建立了一种疲劳损伤函数表达式:

$$\frac{dD}{dN} = [1-(1-D)^{1+\gamma}]^\alpha \left[\frac{\sigma}{M(1-D)}\right]^\gamma \quad (7.5)$$

将式 (7.5) 积分可得

$$D(N) = 1 - \left[1 - \left(N(1+\gamma)(1-\alpha)\left(\frac{\sigma}{M}\right)^\gamma\right)^{\frac{1}{1-\alpha}}\right]^{\frac{1}{1+\gamma}} \quad (7.6)$$

当 $D(N) = 1$, $N = N_f$ 时, 式 (7.6) 可变形得疲劳寿命方程:

$$N_f = \frac{1}{(1+\gamma)(1-\alpha)} \left(\frac{\sigma}{M}\right)^{-\gamma} \quad (7.7)$$

式中, α 和 γ 是与温度、应力幅值、平均应力等相关的材料参数。

令 $k = \dfrac{M^\gamma}{(1+\gamma)(1-\alpha)}$, $n = \gamma$, 将式 (7.7) 变换为

$$N_f = k\left(\frac{1}{\sigma}\right)^n \quad (7.8)$$

式中, N_f 为试件的疲劳寿命; k, n 为疲劳方程的拟合参数。

令 $k = \dfrac{S_t^{-\gamma}}{(1+\gamma)(1-\alpha)(M)^{-\gamma}}$, $n = \gamma$, 式 (7.7) 也可变换为

$$N_f = k\left(\frac{1}{t}\right)^n \quad (7.9)$$

式中, S_t 为静载强度值; t 为应力比, $\sigma = tS_t$。

式 (7.8) 和式 (7.9) 即为广泛采用的疲劳方程表达形式, 即所谓的 S-N 疲劳方程。

2. 基于传统 S-N 疲劳方程的沥青混合料疲劳试验结果对比分析

基于传统疲劳试验方法, 首先根据规范开展不同应力状态下沥青混合料静载强度试验, 得到直接拉伸、单轴压缩及间接拉伸的强度分别为 1.12MPa、11.21MPa 及 2.28MPa。然后选取不同应力水平开展疲劳试验, 本节根据前期试探试验结果, 直接拉伸和间接拉伸疲劳试验的应力水平定为 0.25MPa、0.5MPa、1MPa 和 1.5MPa; 单轴压缩疲劳试验的应力水平定为 2MPa、2.5MPa、3MPa 和 3.5MPa。剔除严重偏离疲劳曲线的试验点后, 不同应力状态下沥青混合料疲劳试验结果及根据传统 S-N 疲劳方程拟合结果如图 7.5、表 7.4 和表 7.5 所示。

7.2 基于屈服准则思想不同应力状态下沥青混合料疲劳特性的归一化

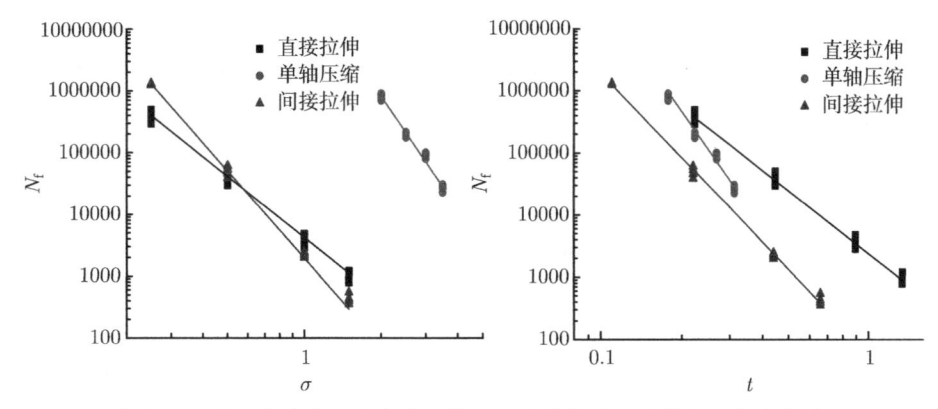

图 7.5 基于应力水平和应力比的不同应力状态下疲劳方程拟合曲线

表 7.4 基于应力水平的不同应力状态下疲劳方程拟合参数

应力状态	k	n	R^2
直接拉伸	4216	3.28	0.994
单轴压缩	4.94819×10^7	5.96	0.989
间接拉伸	1954	4.68	0.981

表 7.5 基于应力比的不同应力状态下疲劳方程拟合参数

应力状态	k	n	R^2
直接拉伸	2898	3.28	0.954
单轴压缩	29.93	5.90	0.981
间接拉伸	41.91	4.68	0.993

由试验结果及拟合结果可知：

(1) 选取应力水平为 1.5MPa 开展直接拉伸疲劳试验时，很明显，该应力水平大于按规范方法测得的沥青混合料直接拉伸强度值，名义应力比为 1.34，大于 1。按传统应力比与疲劳寿命的关系分析，则在此应力比下，沥青混合料的拉伸疲劳寿命应小于 1。然而实际试验结果是在此应力水平下，沥青混合料的平均拉伸疲劳寿命为 993 次。故传统的未考虑加载速度对强度影响的疲劳应力比的确定方式是不对的，会对疲劳寿命的预测带来很大的误差。根据式 (7.1) 可知，当应力水平提高时，疲劳试验过程中的加载速度也相应提高，根据前面的研究成果可知，沥青混合料的强度随加载速度的增大而增大，故在应力水平为 1.5MPa 时开展直接拉伸应力水平，其真实应力水平并不是 1.34，而约是 0.33。

(2) S-N 疲劳方程参数 n 表示疲劳性能对应力状态的敏感性，n 值越大，疲劳寿性能对应力的变化越敏感。同种荷载模式下，两种 S-N 疲劳方程拟合得到的参数 n 值虽几乎相同，但不同应力状态下拟合的 n 值不同，均为单轴压缩 > 间接拉

伸 > 直接拉伸，反映同种材料的疲劳性能对应力状态具有不同的敏感性，这与实际情况不符，且究竟是哪个参数值更能准确地表示疲劳性能对应力状态的敏感性无从得知。

(3) S-N 疲劳方程参数 k 反映疲劳曲线的线位，由拟合结果可知，不同应力状态的 k 值各不相同，使得无法对沥青混合料在不同应力状态下的疲劳性能进行对比分析，进而对其疲劳性能进行准确的评价。而且，不同材料、不同加载频率和不同应力状态下的沥青混合料疲劳试验结果采用传统 S-N 疲劳方程进行拟合得到的 k 值也各不相同，无法对其疲劳性能进行比较。

综上所述，采用传统的 S-N 疲劳方程分析沥青混合料的疲劳性能存在明显的误差，且不同应力状态下沥青混合料的两种 S-N 疲劳方程均展现出较大的差异性，导致无法对不同试验方法所得的沥青混合料疲劳性能进行科学评价。故有必要建立一种考虑真实应力比的不同应力状态下沥青混合料疲劳特性的归一化模型，以准确地评价沥青混合料的疲劳性能。

7.2.3 基于屈服准则与真实应力比思想的不同应力状态下沥青混合料疲劳特性的归一化模型的建立

1. 不同应力状态下疲劳应力路径的确定

不同应力状态下疲劳试验在应力控制模式下以初始应力水平作为疲劳峰值，不同应力状态下疲劳试验的初始状态在强度屈服面中坐标如表 7.6 所示。

表 7.6 不同应力状态下的疲劳初始点坐标

应力状态	应力水平	I_1	$\sqrt{J_2}$
直接拉伸	0.25	0.25	0.144
	0.5	0.5	0.289
	1	1	0.577
	1.5	1.5	0.866
单轴压缩	2	−2	1.155
	2.5	−2.5	1.443
	3	−3	1.732
	3.5	−3.5	2.021
间接拉伸	0.25	−0.5	0.52
	0.5	−1	1.041
	1	−2	2.082
	1.5	−3	3.122

不同应力状态下疲劳初始点在不同加载速率下的疲劳应力路径表示如图 7.6 所示。

7.2 基于屈服准则思想不同应力状态下沥青混合料疲劳特性的归一化

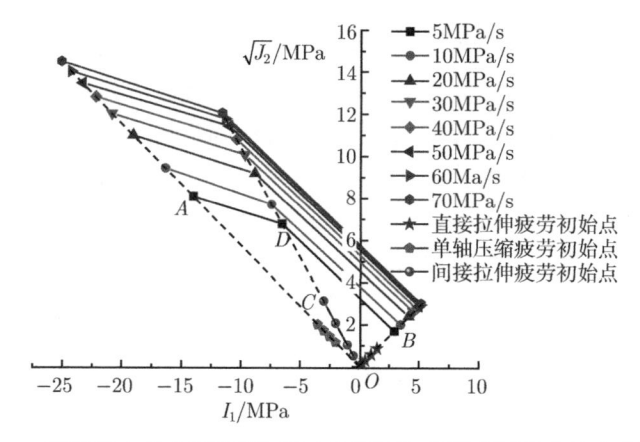

图 7.6 不同应力状态下疲劳初始点在不同加载速率下的疲劳应力路径

图 7.6 中点 $O(0,0)$ 为坐标原点，即为无施加任何荷载时的应力状态；点 $A(I_c, \sqrt{J_{2c}})$ 表示的是抗压破坏时材料或结构内部峰值应力点的屈服状态；点 $B(I_t, \sqrt{J_{2t}})$ 表示的是抗拉破坏时材料或结构内部峰值应力点的屈服状态；从点 A、点 B 的定义及其纵横坐标的大小可以看出：所有抗压强度破坏点的屈服状态点均在 OA 线上，所有抗拉强度破坏点的屈服状态点均在 OB 线上。

点 $C(I_1, \sqrt{J_2})$ 则为给定的一般应力状态下材料或结构内部所处的剪应力强度状态点，本研究即对应于疲劳试验无损状态时材料或结构内部的初始应力状态，随着加载次数的增加，材料或结构内部的损伤也将逐渐增加，对于均质、各向同性假设，材料或结构内部各点的三个主应力也将随着该点损伤的增大而等比例增大，因此疲劳试验时不同加载次数下的应力状态点 $(I_{1i}, \sqrt{J_{2i}})$ 与坐标原点连线的斜率 $\arctan(\sqrt{J_{2i}}/I_{1i}) = \arctan(\sqrt{J_2}/I_1)$ 是相等的，不会随加载次数的变化而发生变化，也就是说，基于屈服准则的思想，不同加载次数下的应力状态点 $(I_{1i}, \sqrt{J_{2i}})$ 将沿着 OC 射线轨迹上移，称之为疲劳轨迹线，即疲劳应力路径，直至与屈服面 AB 相交于破坏点 $D(I_{1N_f}, \sqrt{J_{2N_f}})$。

定义不同应力状态下疲劳应力路径方程为

$$\sqrt{J_{2i}} = kI_{1i} \tag{7.10}$$

对不同应力状态下疲劳过程始终点进行线性拟合，拟合参数如表 7.7 所示。

表 7.7 不同应力状态下疲劳应力路径方程参数

应力状态	k
直接拉伸	$\sqrt{3}/3$
间接拉伸	$-\sqrt{39}/6$
单轴压缩	$-\sqrt{3}/3$

2. 基于屈服准则思想的疲劳特性分析新方法

在现行的沥青路面设计体系中，沥青路面的荷载效应是通过轴载换算将其等效为标准轴载作用次数加以考虑，轴载换算方法则是基于 Miner 线性疲劳损伤理论推导出来的，该理论忽略了疲劳破坏过程中材料本身损伤不断加剧所产生的非线性演化特征，无法考虑加载历史变化引起的损伤累计非线性效应，得到的结论是相同的荷载对无损伤路面与已损伤路面的作用效应是相同的，这一结论显然低估了荷载的作用。上述这些方面的不足，不仅严重影响了路面疲劳寿命设计的准确性，而且对荷载作用效应的分析亦产生了很大的偏差。

研究发现：传统疲劳方程不能反映强度破坏特征，即名义应力比为 1 时不能对应疲劳寿命为 1 的强度破坏，主要是因为传统的疲劳试验及分析没有考虑加载速率的影响；以名义应力比为自变量的疲劳方程与实际偏差较大。现行沥青路面设计规范在使用 S-N 疲劳方程时将其后延到疲劳寿命为 1 的点，认为此时根据疲劳方程计算得到的拉应力就是其疲劳强度，并由此来计算抗拉强度结构系数，抗拉强度结构系数的取值非常重要，直接影响结构层层底容许拉应力的取值和最终的路面设计厚度，陈立杰等通过研究指出传统 S-N 疲劳曲线在宽应力比范围内并不呈现出明显线性关系，由此将疲劳方程后延得到的疲劳强度值是不合适的，据此计算出来的抗拉强度结构系数也就存在较大的偏差，导致沥青路面抗疲劳设计的精准度大打折扣。

对不同加载方式、试件形状、试件尺寸下的沥青混合料疲劳试验，试件内部将会产生不同的应力状态，而不同的应力状态将直接导致不同的疲劳寿命试验结果，这也正是前述不同试验方法下疲劳试验结果差异性较大的症结所在。因此，可采用前述的屈服准则思想，利用不同应力状态下强度屈服面和不同应力状态下疲劳应力路径，开发出一种基于屈服准则思想的疲劳特性分析新方法。

如图 7.6 所示，一方面，轨迹线上初始状态点 C 到破坏状态点 D 的距离即 CD 的长短表征了其抗疲劳破坏的能力，CD 越长，其抗疲劳能力越强，因此，可用 OC 与 OD 的长度之比来表征其抗疲劳破坏的能力，即

$$\Delta_1 = \frac{D_{OC}}{D_{OD}} \tag{7.11}$$

另一方面，破坏点 D 的纵坐标即剪应力强度 $\sqrt{J_{2N_f}}$ 表征了在对应疲劳试验条件下，材料或结构所具有的抗破坏的能力，对于确定的屈服面条件，即剪应力强度 $\sqrt{J_{2N_f}}$ 一定的情况下，疲劳试验时的初始剪应力强度 $\sqrt{J_{2i}}$ 越小，其抗疲劳性能越强，因此，可用点 C 与点 D 的纵坐标之比来表征其抗疲劳破坏的能力，即

$$\Delta_2 = \frac{\sqrt{J_2}}{\sqrt{J_{2N_f}}} \tag{7.12}$$

7.2 基于屈服准则思想不同应力状态下沥青混合料疲劳特性的归一化

从以上分析可以看出,式 (7.11)、式 (7.12) 均具有明确的力学物理意义,同时根据图 7.6 的几何意义可知,二者的数值大小也是相等的,即

$$\Delta = \Delta_1 = \Delta_2 = \frac{D_{OC}}{D_{OD}} = \frac{\sqrt{J_2}}{\sqrt{J_{2N_f}}} \tag{7.13}$$

式 (7.13) 表征了疲劳试验时材料或结构所处的初始应力状态 (与应力水平有关) 与其对应的抗力 (剪应力强度) 的相对大小,疲劳试验时,每一个应力水平或应变水平对应于一个 Δ,不同的 Δ 对应不同的疲劳寿命,通过建立 Δ 与疲劳寿命 N_f 的对应关系,即可建立不同应力状态下沥青混合料的疲劳方程。

$$N_f = r_1 (\Delta)^{-r_2} \tag{7.14}$$

对于极端加载情况,当 Δ 等于 1 时,疲劳初始剪应力强度等于破坏点剪应力强度,即疲劳试验应力水平等于其疲劳动载强度,因此,疲劳试验时试件将一次性破坏,即 $N_f=1$。所以方程应满足 $\Delta=1$,$N_f=1$ 这个 "边界条件"。将 $\Delta=1$,$N_f=1$ 代入式 (7.14) 中得 $r_1=1$,即

$$N_f = (\Delta)^{-r_2} \tag{7.15}$$

而目前基于应力水平和名义应力比建立的沥青混合料 S-N 传统疲劳方程中,k 均不等于 1,这也说明基于应力水平和名义应力比建立的沥青混合料疲劳方程是不能后延到 $N_f=1$ 的。

3. 不同应力状态下疲劳特性的归一化

沥青混合料是一种典型的黏弹性材料,不同加载速度与温度下的沥青混合料具有不同的强度,亦具有不同的屈服面。疲劳试验时,不同的应力水平对应于不同的疲劳加载速率,进而对应于不同加载速率下的强度屈服面,因此,需要通过确定不同应力状态的疲劳应力水平对应下的屈服面,进而建立 Δ 与疲劳寿命 N_f 的对应关系 $N_f = (\Delta)^{-r_2}$。

将直接拉伸、间接拉伸及单轴压缩三种应力状态下疲劳初始点分别沿着对应应力状态下的疲劳应力路径交于对应加载速率下的强度屈服面,得到疲劳初始剪应力强度 $\sqrt{J_2}$ 与破坏点剪应力强度 $\sqrt{J_{2N_f}}$ 比值 Δ,见表 7.8。

表 7.8 不同应力状态下疲劳试验剪应力强度比 Δ

应力状态	$\sqrt{J_2}$	$\sqrt{J_{2N_f}}$	Δ
直接拉伸	0.144	1.703	0.085
	0.289	2.013	0.143
	0.577	2.401	0.24
	0.866	2.628	0.33

续表

应力状态	$\sqrt{J_2}$	$\sqrt{J_{2N_f}}$	Δ
间接拉伸	0.52	6.783	0.077
	1.04	7.71	0.135
	2.082	9.18	0.227
	3.122	10.07	0.31
单轴压缩	1.155	12.81	0.09
	1.443	13.457	0.107
	1.732	14.011	0.124
	2.021	14.496	0.139

将表 7.8 得到的不同应力状态下剪应力强度比与不同应力状态下沥青混合料疲劳寿命建立关系，如表 7.9 所示。

表 7.9　不同应力状态下疲劳寿命与剪应力强度比关系

| 直接拉伸 || 间接拉伸 || 单轴压缩 ||
Δ	N_f	Δ	N_f	Δ	N_f
0.085	294106	0.077	1301910	0.09	698652
	421718		1310276		895372
	390179		1281993		848480
	489512		1240976		747376
0.143	47879	0.135	53822	0.107	207016
	29987		61260		175582
	50346		38986		214563
	36304		46180		198745
0.24	3447	0.227	2159	0.124	79913
	4790		2338		87997
	3614		1989		100212
	2891		2456		96147
0.33	791	0.31	356	0.139	30436
	1212		551		22696
	1114		435		26120
	856		398		27685

根据基于屈服准则思想的疲劳特性分析新方法，将表 7.9 中不同应力状态下疲劳寿命与剪应力强度比在双对数坐标中进行曲线拟合，如图 7.7 所示。

7.2 基于屈服准则思想不同应力状态下沥青混合料疲劳特性的归一化

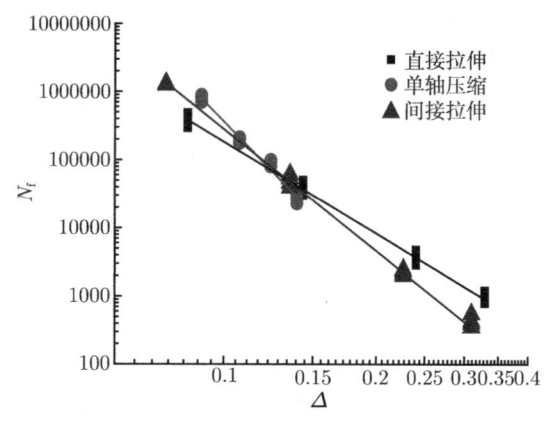

图 7.7　基于屈服准则思想的不同应力状态下疲劳新方程

如图 7.2 所示, 不同应力状态下的沥青混合料疲劳试验结果在 $(\Delta \sim N_{\rm f})$ 双对数坐标系中均表现出很好的线性关系, 拟合参数如表 7.10 所示。

表 7.10　不同应力状态下疲劳方程拟合参数

应力状态	r_2	相关系数
直接拉伸	5.226	0.955
间接拉伸	5.627	0.952
单轴压缩	5.478	0.999

与传统 S-N 疲劳曲线对比, 基于疲劳特性分析新方法的不同应力状态下的疲劳曲线差异性已大大降低了, 且把不同应力状态下的疲劳数据点作为一个整体来看, 已很难区别开来, 数据点非常接近, 可以进行归一化处理。将不同应力状态下疲劳试验结果 $N_{\rm f}$ 与 Δ 在双对数坐标中同时进行拟合, 得到一条归一化疲劳方程, 如图 7.8 所示。

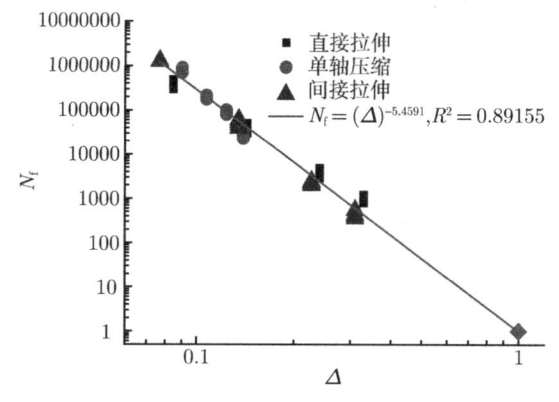

图 7.8　不同应力状态下疲劳特性归一化方程

不同应力状态下疲劳特性归一化方程 $N_f = (\Delta)^{-5.4591}$ 在双对数坐标系中表现出很好的线性关系，且相关系数较高，达到了将不同应力状态下疲劳特性归一化的目标。由于直接拉伸、单轴压缩与间接拉伸三种疲劳试验加载方式不同，且试件成型方式与形状也不同，所以与传统方法相比，新方法减小甚至消除了加载方式、试件形状、试件尺寸对疲劳试验结果的影响，这种新的疲劳分析方法为不同加载方式、试件形状、试件尺寸下疲劳试验结果的对比提供了可能，实现了对不同疲劳试验方法试验结果的统一，为实现从材料疲劳到结构疲劳的科学转化提供了理论、方法与技术依据。

7.3 与真实应力比疲劳方程的比较

沥青混合料是一种典型的黏弹性材料，其强度与加载速率和温度密切相关。真实应力比疲劳方程考虑了加载速率对强度的影响，可将不同加载频率(加载速率)下的疲劳曲线进行归一化。长沙理工大学的吕松涛定义名义应力比用 t_{dz} 表示，定义真实应力比用 t_s 表示，确定名义应力比时须首先进行固定加载速率下的沥青混合料标准静载强度试验，确定真实应力比时须进行不同加载速率下的动载强度 S_{dz} 试验，因此，真实应力比 t_s 可表示为

$$t_s = \sigma/S_{dz} \tag{7.16}$$

式中，σ 为疲劳试验施加的应力水平；S_{dz} 为与加载频率和应力水平相对应的加载速率下的疲劳动载强度。真实应力比与疲劳寿命的疲劳方程为

$$N_f = (t_s)^a \tag{7.17}$$

进一步分析 Δ 的物理意义：

$$\Delta = \frac{D_{OC}}{D_{OD}} = \frac{\sqrt{J_2}}{\sqrt{J_{2N_f}}} \tag{7.18}$$

在一维应力状态下：

$$J_2 = \frac{1}{6}\left[(\sigma_1 - \sigma_2)^2 + (\sigma_2 - \sigma_3)^2 + (\sigma_3 - \sigma_1)^2\right] = \frac{1}{3}\sigma^2 \tag{7.19}$$

$$J_{2N_f} = \frac{1}{3}\sigma_{1s}^2 \tag{7.20}$$

因此

$$\Delta = \frac{D_{OC}}{D_{OD}} = \frac{\sqrt{J_2}}{\sqrt{J_{2N_f}}} = \frac{\sigma_1}{\sigma_{1s}} = t_s \tag{7.21}$$

式 (7.21) 即为一维应力状态下基于屈服准则思想的表征其抗疲劳破坏能力的表达式，这与真实应力比的定义完全一致，因此，在均质、各向同性、线性弹性的假设前提下，真实应力比的思想同样可以推广到其他应力状态，或者说，不同应力状态下疲劳特性的归一化就是真实应力比在三维空间中的推广。

7.4 结　　论

(1) 对不同应力状态下沥青混合料进行疲劳试验，得到了基于两种 S-N 疲劳方程的不同应力状态下疲劳试验结果具有较大的差异性，导致使用不同试验方法的抗疲劳性能无法对比评价。

(2) 对不同应力状态下沥青混合料进行与疲劳试验加载速率对应的强度试验，分别得到不同应力状态在不同加载速率下的强度值，根据 Desai 强度屈服面模型和不同加载速率下不同应力状态的强度值，建立了不同加载速率下的强度屈服面。

(3) 基于屈服准则思想，疲劳试验时的初始应力状态 $(I_1,\sqrt{J_2})$ 与其对应加载速度下的极限破坏状态时的 $(I_{1N_f},\sqrt{J_{2N_f}})$ 决定了沥青混合料的抗疲劳性能，提出了以疲劳轨迹线上的距离之比以及初始剪应力强度 $\sqrt{J_{2i}}$ 与剪应力强度 $\sqrt{J_{2N_f}}$ 之比作为疲劳性能评价指标。在此基础上建立了一种疲劳寿命 N_f 关于剪应力强度比 Δ 的基于屈服准则思想的疲劳特性分析新方法，与传统疲劳方法相比，新方法减少甚至消除了加载方式、试件形状、试件尺寸对疲劳试验结果的影响，为实现从材料疲劳到结构疲劳的科学转化提供了理论、方法与技术依据。

(4) 本章的疲劳试验在一种沥青材料一种温度条件下进行，只有三种应力状态，且分别只有一种尺寸，对于不同沥青材料、温度、老化时间、其他应力状态和其他试件尺寸的疲劳试验结果还需要进一步的研究，疲劳特性的归一化还有待进一步的深入研究。

参 考 文 献

[1] Kim Y R, Lee H J, Little D N. Fatigue characterization of asphalt concrete using viscoelasticity and continuum damage theory[J]. Journal of the Association of Asphalt Paving Technologists, 1997, 66

[2] Lundström R, Isacsson U. Characterization of asphalt concrete deterioration using monotonic and cyclic tests[J]. International Journal of Pavement Engineering, 2003, 4(3):143-153

[3] Benedetto H D, Baaj H, Roche C D L, et al. Fatigue of bituminous mixtures[J]. Materials & Structures, 2004, 37(3):202-216

[4] 吕松涛. 基于非线性疲劳损伤的沥青路面轴载换算 [J]. 工程力学, 2012, 29(10): 268-274

[5] Kim J, West R C. Application of the viscoelastic continuum damage model to the indirect tension test at a single temperature. Journal of Engineering Mechanics, 2010, 136(4): 496-505

[6] Benedetto H D, Roche C D L, Baaj H, et al. Fatigue of bituminous mixtures. Materials & Structures, 2004, 37(3): 202-216

[7] 吕松涛, 郑健龙. 基于耗散能理论的老化沥青混合料疲劳方程 [J]. 中外公路, 2012, 32(3):284-286

[8] 吕松涛. 用真实应力比表征的老化沥青混合料疲劳性能 [J]. 公路交通科技, 2012, 29(10):1-6.

[9] Li N, Molenaar A A A, Ven M F C V D, et al. Characterization of fatigue performance of asphalt mixture using a new fatigue analysis approach[J]. Construction & Building Materials,2013,45(45):45-52

[10] Li N, Molenaar A A A, Pronk A C, et al. Effect of Specimen Size on Fatigue Behavior of Asphalt Mixture in Laboratory Fatigue Tests[M]// 7th RILEM International Conference on Cracking in Pavements. Amsterdam: Springer, 2012:827-836

[11] Li N, Molenaar A A A, Pronk A C, et al. Investigation into the Size Effect on Four Point Bending Fatigue Tests[M]. Proceedings of the 3rd Workshop on 4PB, Davis, California, 2012:444-489

[12] Akhaveissy A H, Desai C S, Mostofinejad D, et al. FE analysis of RC structures using DSC model with yield surfaces for tension and compression[J]. Computers & Concrete, 2013, 11(2): 123-148

[13] Mannan U A, Islam M R, Tarefder R A. Effects of recycled asphalt pavements on the fatigue life of asphalt under different strain levels and loading frequencies[J]. International Journal of Fatigue, 2015, 78: 72-80

第 8 章 结论与展望

8.1 主 要 结 论

为了认识重复荷载作用下沥青混合料疲劳损伤的产生、演化及累计的过程,揭示其强度和刚度衰变规律,开展了沥青混合料非线性疲劳损伤特性研究。从疲劳方程的角度描述了沥青混合料的疲劳特性,建立了传统疲劳方程和基于真实应力比的疲劳方程,并应用真实应力比疲劳方程提出了计算沥青面层抗拉强度结构系数的新方法;通过直接拉伸疲劳试验及剩余强度试验,揭示了刚度和剩余强度的衰变规律,分别以刚度和剩余强度定义的损伤变量,建立了能考虑临界损伤的非线性疲劳损伤修正模型,分别构建了沥青混合料基于刚度和剩余强度的损伤演化方程;分析了基于刚度和剩余强度衰变定义的损伤变量的差异,建立了基于剩余强度和刚度定义的损伤变量 D_s 和 D_f 的相关函数关系;最后将沥青混合料的非线性疲劳损伤特性研究成果应用到沥青路面设计轴载换算中,建立了一种能考虑损伤程度(或加载历史)影响的轴载换算新方法。获得了如下主要结论:

(1) 速度特性试验说明加载速率对沥青混合料强度影响显著,动载强度随加载速率可近似表示为幂函数关系 $S = 2.583v^{0.2}$,揭示了沥青混合料的强度随加载速率变化的本质特性;通过引入动载强度和真实应力比的概念,建立了基于真实应力比的疲劳方程 $t_s = N_f^{-0.218}$。基于真实应力比的疲劳方程不仅反映了沥青混合料的重复荷载作用下的疲劳性质,而且反映了一次荷载作用下的强度破坏性质,从而揭示了强度破坏和疲劳破坏的内在联系。

(2) 应用真实应力比疲劳方程建立了沥青面层抗拉强度结构系数计算新方法,由真实应力比疲劳方程可以近似后延到 $N_f = 1$ 时 $t_s = 1$,用动载强度 S_{dz} 取代极限抗拉强度 σ_1,动载强度是随加载速率和温度而变化的,符合沥青混合料本身的黏弹性性质,因此新方法比原有方法更加科学合理。

(3) 不同应力水平下的应力应变滞回曲线变化规律表明,疲劳破坏时累计耗散能并不是常量,与应力水平有关。沥青混合料累计耗散能与疲劳寿命之间存在良好的关系,耗散能是分析和预测沥青混合料疲劳特性的有效方法。

(4) 建立了动模量幂函数衰变模型 $E(N) = (E_0 - E_{\min})(1 - N/N_f)^m + E_{\min}$,动模量衰变具有确定的非线性特性,前一阶段衰变速度较稳定,在寿命比 90% 左右时衰变速度加快,进入急剧衰变阶段;衰变规律表明应力水平越大动模量随寿命比衰变得越快，衰变参数 m 随应力水平增大而增大。

(5) 获取了以动模量定义的临界损伤，临界损伤随真实应力比增大而减小，可近似表示为 $D_c = 0.53 - 1.26t_s$。

(6) 疲劳破坏全过程分为两个阶段：疲劳损伤累计阶段即循环荷载下的疲劳损伤累计过程，以及强度破坏阶段即最后一次加载的强度破坏过程；提出了一种能考虑临界损伤的非线性疲劳损伤修正模型

$$D = D_c \left[1 - \left(1 - \frac{N}{N_f}\right)^m \right]$$

通过不同应力水平的疲劳试验数据，验证了非线性疲劳损伤修正模型，构建了基于刚度（动模量）衰变的非线性疲劳损伤演化方程：

$$D_f(N) = \left(0.53 - 0.27\sigma^{0.8}\right) \left[1 - \left(1 - \frac{N}{N_f}\right)^{0.29 \cdot \sigma^{0.67}} \right]$$

(7) 通过两级荷载下的疲劳试验，损伤累计受到加载次序的影响，验证了沥青混合料疲劳损伤累计的非线性。由两级荷载下的疲劳试验结果发现：从低应力到高应力加载时 $N_1/N_{f1} + N_2/N_{f2} < 1$；而从高应力到低应力加载时 $N_1/N_{f1} + N_2/N_{f2} > 1$；给出了两级荷载加载和损伤演化的路径图，直观而合理地解释了两级荷载下的疲劳试验结果。

(8) 建立了剩余强度幂函数退化模型 $S_r(N) = (S_0 - \sigma_{\max})(1 - N/N_f)^s + \sigma_{\max}$，揭示了不同应力水平下剩余强度的衰变规律；构建了基于剩余强度的沥青混合料疲劳损伤演化方程：

$$D_s(N) = \left(1 - 0.213 \cdot \sigma^{0.8}\right) \left[1 - (1 - N/N_f)^{0.156} \right]$$

(9) 相同材料同等寿命比的条件下基于剩余强度定义的损伤要比基于刚度的大；基于刚度（动模量）定义的损伤变量，由有效应力等价原理推导得到，在理论上还不完善，刚度即变形特性属于一种对内部结构缺陷或损伤分布反应钝感的材料特性；而基于剩余强度来度量疲劳损伤有着天然的破坏准则，与损伤的原始定义吻合，属于一种对内部结构缺陷或损伤分布反应敏感的材料特性，因此选用组织敏感量剩余强度作为疲劳损伤评价参数比组织不敏感量刚度更具有优越性。

(10) 统一了基于剩余强度和刚度的损伤变量定义方法，基于刚度和剩余强度关联的损伤曲线能较好地预测沥青混合料的损伤演化规律；关联系数 ω 可认为是一材料常数，提出了对以刚度（动模量）定义的损伤变量的修正式：

$$D = \left(1 - \frac{E}{E_0}\right)^{0.646}$$

基于刚度和剩余强度关联的损伤，一方面与单独基于刚度定义的损伤相比准确性得到提高，另一方面与单独基于剩余强度定义的损伤相比大大降低了费用和试验工作量，省时省力。

(11) 应用沥青混合料的非线性疲劳损伤特性，建立了一种能够考虑损伤程度或加载历史影响的沥青路面轴载换算新方法，其标准轴载换算公式为

$$N = \sum_{i=1}^{K} C_1 \cdot C_2 \cdot n \cdot \left(\frac{P_i}{P_s}\right)^{4.35} \cdot B$$

并绘制了不同轴载修正系数 B 随年限变化的诺模图，算例分析表明传统轴载换算方法低估了累计轴载作用次数。

研究成果对于推进沥青路面轴载换算方法的发展，完善沥青路面设计方法，提高沥青路面耐久性和设计水平有重要意义。

8.2 创 新 点

(1) 建立了沥青混合料基于真实应力比的疲劳方程，该方程既可以体现重复加载的疲劳破坏，又可以涵盖一次加载的强度破坏，从而揭示了强度破坏和疲劳破坏的内在联系；以此为基础，建立了一种沥青面层抗拉强度结构系数计算新方法。

(2) 提出了刚度和剩余强度关联的损伤变量修正公式，统一了基于剩余强度和刚度的损伤变量定义方法。

(3) 提出了能考虑临界损伤的疲劳损伤修正模型，构建了基于剩余强度的沥青混合料非线性疲劳损伤方程，以此为基础，建立了一种能够考虑损伤程度或加载历史影响的沥青路面轴载换算新方法。

8.3 不足与进一步工作构想

本书基于刚度和剩余强度对沥青混合料非线性疲劳损伤做了一定的探讨，影响疲劳性能的因素多且非常复杂，本书做的工作很有限，需要做的工作还很多，对沥青混合料非线性疲劳损伤特性进一步研究的建议如下：

(1) 本书加载方式采用的单轴直接拉伸疲劳，受力简单而均匀；但难以模拟路面的复杂受力状态，需要进一步研究复杂三维应力下的沥青混合料非线性疲劳损伤特性。

(2) 本书从材料力学性能衰变的宏观角度，分析了沥青混合料的非线性疲劳损伤特性，尚缺少从细观力学角度对疲劳损伤特性的分析，在描述疲劳损伤上建立宏细观指标间的联系，以及强度和刚度衰变的细观机理还有待进一步研究。

附　录

附　录

Durability of Innovative Construction Materials and Structures
Comparisons of synchronous measurement methods on various moduli of asphalt mixtures

Songtao Lv, Chaochao Liu *, Hui Yao, Jianlong Zheng

National Engineering Laboratory of Highway Maintenance Technology, Changsha University of Science & Technology, 410004 Hunan, PR China

HIGHLIGHTS

- Two synchronous measurement methods of different moduli for asphalt mixture were proposed.
- The effectiveness of two synchronous measurement methods was verified.
- The correlation and difference of moduli obtained by four test methods were analyzed.

GRAPHICAL ABSTRACT

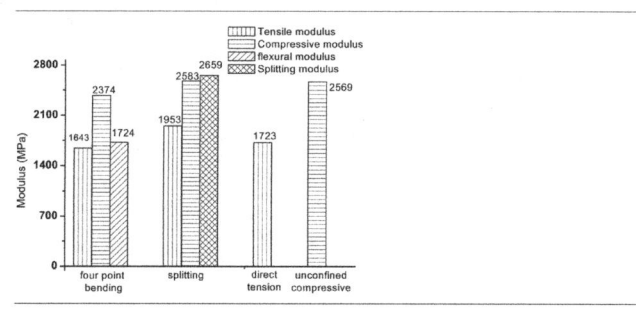

ARTICLE INFO

Article history:
Received 13 July 2017
Received in revised form 16 September 2017
Accepted 28 September 2017
Available online 6 October 2017

Keywords:
Road engineering
Asphalt mixture
Modulus test
Tensile moduli
Compressive moduli

ABSTRACT

Two new test methods were proposed to measure the different moduli of asphalt mixtures simultaneously based on four-point bending and indirect tensile tests. The new calculating formulas were derived for tensile and compressive moduli of asphalt mixtures under four-point bending loading model, which combining the equilibrium condition and the plane hypothesis in elastic mechanics theory. Meanwhile, on the basis of the test principle of indirect tensile moduli and Hooke's law in two-dimensional stress states, the new calculating formulas were derived in indirect tensile loading model. The moduli tests of four-point bending, indirect tensile, direct tension and unconfined compression were carried out separately to verify effectiveness of the new methods. The results of tensile and compressive moduli from the two new methods were compared with the direct tension moduli tests and unconfined compression moduli tests. The correlations among them were analyzed. The result indicates that the tensile and compression moduli of asphalt mixtures show a significant difference, and can be obtained by two methods simultaneously. The two new methods realize the synchronous measuring of various moduli of asphalt mixtures.

© 2017 Elsevier Ltd. All rights reserved.

1. Introduction

Multiplayer elastic system theory is the basic theory of asphalt pavement design method in the most countries [1,2]. Practice has proved that more than 100,000 km expressway and millions kilometers ordinary road were built according to the Chinese asphalt pavement design method. It has made an important contribution to the development of Chinese transportation [3]. However, there is no doubt that there remains a lot of in-adaptation, irrational and ineligible problems of the current asphalt pavement design theory and method [4].

Construction and Building Materials, 2018, 158: 1035-1045.

The major problems in design parameter of the current asphalt pavement design method are as follows:

(1) The current asphalt pavement design method of the most parts of the world adopts the multiplayer elastic system theory which on the basis of the hypothesis that the tensile and compressive moduli of the pavement material are equivalent [4,5], and only unconfined compressive moduli are used as design parameter during the structural design. However, lots of experimental results have proved that the tensile and compressive moduli of asphalt mixture material or semi-rigid base course materials are different, and the compressive moduli are usually much larger than the tensile moduli [6,7]. In fact, the actual stress states of pavement structure layers are that the tensile stress and compressive stress coexist in the pavement structure layers [8], and the stress states are upper compression and lower tension [9,10]. Therefore, it will cause large errors in the calculation results of pavement design which leads to overestimation of deformation resistance and resisting power of pavement and makes the design unsafe if only unconfined compressive moduli are used as design parameter during the mechanical calculation of pavement design, equating the tensile and compressive moduli. Those really affect the performance and service life of pavement negatively.
(2) The stress states of asphalt mixture during the experiments of obtaining moduli don't match with the stress states of asphalt pavements [11]. The general moduli test methods of pavement materials are moduli tests of four-point bending, indirect tensile and unconfined compression [12]. However, the stress states into materials are defined as tension, compression and the various combinations of them, without flexural tensile stress state or indirect tensile stress state [13], which means the flexural tensile moduli and indirect tensile moduli obtained by experiments are not corresponding to the stress state of the material. Therefore, it will cause large errors in the calculation results of pavement design if the flexural tensile moduli and indirect tensile moduli which are the macroscopic mechanical response of materials [14,15] were used as design parameters. Furthermore, the calculation models of the flexural tensile and indirect tensile moduli are both deduced on the basis of the hypothesis that the tensile and compressive moduli of the asphalt mixtures are equal, ignoring the dissimilarity between them [16]. And different moduli are obtained via different test methods; it means not only the waste of materials, labors, and capital but the impossibility of comparisons among the moduli obtained respectively. Which parameter could reflect the mechanical properties of asphalt mixture materials is still undetermined.

This paper proposed two new tests and calculation methods to measure the different moduli of asphalt mixtures simultaneously, one for the tensile, compressive and flexural tensile moduli which is based on the four-point bending test, and the calculation formula was derived which combining the equilibrium condition and the plane hypothesis in elastic mechanics theory. Another for the tensile, compressive and indirect tensile moduli of asphalt mixtures, which is based on the indirect tensile test, and the calculation formula was derived on the Hooke's law in two-dimensional stress states. The difference of tensile and compressive moduli were taken account into both two new methods, and the tensile and compressive moduli were obtained not under a simple stress state, the stress states of materials in the moduli tests of four-point bending and indirect tensile are more similar to a real stress states of pavement materials. The moduli tests of four-point bending, indirect tensile, direct tension and unconfined compression were carried out separately with the Material Test System (MTS). The results obtained by new & original methods are compared, and the correlations of them were analyzed. This paper can provide theoretical supports and method basis to optimize the design parameters of asphalt pavement structures.

2. Sample preparations

2.1. Materials

In this paper, the moduli tests of four-point bending, indirect tensile, direct tension and unconfined compression were carried out separately to verify the new methods. In order to reduce the discreteness of experimental results, the asphalt mixtures (fine-grained AC-13C) were taken as research object, which were composed of SBS modified asphalt binders, limestone aggregates, and limestone powders. The performance indexes of SBS modified asphalt are shown in Table 1, the physical and chemical properties of aggregates are shown in Table 2 and the dense skeleton type gradation of aggregate were chosen according to "Specifications for Design of Highway Asphalt Pavement" [5], the detail information is presented in Fig. 2. The optimum asphalt ratio were determined by Marshall Tests, the test results are displayed in Table 3.

The dense skeleton type gradation of aggregate was shown as Fig. 1.

2.2. Specimen manufacture

According to the specifications and test methods of bitumen and bituminous mixtures for highway engineering (JTG E20-2011) [17], samples 400 mm × 300 mm × 80 mm were made through the experiment of vibrating compaction. Then, the beam specimens were cut from block samples to the size of 360 mm × 50 mm × 50 mm for four-point-bending test and directly tensile test, as the Fig. 2(a), (c); the cylindrical specimens were drilled from block samples to the size of Φ100 mm × 80 mm for the unconfined compressive moduli test, as the Fig. 2(b); and the indirect tensile specimens were prepared by sliced the top and bottom surface of the specimens of unconfined compressive moduli test to the size of Φ100 mm × 60 mm, as the Fig. 2(d). All the specimens were preserved in a thermostat of 15 °C after the smoothing of the surface and pasted with strain gauge for the following experiment. There were five parallel tests for each moduli test.

3. Moduli test

3.1. Experiment condition

The static moduli of pavement material is calculated with the loads applied to the material and the corresponding rebound

Table 1
Performance Index of SBS (I-D) modified asphalt.

Technical indexes	Result	Specification
Penetration 25 °C, 100 g, 5 s (0.1 mm)	55.91	30–60
Ductility 5 cm/min, 5 °C (cm)	34.22	$\geq$20
Softening point TR&B (°C)	79.39	$\geq$60

Table 2
Physical and chemical properties of aggregates.

Items	Crushing value	Content of needle-like particles	Content of SiO$_2$	Apparent density
Value	10.8	7.8	1.79	2.578
Specification	$\leq$26	$\leq$20	/	/

附 录

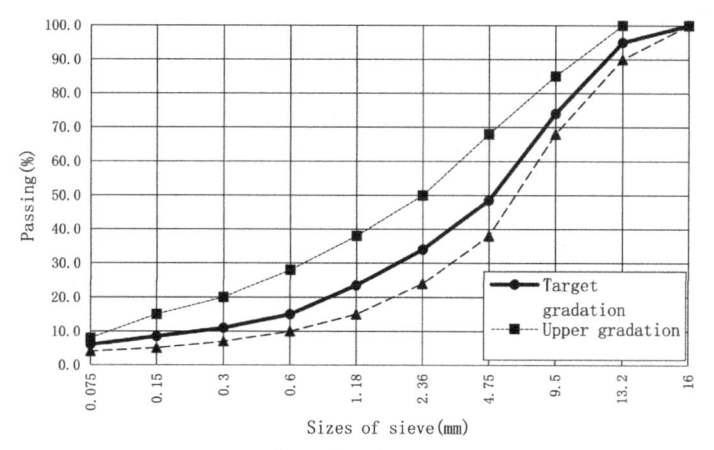

Fig. 1. Gradation of Aggregate.

Fig. 2. Test specimens for various tests and the adhesive method of strain gauge: (a) four-point bending test specimen, (b) indirect tensile test specimen, (c) direct tensile test specimen, (d) unconfined compressive test specimen.

Table 3
Marshall Test results at optimal asphalt content.

Asphalt aggregate ratio (%)	Bulk specific gravity (g cm^{-3})	Volume of air voids VV (%)	Voids filled with asphalt VFA (%)	Voids in mineral aggregate VMA/%	Marshall stability (kN)	Flow value (0.1 mm)
5.2%	2.54	4.51	67.20	16.11	12.71	27.89

deformation, under the condition of step loading and unloading. In order to inter-compare the moduli obtained by different methods, the test conditions were unified. The moduli test were conducted using Material Test System (MTS), the strain were measured by strain gauge and the data acquisition system of dynamic strain. The temperature of test was fixed at 15 °C which controlled by environmental chamber, as Fig. 2(a), and the loading rate was 0.4 MPa/s based on the general test condition according to the specifications and test methods of bitumen and bituminous mixtures for highway engineering (JTG E20-2011) [17]. In this paper the magnitude of the seven stages loading in the moduli test procedure are 0.1P, 0.2P ...0.7P, P is the homologous damage load of material, and dynamic strain collection system was selected uniformly to collect and record test data. The loading procedure was 1) Taking 0.2P as pre-compaction load to pre-process the specimen at the loading rate of 0.4 MPa/s, and unload after a minute at the same loading rate; 2) Loading the first stage loading at the loading rate of 0.4 MPa/s, and unload to zero immediately when the loading reached 0.1P, remaining no load for 30 s. 3) Carrying second to seventh stage loading in step two.

Each moduli tests were shown as Fig. 3.

3.2. Tensile and compressive resilient moduli test by four-point bending method

3.2.1. Calculation formula

The new tensile and compressive resilient moduli calculation models of four-point bending method were derived respectively on the basis of combining the equilibrium condition and the plane hypothesis in elastic mechanics [12,18], the tensile and compressive strains used in the derivation process of the calculation models were the tensile strain at the bottom of specimen and the compressive strain at the top of specimen. The derivation process of the calculation models is described in detail as follows.

The specimen's dimensions of four-point bending moduli test are represent by L for length, b for width and h for height, the loads applied to the specimens is P. The force diagram of specimen are shown in Fig. 4(a); and stress distributions of tensile and compressive in the cross-section of specimen are shown in Fig. 4(b), (c).

There is a neutral plane, without tensile or compressive stress as the Fig. 4(a) shown. Taking a micro area unit paralleling to the neutral plane as shown in Fig. 4(b), (c), $dA = bdx$. The bending

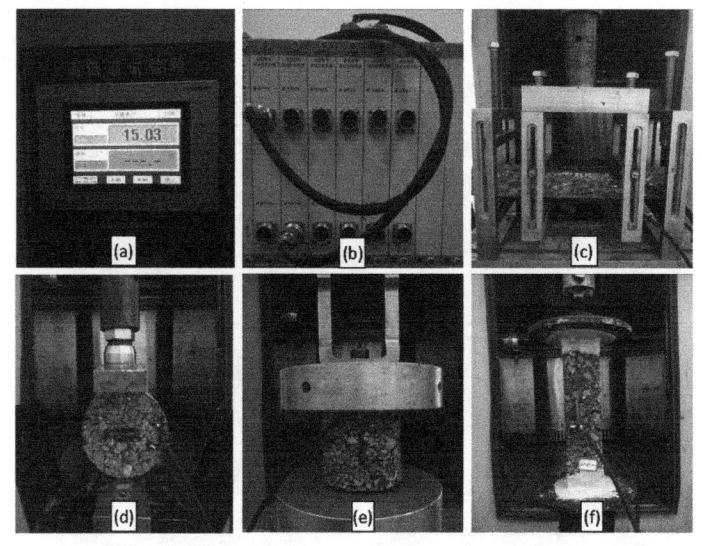

Fig. 3. The diagram of test equipment: (a) environmental chamber, (b) the data acquisition system of strain, (c) four-point bending test, (d) indirect tensile test, (e) unconfined compressive test, (f) direct tensile test.

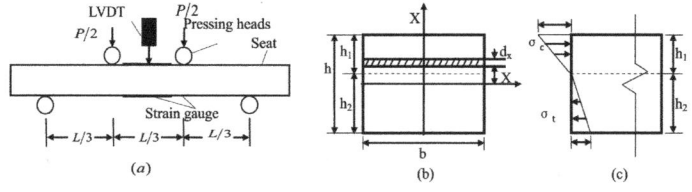

Fig. 4. (a) The force diagram of specimen (b), (c) the stress distributions of tensile and compressive in the cross-section of specimen.

moment on the mid-span cross-section caused by the internal stress can be expressed as:

$$M = \int_0^{h_1} \frac{\sigma_c}{h_1} bx^2 dx + \int_{-h_2}^{0} \frac{\sigma_t}{h_2} bx^2 dx \qquad (1)$$

After integration, there are:

$$M = \sigma_c bh_1^2/3 + \sigma_t bh_2^2/3 = E_c \varepsilon_c bh_1^2/3 + E_t \varepsilon_t bh_2^2/3 \qquad (2)$$

The plane hypothesis:

$$\varepsilon_t/h_2 = \varepsilon_c/h_1 \qquad (3)$$

And the equilibrium condition:

$$\int_0^{h_1} \frac{\sigma_c}{h_1} bxdx = \int_{-h_2}^{0} \frac{\sigma_t}{h_2} bxdx \Rightarrow \sigma_c h_1 = \sigma_t h_2 \qquad (4)$$

According to $E_c = \sigma_c/\varepsilon_c, E_t = \sigma_t/\varepsilon_t$ and moment $M = PL/6$, combining the formula (2)–(4), the formulas of tensile and compressive moduli test by four-point bending method were proposed as follows:

$$E_c = \frac{\sigma_{cmax}}{\varepsilon_{cmax}} = \frac{3M}{bh_2 h \varepsilon_c} = \frac{PL(\varepsilon_t + \varepsilon_c)}{2b\varepsilon_c^2 h^2} \qquad (5)$$

$$E_t = \frac{\sigma_{tmax}}{\varepsilon_{tmax}} = \frac{3M}{bh_2 h \varepsilon_t} = \frac{PL(\varepsilon_t + \varepsilon_c)}{2b\varepsilon_t^2 h^2} \qquad (6)$$

where, σ_c is the compressive stress, ε_c is the corresponding compressive strain at the top of specimen compressive strain of the upper surface; σ_t is the tensile stress ε_t is the corresponding tensile strain at the bottom of specimen; E_c is the compressive moduli, E_t is the tensile moduli; other symbols are the same meanings as above.

And the formula of flexural moduli was given in the specifications and test methods of bitumen and bituminous mixtures for highway engineering (JTG E20-2011) [17]:

$$E_f = \frac{23PL^3}{108bh^3 w} \qquad (7)$$

where E_f is the flexural moduli; w is the deflection; other symbols are the same meanings as above.

The parameters, like the length of specimen L, the thickness h and the height of specimen b are known, and the load P, midspan deflection, w compressive strain ε_c and tensile strain ε_t were obtained by tests. And bring all parameters into the formula to get the moduli.

3.2.2. Tests and results

P_b is 1.523 KN obtained by strength test according to the specifications and test methods of bitumen and bituminous mixtures for highway engineering (JTG E20-2011) [17], under the four-point bending load condition. The magnitudes of seven stage loading in the moduli test procedure are $0.1P_b, 0.2P_b \ldots 0.7P_b$, and the loading rate is 0.4 MPa/s (in order to be operable, the loading rate was converted to 1.002 KN/min). On the basis of flexural moduli test, two strain gauges were pasted on the middle position of bottom of specimen to measure the tensile strain, two strain gauges were pasted on the middle position of top of specimen to measure the compressive strain, and the deflection of the specimen were measured by LDVT. The adhesive method of strain gauge and the test procedure diagram were shown as Fig. 3(c).

Real-time situation of load application and strain acquisition were shown as Fig. 5.

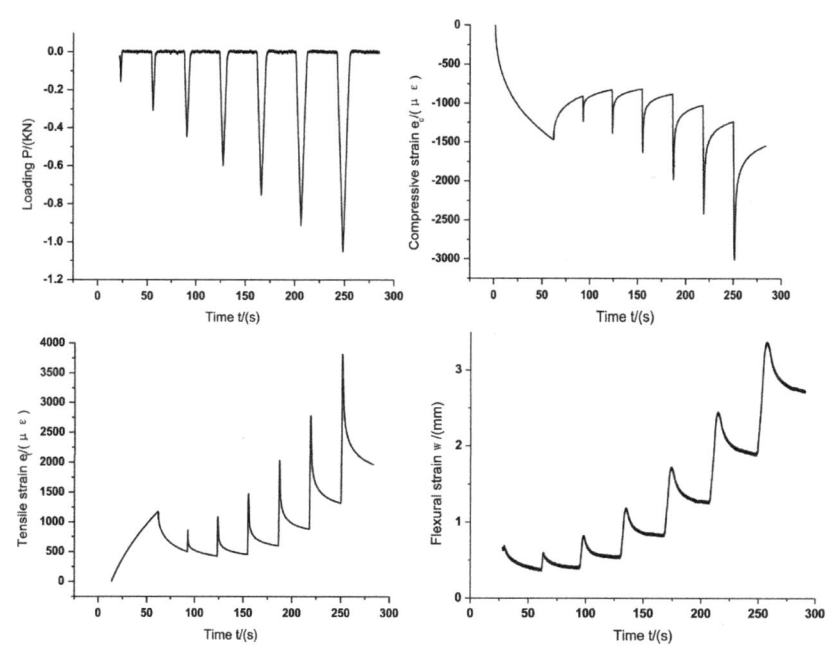

Fig. 5. Real time data acquisition of step load, compressive strain and tensile strain of four-point bending synchronous measurement test.

Table 4
The tensile and compressive resilient moduli in each loading levels of four-point bending tests.

Loading grades	Loading P_i (kN)	Compressive strain magnitude ($\mu\varepsilon$)	Tensile strain magnitude ($\mu\varepsilon$)	Deflection (mm)	Compressive resilient moduli (MPa)	Tensile resilient moduli (MPa)	Flexural resilient moduli (MPa)
2	0.2971	279.2	309.3	0.1354	2692	2193	2019
3	0.4569	461.8	588.6	0.2201	2587	1593	1829
4	0.6092	684.2	857.4	0.3274	2407	1533	1712
5	0.7615	899.7	1187.4	0.3904	2197	1261	1674
6	0.9138	1189.3	1548.2	0.5201	2122	1252	1616
7	1.0658	1460.9	1874.8	0.6297	1999	1214	1557
Average	/	/	/	/	2334	1507	1735

Table 5
The tensile and compressive resilient moduli of parallel tests for four-point bending tests.

Parallel tests	Tensile resilient moduli (MPa)	Compressive resilient moduli (MPa)	Flexural resilient moduli (MPa)
1	1508	2334	1735
2	1929	2598	1412
3	1367	2180	1751
4	1781	2271	1704
5	1771	2491	2022
Average value	1671	2375	1724
Variation coefficient	0.121	0.066	0.112

Origin correction method was taken to measure the moduli, the average value of resilience moduli at 2–7 grades loading was taken as the moduli value according to the Test Method for Static Moduli of resilience, which introduced in the specifications and test methods of bitumen and bituminous mixtures for highway engineering (JTG E20-2011) [17]. One sample test results were presented in Table 4, the loading and strains were gotten by Material Test System, and the moduli were calculated by formula (5) and (6).

The results of all five parallel moduli tests were summarized in Table 5.

3.3. Tensile and compressive resilient moduli test by indirect tensile method

3.3.1. Calculation formula

On the basis of the test principle of indirect tensile moduli and Hooke's law in two-dimensional stress states [19,20], the tensile and compressive moduli calculating formulas were derived in indirect tensile loading model. The tensile strain used in the derivation process of the calculation models were the transverse strain of specimen, as the Fig. 6(a) shown, and the compressive strain were the vertical strain of specimen. The derivation process of the calculation models were described in detail as follows.

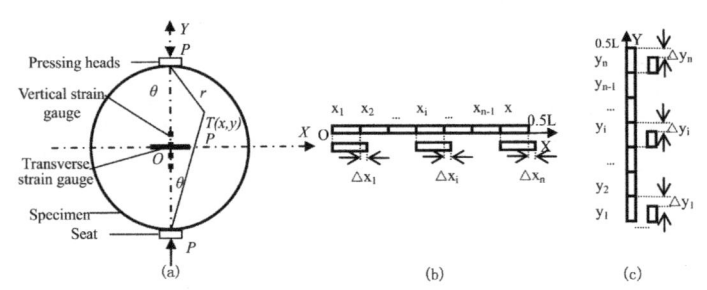

Fig. 6. (a) The force diagram of specimen, (b) Calculation diagram of the strain gauge deformation in the horizontal direction (c) Calculation diagram of the strain gauge deformation in the vertical radial.

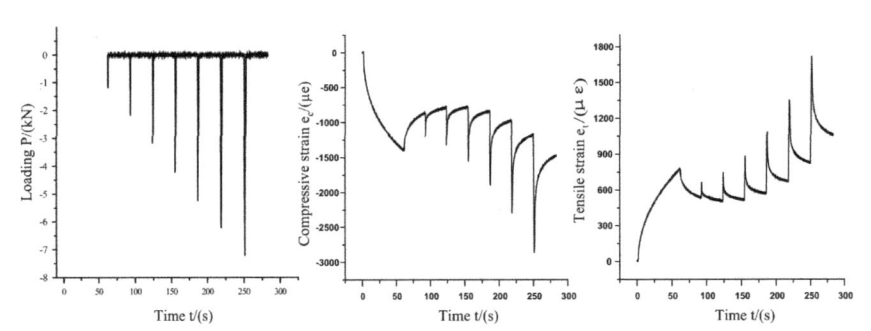

Fig. 7. Real time data acquisition of step load, compressive strain and tensile strain of indirect tensile synchronous measurement test.

The specimen's dimensions of indirect tensile moduli test are represent by D for diameter, L for height, and l is the length of strain gauge, the loads applied to the specimens is P. On the basis of plane stress states, Jian-hong YE etc. obtained the stress analytical equation of any point (T(x,y)) of Brazil disk at rectangular coordinates, according to the Airy stress function and the Principle of linear elastic superposition [21,22]. The stress analytical equations were as follows.

$$\begin{cases} \sigma_x = \frac{2P}{\pi L}\left(\frac{\sin^2\theta_1 \cos\theta_1}{r_1} + \frac{\sin^2\theta_2 \cos\theta_2}{r_2}\right) - \frac{2P}{\pi DL} \\ \sigma_y = \frac{2P}{\pi L}\left(\frac{\cos^3\theta_1}{r_1} + \frac{\cos^3\theta_2}{r_2}\right) - \frac{2P}{\pi DL} \\ \tau_{xy} = \frac{2P}{\pi L}\left(\frac{\sin\theta_1 \cos^2\theta_1}{r_1} - \frac{\sin\theta_2 \cos^2\theta_2}{r_2}\right) \end{cases} \quad (8)$$

So, according to the analytical equations of elastic mechanical problems based on plane stress problems and the geometric characteristics of OX axis and OY axis, the stress states of any point of OX axis or OY axis were obtained as follows.

The point of OX axis:

$$\begin{cases} \sigma_x(x) = \frac{2P}{\pi DL} \times \left[1 - \frac{16D^2 x^2}{(4x^2+D^2)^2}\right] \\ \sigma_y(x) = \frac{2P}{\pi DL} \times \left[1 - \frac{4D^4}{(4x^2+D^2)^2}\right] \\ \tau_{xy}(x) = 0 \end{cases} \quad (9)$$

The point of OY axis:

$$\begin{cases} \sigma_x(y) = \frac{2P}{\pi DL} \\ \sigma_y(y) = \frac{2P}{\pi DL} \times \left[1 - \frac{D^2}{R^2-y^2}\right] \\ \tau_{xy}(y) = 0 \end{cases} \quad (10)$$

where, $\sigma_x(x)$ is the tensile stress of any point of OX axis, $\sigma_y(x)$ is the compressive stress of any point of OX axis, $\tau_{xy}(x)$ is the sheer stress of any point of OX axis, $\sigma_x(y)$ is the tensile stress of any point of OY axis, $\sigma_y(y)$ is the compressive stress of any point of OY axis, $\tau_{xy}(y)$ is the sheer stress of any point of OY axis.

According to Hooke's law in two-dimensional stress states, and the difference between the tensile and compressive moduli, the relationship between stress and strain could be expressed as follows.

$$\begin{cases} \varepsilon_x(x) = \frac{\sigma_x(x)}{E_x} - \frac{\mu \sigma_y(x)}{E_y} \\ \varepsilon_y(y) = \frac{\sigma_y(y)}{E_y} - \frac{\mu \sigma_x(y)}{E_x} \end{cases} \quad (11)$$

Combining the formula (9)-(11), the strain formula of any point of OX axis or OY axis were obtained as follows.

The tensile strain of the any point of OX axis:

$$\varepsilon_x(x) = \frac{2P}{\pi DL}\left\{\frac{1}{E_x}\left[1 - \frac{16D^2 x^2}{(4x^2+D^2)^2}\right] - \frac{\mu}{E_y}\left[1 - \frac{4D^4}{(4x^2+D^2)^2}\right]\right\} \quad (12)$$

The compressive strain of any point of OY axis:

$$\varepsilon_y(y) = \frac{2P}{\pi DL}\left\{\frac{1}{E_y}\left(1 - \frac{D^2}{R^2-y^2}\right) - \frac{\mu}{E_x}\right\} \quad (13)$$

When the specimen was under loads, the changes of gauges were described as Fig. 6(b), (c). The distance from the center of specimen, also the center of the gauge, to the end of the gauge which was $l/2$, was divided in n parts on the basis of the theory of differential calculus, and the length of each part of horizontal direction was marked by $x_1, x_2, ..., x_n$; the length of each part of vertical direction was marked by $y_1, y_2, ..., y_n$. Then, it was obvious that:

$$\begin{cases} \sum_{i=1}^{n} x_i = \frac{l}{2} \quad (i=1,2,...,n) \\ \sum_{i=1}^{n} y_i = \frac{l}{2} \quad (i=1,2,...,n) \end{cases} \quad (14)$$

It is obvious that the bigger the n, the shorter the x_i and y, and when the n was big enough, the stress and strain of part i could be considered homogeneous and equivalent. The transverse and longitudinal micro-deformation of part i was expressed as follows.

$$\begin{cases} \Delta x_x(i) = \varepsilon_x(i) \times x_i \quad (i=1,2,...,n) \\ \Delta y_y(i) = \varepsilon_y(i) \times y_i \quad (i=1,2,...,n) \end{cases} \quad (15)$$

Then, the total deformation of the transverse and longitudinal gauge, Δu and Δv, are twice of the deformation of the part from the center of specimen to the end of the gauge respectively. It was shown as follows.

$$\begin{cases} \Delta u = 2\sum_{i=1}^{n}\Delta x_x(i) = 2\sum_{i=1}^{n}(\varepsilon_x(i) \times x_i) \\ \Delta v = 2\sum_{i=1}^{n}\Delta y_y(i) = 2\sum_{i=1}^{n}(\varepsilon_y(i) \times y_i) \end{cases} \quad (16)$$

According to the formula (11), the strain function, both of transverse and longitudinal direction, were continuous in the domain of the length of strain gauges. Then, after integration, the total deformation of the transverse and longitudinal gauge, Δu and Δv, could be gotten as follows approximately.

$$\begin{cases} \Delta u = 2\int_0^{\frac{l}{2}} \varepsilon_x(x)dx \\ \Delta v = 2\int_0^{\frac{l}{2}} \varepsilon_y(y)dy \end{cases} \quad (17)$$

Calculate the definite integral of formula (17), after bringing the formula (11) in the formula (17), and the total deformation of the transverse and longitudinal gauge, Δu and Δv, were obtained as follows (the value of total deformation of the gauge was taken positive value uniformly in the calculation).

$$\begin{cases} \Delta u = \frac{4P}{\pi L}\left[\left(\frac{\mu}{E_y} - \frac{1}{E_x}\right)\arctan\left(\frac{l}{D}\right) + \left(\frac{\mu}{E_y} + \frac{1}{E_x}\right) \times \frac{Dl}{l^2+D^2} + \left(\frac{1}{E_x} - \frac{\mu}{E_y}\right) \times \frac{l}{2D}\right] \\ \Delta v = \frac{4P}{\pi L}\left[\left(\frac{1}{E_y} - \frac{\mu}{E_x}\right) \times \frac{l}{2D} - \frac{1}{E_y}\ln\left(\frac{D-l}{D+l}\right)\right] \end{cases} \quad (18)$$

Solve the equation of the tensile moduli E_x and the compression moduli E_y according to formula (18), and E_x, E_y were obtained as follows.

$$E_x = \frac{4P}{\pi L} \times \frac{\left(\frac{Dl}{D^2+l^2} - \arctan\frac{l}{D} + \frac{l}{2D}\right) \times \left(\frac{l}{2D} - \ln\frac{D-l}{D+l}\right) + \frac{l}{2D} \times \left(\frac{Dl}{D^2+l^2} + \arctan\frac{l}{D} - \frac{l}{2D}\right) \times \mu^2}{\left(\frac{l}{2D} - \ln\frac{D-l}{D+l}\right) \times \varepsilon_h l - \mu \times \left(\frac{Dl}{D^2+l^2} + \arctan\frac{l}{D} - \frac{l}{2D}\right) \times \varepsilon_v l} \quad (19)$$

$$E_y = \frac{4P}{\pi L} \times \frac{\left(\frac{Dl}{D^2+l^2} - \arctan\frac{l}{D} + \frac{l}{2D}\right) \times \left(\frac{l}{2D} - \ln\frac{D-l}{D+l}\right) + \frac{l}{2D} \times \left(\frac{Dl}{D^2+l^2} + \arctan\frac{l}{D} - \frac{l}{2D}\right) \times \mu^2}{\mu \times \frac{l}{2D} \times \varepsilon_h l + \left(\frac{Dl}{D^2+l^2} - \arctan\frac{l}{D} + \frac{l}{2D}\right) \times \varepsilon_v l} \quad (20)$$

where μ is the Poisson ratio; other symbols are the same meanings as above. The parameters, like the diameter of specimen D, the thickness L, the effective length of gauge l and the Poisson ratio μ are known, and the load P, vertical strain of specimen ε_v and transverse strain of specimen ε_h were obtained by tests. And bring all parameters into the formula to get the moduli.

3.3.2. Test and results

On the basis of indirect tensile moduli test, P_s is 10.32 kN obtained by strength test according to the specifications and test methods of bitumen and bituminous mixtures for highway engineering (JTG E20-2011) [17], during the homologous damage loading of material under indirect tensile load condition. The magnitudes of the seven stage loading in the moduli test procedure are $0.1P_s, 0.2P_s \ldots 0.7P_s$, and the loading rate is 0.4 MPa/s (in order to be operable, the loading rate was converted to 361.9 kN/min). The adhesive methods of strain gauge used to measure the compressive and tensile strain are shown as Fig. 2(d) and the test procedure diagram are shown as Fig. 3(d). The Real-time situation of loading application and strain acquisition is shown as Fig. 7.

The results of one indirect tensile test sample results were presented in Table 6, the loading and strains were gotten by Material Test System, and the moduli were calculated by formula (19) and (20).

The results of all five parallel moduli tests were summarized in Table 7.

3.4. Direct tension test and unconfined compression test

3.4.1. Calculation formula

The formulas of tensile moduli obtained by direct tension test and the compression moduli obtained by unconfined compression test were presented in the specifications and test methods of bitumen and bituminous mixtures for highway engineering (JTG E20-2011) [17], as follows.

$$E_c = \frac{4P}{\pi d^2 \varepsilon_c} \quad (21)$$

$$E_t = \frac{P}{bh\varepsilon_t} \quad (22)$$

where d is the diameter of the compressive moduli test specimen; b is the width of the tensile moduli test specimen; h is the height of the tensile moduli test specimen and other symbols are the same meanings as above.

3.4.2. Test and results

The homologous damage loads of material under compressive and tensile load condition were 38.92 kN and 1.22 kN respectively, obtained by strength test according to the specifications and test methods of bitumen and bituminous mixtures for highway engineering (JTG E20-2011) [17], so the magnitude of the seven stage loading in the moduli test procedure are 0.1P, 0.2P, ..., 0.7P, and the loading rate were 0.4 MPa/s (in order to be operable, the loading rate was converted to 361.9 kN/min and 6 kN/min respectively). The adhesive methods of strain gauge used to measure the compressive and tensile strain were shown as Fig. 2(b), (c), and the test procedure diagram were shown as Fig. 3(e), (f).

Real-time situation of load application and strain acquisition were shown as Fig. 8.

The results of one tensile test sample and compressive test sample were presented in Table 8, the loading and strains were gotten by Material Test System, and the compressive and tensile moduli were calculated by formula (21) and (22).

The results of all five parallel moduli tests were summarized in Table 9.

4. Comparison and analysis of the test methods and test results

All the moduli average values obtained by four test methods are plotted in Fig. 9.

4.1. Comparison of the moduli obtained by two synchronous measurement test with the direct tensile test, unconfined compression test

As Fig. 9.shown:

a) The tensile, compressive and flexural moduli measured by four-point bending synchronous measurement method were 1643.43 MPa, 2374.95 MPa, 1724.73 MPa respectively, and the deviation of tensile moduli measured by four-point bending synchronous measurement method and direct tensile method were 4.6%, as the average value of direct tensile moduli was 1723.0 MPa. The deviation of compressive moduli measured by four-point bending synchronous measurement method and unconfined method were 7.6%, as the average value of unconfined compressive moduli was 2569.3 MPa. Both of the compressive moduli and tensile moduli measured by four-point bending synchronous measurement method were smaller than the moduli of direct tensile test and unconfined compressive test, the main reason for this phenomenon lies in the loading rate. The formu-

Table 7
The results of five parallel indirect tensile moduli tests.

Parallel tests	Tensile resilient moduli (MPa)	Compressive resilient moduli (MPa)	Indirect tensile resilient moduli (MPa)
1	2105	2519	2757
2	2097	2593	2718
3	2041	2539	2589
4	1706	2551	2597
5	1820	2659	2639
Average value	1953	2572	2660
Variation coefficient	0.083	0.019	0.025

Table 6
The tensile and compressive resilient moduli in each loading levels for one indirect tensile moduli test sample.

Loading grades	Loading P_i (kN)	Tensile strain magnitude (με)	Compressive magnitude strain (με)	Compressive resilient moduli (MPa)	Tensile resilient moduli (MPa)
2	2.274	205	516	2241	1902
3	3.360	260	655	2610	2191
4	4.224	340	810	2632	2270
5	5.294	411	1089	2501	2257
6	6.232	478	1237	2561	2228
7	7.223	654	1393	2570	1783
Average	/	/	/	2519	2105

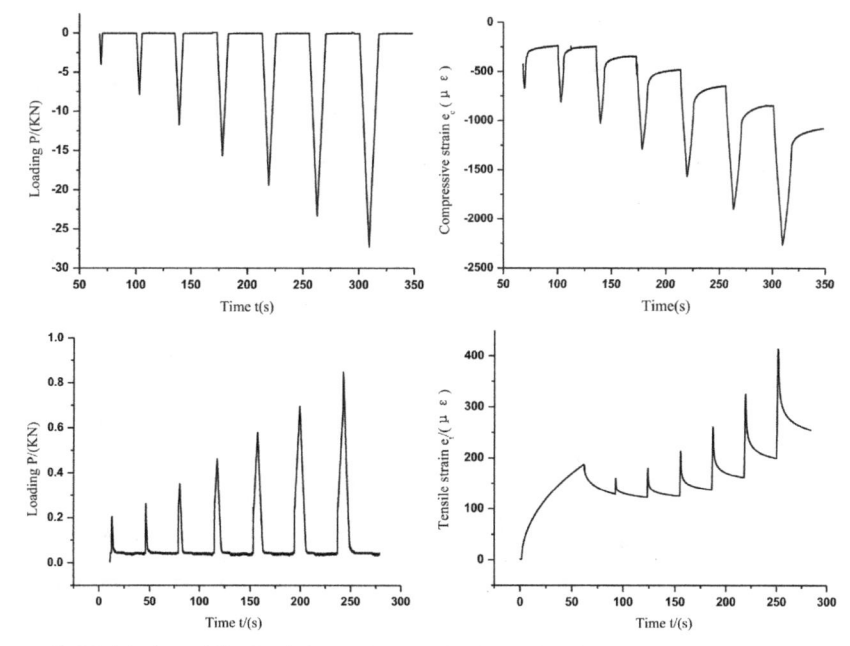

Fig. 8. Real time data acquisition of step load, compressive strain and tensile strain of unconfined compressive and direct tensile test.

Table 8
The tensile and compressive resilient moduli in each loading levels for one tensile and unconfined compressive moduli test sample.

Loading grades	Tensile loading P_i (kN)	Tensile strain magnitude (με)	Tensile resilient moduli (MPa)	Compressive loading P_i (kN)	Compressive strain magnitude (με)	Compressive resilient moduli (MPa)
2	0.262	67	1565	7.848	467	2137
3	0.352	84	1674	11.755	675	2218
4	0.461	102	1807	15.665	805	2478
5	0.581	120	1934	19.505	951	2613
6	0.695	132	2093	23.424	1043	2860
7	0.848	156	2177	27.242	1185	2927
Average value	/	/	1875	/	/	2539

Table 9
The results of five parallel tensile and unconfined compressive moduli tests.

Parallel tests	Tensile resilient moduli (MPa)	Compressive resilient moduli (MPa)
1	1875	2539
2	1801	2486
3	1505	2798
4	1711	2319
5	1723	2705
Average value	1723	2569
Variation coefficient	0.067	0.095

las of converting the loading rates were difference, Although the loading rates were all 0.4 MPa/s, the loading rate of four-point bending synchronous measurement test was calculated by the formula of calculating the four-point bending strength, so, the loading rates of compression on the top surface and tension on the down surface of specimen were not 0.4 MPa/s, they were less than 0.4 MPa/s. According to the speed dependence of the moduli of asphalt mixture [23], the moduli value obtained by four-point bending synchronous measurement method were less than the moduli obtained by direct tensile and unconfined compressive test. The above studies proved that the four-point bending synchronous measurement method made it possible to obtain the tensile moduli and compressive moduli simultaneously, but more works needed to determine the loading rates.

b) The tensile, compressive and indirect tensile moduli measured by indirect tensile synchronous measurement method were 1953.8 MPa, 2582.2 MPa, 2659.9 MPa, and the deviation of tensile moduli measured by indirect tensile synchronous measurement method and direct tensile method were 11.7%, the deviation of compressive moduli measured

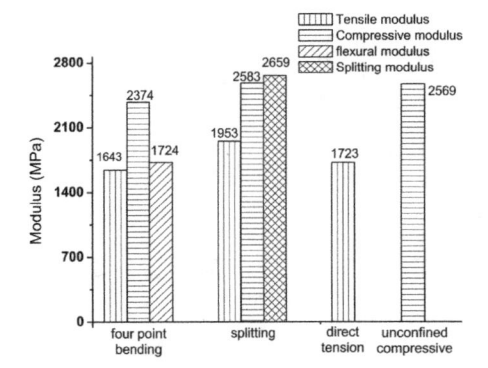

Fig. 9. The moduli average values obtained by this four test methods.

by indirect tensile synchronous measurement method and unconfined method were 0.5%. Both of the compressive moduli and tensile moduli measured by indirect tensile synchronous measurement method were larger than the moduli of direct tensile test and unconfined compressive test due to: 1) the same as the reason of four-point bending synchronous measurement method; 2) Compared with the direct tensile and unconfined compressive test which the test points of specimen were under one-dimensional stress state, the stress states of the test points of indirect tensile specimen were more complex for which were under two-dimensional stress states, and lots of researches indicated that different moduli values of asphalt mixture would be gotten under different stress conditions [23]. However, it's common for pavement material to sustain tensile and compressive stress simultaneously, therefore, the stress of indirect tensile specimen were much closer to the actual stress states of pavement material, and the moduli obtained by indirect tensile synchronous measurement method could reflect the deformation resistance of pavement material under the actual stress states more veritably.

4.2. Analysis of the difference between tensile and compressive moduli of asphalt mixture

The results of four-point bending synchronous measurement test in Tables 5 and 10 indicated that the compressive, tensile and flexural moduli of asphalt mixture were obtained synchronously, the average values of compressive, tensile and flexural moduli were 2374.9 MPa, 1643.4 MPa, 1724.7 MPa respectively; the variation coefficient of them were 0.066, 0.141, 0.112 severally; the ratio of compressive and tensile moduli was 1.45.

The results of indirect tensile synchronous measurement test in Tables 7 and 10 indicated that the compressive, tensile and indirect tensile moduli of asphalt mixture were obtained synchronously, the average values of compressive, tensile and indirect tensile moduli were 2582.2 MPa, 1953.8 MPa, 2659.9 MPa respectively; the variation coefficient of them were 0.083, 0.019, 0.025 respectively; the ratio of compressive and tensile moduli was 1.32.

And the average value of unconfined compressive test was 2569.3 MPa, the average value of direct tensile test was 1723.0 MPa, and the ratio of compressive and tensile moduli was 1.49.

The results of unconfined compressive moduli test, direct tensile moduli test, four-point bending synchronous measurement test and indirect tensile synchronous measurement test all indicated that there were differences between the compressive and tensile moduli of asphalt mixture.

The ratio of compressive and tensile moduli obtained by four-point bending synchronous measurement method were close to the direct tensile and unconfined compressive test, and the ratio of compressive and tensile moduli obtained by indirect tensile synchronous measurement method were different from them. Because that the test points of direct tensile, unconfined compressive and four-point bending specimen were under one-dimensional stress states, and the test points of indirect tensile specimen were under two-dimensional stress states [24], the resistance of tensile and compressive deformation of the test points would interact each other. Therefore, the moduli obtained by four-point bending synchronous measurement method were the reflection of deformation resistance of material itself, and the moduli obtained by indirect tensile synchronous measurement method were the reflection of deformation resistance of pavement material under the actual stress states.

4.3. Comparison of the two synchronous measurement methods

The synchronous testing of asphalt mixture moduli was realized by the two new measurement methods developed in this paper. However, the results of these two measurement methods were different, the average ratio of tensile moduli measured by these two measurement methods was 0.84, and the average ratio of compressive moduli was 0.92, both of the compressive moduli and tensile moduli measured by indirect tensile synchronous measurement method were larger than the four-point bending synchronous measurement method's. Two factors cause this phenomenon.

One is that the loading rates were calculated by different formulas, the loading rate of four-point bending test was calculated with the formula of calculating the four-point bending strength, and the loading rate of indirect tensile test was calculated with the formula of calculating the indirect tensile strength, both of the loading rates of these two tests were not the loading rates of the test points. So, even the loading rate of the tests was unified in 0.4 MPa/s, the loading rates of the test point were not unified.

Another is that the stress states of the test points of these two tests were different. The test points of four-point bending

Table 10
The ratio of compressive and tensile moduli obtained by four moduli tests.

Parallel tests	Ratio of compressive and tensile moduli obtained by four-point bending synchronous measurement test	Ratio of compressive and tensile moduli obtained by indirect tension synchronous measurement test	Ratio of compressive and tensile moduli obtained by tension and unconfined compressive test
1	1.55	1.20	1.35
2	1.35	1.24	1.38
3	1.59	1.24	1.86
4	1.34	1.49	1.35
5	1.43	1.45	1.56
Average value	1.45	1.32	1.49

specimen were under one-dimensional stress states, and the test points of indirect tensile specimen were under two-dimensional stress states. The moduli obtained by four-point bending synchronous measurement method were the reflection of deformation resistance of material itself which much closer to the moduli obtained by direct tensile and unconfined compressive test, and the moduli obtained by indirect tensile synchronous measurement method were the reflection of deformation resistance of pavement material under the actual stress states, which has important reference significance to the design of asphalt pavement structure as it's very common for pavement material to sustain tensile and compressive stress simultaneously.

In conclusion, the synchronous testing of asphalt mixture moduli was realized by the two new measurement methods developed in this paper, and the materials, labors, and capital were saved. Better yet, by considering the stress sates, the moduli obtained by indirect tensile synchronous measurement method could reflect the deformation resistance of pavement material under the actual stress states more veritably.

5. Conclusions

(1) The synchronous test of asphalt mixtures was realized for the moduli by two new measurement methods developed in this paper. With these synchronous measurement methods, the efficiency of moduli parameters measuring was improved greatly, and experimental resources were saved.

(2) The ratio of compressive and tensile moduli were in the range of 1.3–1.6 according to the test result. It indicates that there was a difference between the compressive and tensile moduli of asphalt mixture under static loading states. It is irrational to equate the compressive and tensile moduli in the design of pavement structures.

(3) The test points of four-point bending specimen are in a one-dimensional stress state, and that is approximate to a stress state of direct tensile and unconfined compressive specimens.

(4) The moduli obtained by the indirect tensile synchronous measurement method are closer to the moduli of pavement materials in the actual stress state. This has an important reference and significance for a design of asphalt pavement structures. Further research is also required in the near future.

Acknowledgements

This work was supported by National Natural Science Foundation of China (51578081, 5160858), Chinese Academy of Engineering Consulting Research Project (2017-XY-17), The Ministry of Transport Construction Projects of Science and Technology (2015318825120), Key Projects of Hunan Province-Technological Innovation Project in Industry (2016GK2096), National Engineering Laboratory Open Fund Project (kfh160102), and Scientific and Technological Innovation Project of Hunan Province for University Graduate Students (CX2017B457).

References

[1] Y. Gao, D. Geng, X. Huang, G. Li, Degradation evaluation index of asphalt pavement based on mechanical performance of asphalt mixture, Constr. Build. Mater. 140 (2017) 75–81.
[2] Jin'an SHEN, Overseas Asphalt Pavement Design Method Confluence, Communication Press, Beijing, China, 2004.
[3] Jian-long ZHENG, New structure design of durable asphalt pavement based on life increment, China J. Highway Transp. 27 (01) (2014) 1–7.
[4] Zu-kang YAO, Asphalt Pavement Structure Design, Communications Press, Beijing: China, 2011.
[5] JTG D50-2006, Specifications for Design of Highway Asphalt Pavement[S], 2006.
[6] Hong-wu ZHANG, Liang ZHANG, Qiang GAO, The parametric variational principle and finite element method for material with different moduli in tension and compression, Eng. Mech. 29 (8) (2012) 22–117.
[7] Xiang Shu, Baoshan Huang, Predicting dynamic moduli of asphalt mixtures with differential method, Road Mater. Pavement Des. 10 (2) (2009) 337–359, https://doi.org/10.1080/14680629.2009.9690198.
[8] Sanchez-Silva Mauricio, Castillo Daniel, A methodology to model the uncertainty of material properties in asphalt pavements, J. Mater. Civil Eng. 26 (3) (2014) 440–448, https://doi.org/10.1061/(ASCE)MT.1943-5533.0000841.
[9] Wu Xiao, Yang Li-jun, The elastic theory solution for curved beam with difference elastic moduli in tension and compression, Eng. Mech. 30 (01) (2013) 76–80.
[10] Jian-long ZHENG, Deflection design standards of asphalt pavement based on state design method, China J. Highway Transp. 25 (4) (2012) 1–9.
[11] Seong-Wan Park, Analysis of stress-dependent behavior in conventional asphalt pavements, KSCE J. Civil Eng. 5 (4) (2001) 387–395, https://doi.org/10.1007/BF02829112.
[12] Song-tao LV, Jie-dong CHEN, Hui ZHANG, Comparative analysis of tensile, compression, flexural static moduli and dynamic moduli of cement-stabilized macadam, J. Highway Transp. Res. Dev. 33 (10) (2016), https://doi.org/10.3969/j.issn. 1002-0268.2016.10.007.
[13] Maryam S. Sakhaeifar, Y. Richard Kim, Blanca E. Garcia Montano, Individual temperature-based models for nondestructive evaluation of complex moduli in asphalt concrete, Constr. Build. Mater. 137 (2017) 117–127.
[14] Bo Yao, Gang Cheng, Xiao Wang, Cheng Cheng, Characterization of the stiffness of asphalt surfacing materials on orthotropic steel bridge decks using dynamic moduli test and flexural beam test, Constr. Build. Mater. 44 (2013) 200–206.
[15] C. Parra a, M. Valcuende, F. Gómez, Indirect tensile strength and moduli of elasticity of self-compacting concrete, Constr. Build. Mater. 25 (2011) 201–207.
[16] F. Mujika, On the difference between flexural moduli obtained by three-point and four-point bending tests, Polym. Test. 25 (2006) 214–220, https://doi.org/10.1016/j.polymertesting.2005.10.006.
[17] JTG E20-2011, Specifications and Test Methods of Bitumen and Bituminous Mixtures for Highway Engineering [S], (2011).
[18] Zhongzheng WANG, Junzuo ZHU, Lei CHEN, et al., The stress calculation method for deep beams with shear-bending coupling distortion under concentrated load, Eng. Mech. 25 (4) (2008) 115–119.
[19] J.H. YE, F.G. WU, J.Z. SUN, Estimation of the tensile elastic moduli using Brazilian disc by applying diametrically opposed concentrated loads, Int. J. Rock Mech. Min. Sci. 46 (03) (2009) 568–576.
[20] Fengqiang Gong, Xibing LI, J. ZHAO, Analytical algorithm to estimate tensile moduli in Brazilian disk indirect tensile tests, Chin. J. Rock Mech. Eng. 29 (5) (2010) 881–891.
[21] Yao-Guang HUANG, Lian-Guo WANG, Jia-rui CHEN, Theoretical analysis of flattened Brazilian indirect tensile test for determining tensile strength of rocks, Rock Soil Mech. 36 (03) (2015) 739–748, https://doi.org/10.16285/j.rsm.2015.03.018.
[22] Jian-hong YE, Yang YANG, Zhong-hua CHANG, Airy stress function method for analytic solution of stress field during Brazilian disc test, J. Eng. Geol. 17 (4) (2009) 528–532, https://doi.org/10.4028/www.scientific.net/AMM.70.87.
[23] Jianlong ZHENG, Songtao LV, Nonlinear fatigue damage model for asphalt mixtures, China J. Highway Transp. 22 (5) (2009) 21–28.
[24] Mohamed Attia, Magdy Abdelrahman, Effect of state of stress on the resilient moduli of base layer containing reclaimed asphalt pavement, Road Mater. Pavement Des. 12 (2011) 79–97, https://doi.org/10.1080/14680629.2011.9690353.

Fatigue performance of aging asphalt mixtures[*)]

Lü Song-tao[1), **)], Luo Zhaohui[1)], Xie Juan[1)]

DOI: dx.doi.org/10.14314/polimery.2015.126

Abstract: Fatigue and aging inevitably exist in asphalt pavement. To reveal fatigue characteristics, strength tests were carried out under different loading rates (v). The rules of dynamic loading strength (S_{dz}) and v were acquired and the real stress ratios corresponding to the fatigue test loading rates were obtained. Fatigue equations describing fatigue life (N_f) as a function of the nominal (t_m) and real (t_s) stress ratios were also acquired. It was discovered that the equations could be extended to the strength failure point ($t_s = 1$, $N_f = 1$) based on the real stress ratio, but not the nominal stress ratio. The equation provided the theoretical method to design a method to assess aging of asphalt pavement.

Keywords: road engineering, asphalt pavement, fatigue, aging, stress ratio.

Odporność zmęczeniowa starzonych mieszanek asfaltowych

Streszczenie: Przeprowadzono testy nawierzchni asfaltowych stosując różne szybkości obciążania (v). Określono zależności matematyczne między wytrzymałością na obciążenia dynamiczne (S_{dz}) i v oraz równania opisujące trwałość zmęczeniową (N_f) w funkcji rzeczywistego współczynnika asymetrii cyklu (t_s) i nominalnego współczynnika asymetrii cyklu (t_m). Stwierdzono, że tylko równanie uwzględniające współczynnik t_s może być stosowane do ekstrapolacji do punktu wytrzymałości na uszkodzenie ($t_s = 1$, $N_f = 1$). Równanie to pozwala na zaprojektowanie teoretycznej metody oceny starzenia się nawierzchni asfaltowej.

Słowa kluczowe: inżynieria drogowa, nawierzchnia asfaltowa, zmiany zmęczeniowe, starzenie, współczynnik asymetrii.

The asphalt pavement has already experienced short-term and long-term aging when the fatigue failure takes place, and the fatigue performance is reflected by the degree of aging in the asphalt mixture. Asphalt pavement should be evaluated under different degrees of aging, but few studies have given sufficient account of the differences in aging degrees, instead using the original asphalt mixture to conduct fatigue tests. This results in large differences from the actual fatigue properties of the pavement. To reduce the differences and reflect the real fatigue performance of the pavement, it's necessary to explore the aging effect on fatigue performance of asphalt mixtures.

According to the methods of asphalt aging tests introduced by Strategic Highway Research Program (SHRP), a loose mixture is heated for four hours at 135 °C with forced ventilation in an oven, which is called short-term oven aging (STOA), and then the formed specimen is heated for five days at 85 °C in the delay oven with forced ventilation, which is called long-term oven aging (LTOA). This is an effective way to simulate the aging that occurs during construction and is used in a laboratory setting [1—4]. Due to the enormous amount of time and the expense of age and fatigue testing on asphalt mixtures, aging factors have not been considered in the majority of research concerning asphalt fatigue properties.

To date, the problems of aging asphalt have not been comprehensively considered when pavement is designed in all parts of the world, so the effects of aging on the life of asphalt pavement have not been studied accurately. The study of fatigue performance in different degrees of aging plays a significant role in improving design parameters and asphalt mixtures, and preventing early damage, as well as improving road performance and extending the life of asphalt pavement.

A major deficiency of the existing design specifications of asphalt pavement in China using the S-N fatigue equation is that the specifications drop the fatigue equation to the value of fatigue life $N_f = 1$, which is the ultimate tensile strength calculated from the fatigue equation when the asphalt mixture is damaged under a single loading. Due to this imprecision, the method to calculate the tensile strength coefficient lacks experimental verifica-

---

[1)] Changsha University of Science & Technology, School of Communication and Transportation Engineering, National Engineering Laboratory of Highway Maintenance Technology, Changsha-410004, P.R. China.

[*)] Material contained in this article was presented at Global Conference on Polymer and Composite Materials, 27—29 May 2014, Ningbo, China.

[**)] Author for correspondence; e-mail: lstcs@126.com

tion based on the artificial ultimate tensile strength. The fatigue equation is derived from the regression analysis, taking into account certain test conditions and scopes of application. For example, the scope of the double logarithmic linear relationship is $N_f = 10^4 - 10^8$ in Pell's research, and this relationship does not exist beyond the scope. There is necessary to perform experimental verification whether the relationship can be extended [5, 6]. Generally speaking, the relationship curve inside or outside of the scope appears as the curved line. In the case of low cycle fatigue, the fatigue curve does not show any clear linear relationship, but an upward convex and curve downward. The ultimate tensile strength values obtained by dropping the fatigue equation to $N_f = 1$ is inaccurate [7].

The traditional stress ratio in the fatigue test is determined by the standard strength value. But the standard strength is tested under the conditions of a fixed loading rate. Asphalt mixtures are a typical viscous-elastic material, whose stiffness and strength indicators are affected significantly by loading rates and temperatures [8—11]. Different loading rates will lead to different strengths. So the inconsistencies in strength are the main reason for the problems of inaccurate calculation. As the loading rate of a standard strength test is much smaller than that of a fatigue test in 1/2 cycle (related to the stress level and loading frequency), there is a greater difference from the strength value corresponding to the fatigue loading rate. The stress ratio (σ/s) based on standard strength is defined as the nominal stress ratio, and the stress ratio determined by the strength value corresponding to the fatigue loading rate is defined as the real stress ratio. That is to say, the stress ratio used in traditional fatigue test analyses is the nominal stress rather than the real stress ratio. Therefore, the strength values derived from the fatigue equation established under the basis of normal stress ratios by using $N_f = 1$ is not the ultimate tensile strength, and it is not accurate for calculating the structure coefficient in tensile strength.

Studies on the fatigue properties of asphalt rarely consider the effects of the loading rate on strength, which is the basis for determining the fatigue stress ratio, and the erroneous results would lead to a distortion of the fatigue equation and does not reflect the strength characteristics of $N_f = 1$ when the stress ratio $\sigma/s = 1$. This is because the loading rate is slow during the standard strength test, but faster during the fatigue test, so the real strength is much higher than the nominal strength obtained by standard strength tests [12—18].

Therefore, the change law in strength with the loading rate is revealed by analyzing the loading rate of the asphalt mixture impact strength, and the fatigue equation of aging asphalt is established based on the real stress ratio, which has important theoretical significance and engineering application value in improving asphalt pavement design.

EXPERIMENTAL PART

Materials

The AC-13C fine-grade asphalt mixture was chosen to the study. Styrene-butadiene-styrene (SBS) modified asphalt (I-D) was used as a binder and the basalt as an aggregate. Both were produced in Nanjing (Jiangsu province, China). The optimum asphalt-aggregate ratio was 5.3 wt % as determined by the method of Marshall proportions for the asphalt mixture.

The characteristics of raw materials (asphalt binder, aggregate, mineral powders) and the mixture for AC-13C asphalt mixture are shown in Tables 1—4.

Table 1. Test results of SBS modified asphalt (I-D)

Property		Test result	Technical requirements (Chinese Standard)
Penetration number (25 °C, 100 g, 5 s), 0.1 mm		56	30 to 60
Penetration index PI		0.533	≥0
Ductility (5 cm/min, 5 °C), cm		34	≥20
Softening temperature (TR&B), °C		79	≥60
Kinematic viscosity (135 °C), Pa·s		2.31	≤3
Flashing temperature, °C		267	≥230
Solubility, %		99.92	≥99
Elastic recovery (25 °C), %		77	≥75
Storage stability segregation — 48 h softening temperature difference, °C		1.5	≤2.5
After STOA residue	Quality change, %	0.1	≤±1.0
	Residue penetration ratio (25 °C), %	73	≥65
	Residue ductility (5 °C), cm	16	≥15

Table 2. Density of mineral (basalt) aggregate

Sieve size, mm	13.2	9.5	4.75	2.36	1.18	0.6	0.3	0.15	0.075	Mineral powders
Density, g/cm³	2.731	2.730	2.729	2.715	2.716	2.717	2.717	2.718	2.719	2.753

Table 3. Mineral aggregate gradation of AC-13C fine-grade asphalt mixture

Mesh size, mm	16	13.2	9.5	4.75	2.36	1.18	0.6	0.3	0.15	0.075
Passing rate, %	100	95	74	48.5	34	23.5	15	11	8.5	6

Table 4. Marshall test results for asphalt mixture at the optimum asphalt aggregate ratio

Asphalt-aggregate ratio, wt %	Bulk specific gravity of asphalt mixture, g/cm³	Void volume, %	Void filled with asphalt, %	Void in mineral aggregate, %	Marshall stability, kN	Marshall flow value, 0.1 mm
5.3	2.455	5.2	67.2	16.1	15.7	27.9

Methods of testing

Using the SHRP method, delayed oven heating was used in the long-term oven aging (LTOA) test, and the test conditions were fixed at the temperature of 85 °C. The aging time was five days. This method simulates the aging degree of the actual pavement for six to nine years. This is not accurate to test the fatigue because the failure does not necessarily occur in 6—9 years of traffic use, and could happen in an earlier or later stage. Therefore, five different aging levels (0, 1, 3, 5, and 7 days) were chosen to simulate the actual aging degrees of the road surface when the fatigue damage happens.

The strength and fatigue tests of asphalt mixtures were performed on the material test system equipment (MTS Landmark®, USA). First, the asphalt mixture was compacted and shaped into a plate specimen measuring 30 × 30 × 5 cm, and then cut into a beam shape that was 25 × 5 × 5 cm. The force and displacement of each stress cycle were captured automatically by the data acquisition system. The corresponding stress and strain values were obtained by calculation, and the time intervals of the data acquisition system were set depending on the experimental conditions. The loading methods in strength and fatigue tests were used with direct tensile tests at the temperature of 15 °C, and the test specimens were stored in an environmental chamber for 24 h beforehand to ensure a consistent temperature inside and outside the specimen.

RESULTS AND DISCUSSION

Speed characteristics of asphalt mixture strength

The results of strength and fatigue test of the original asphalt mixture were taken as examples and the results of the different degrees of aging were analyzed in the same way.

First, the standard direct tensile strength (S_t) test was performed three times in parallel with the loading rate of 5 mm/min, and the mean value obtained was 1.963 MPa. The results are shown in Table 5.

Table 5. Standard direct tensile strength (S_t) test results

Test number	S_t, MPa	Average value, MPa	Standard deviation	Variation coefficient
1	2.101			
2	1.894	1.963	0.120	0.061
3	1.894			

The tensile strength under different v is defined as the dynamic load strength (S_{dz}). The S_{dz} were determined for various loading rates (v) in the range of 0.0037—37 MPa/s, and the results are shown in Table 6. It can be easily seen that v affected S_{dz} of the asphalt mixture significantly, and the maximal S_{dz} is more than six times higher than the minimal in the loading scope.

Table 6. Direct tensile strength (S_{dz}) test results under different loading rates (v)

Test number	v, MPa/s	Sample area, mm²	Destroy load, N	S_{dz}, MPa
1	0.0037	2695.7	2276	0.844
2	0.037	2688.2	3749	1.395
3	0.37	2727.2	5453	2.000
4	1.85	2662.8	7548	2.835
5	3.70	2676.6	7910	2.955
6	7.40	2799.6	10757	3.842
7	10.80	2778.3	11892	4.280
8	13.72	2915.4	13888	4.589
9	17.77	2813.1	13027	4.695
10	21.00	2869.8	13550	4.722
11	24.80	2818.7	13927	4.941
12	29.60	2703.0	13969	5.168
13	33.30	2625.1	13119	4.998
14	37.00	2703.1	14129	5.227

The effect of v on S_{dz} at 15 °C for AC-13C is shown in Fig. 1.

The regression equation between S_{dz} and v has the form:

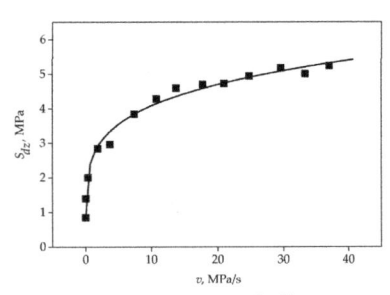

Fig. 1. Direct tensile strength (S_{dz}) versus loading rate v at 15 °C for AC-13C

$$S_{dz} = 2.583v^{0.2} \quad (1)$$
$$R^2 = 0.984$$

According to the fitting results v has significant influence on S_{dz} of asphalt mixtures, and the relationship between them is the power function. The strength corresponding to the loading rate in fatigue tests is defined as fatigue dynamic load strength.

A loading frequency of 10 Hz is typically used in fatigue tests of asphalt mixtures. If the fatigue test is carried out under the stress level of 1 MPa, v value is 20 MPa/s in the process. According to eq. (1), v was approx. 0.25 MPa/s, corresponding to S_t of 1.963 MPa. Value 20 MPa/s was roughly 80 times higher than 0.25 MPa/s. Whereas S_{dz} corresponding to v of 20 MPa/s was 4.703 MPa [from eq. (1)], and was 2.396 times higher than 1.963 MPa. Therefore, the traditional stress ratio used in fatigue tests is not correct, and is just a nominal stress ratio.

Fatigue properties of aging asphalt mixture characterized by real stress ratio

The defined nominal stress ratio is denoted by t_m, and the real stress ratio is denoted by t_s.

The standard static load strength test of asphalt mixtures should be taken first into account for determining t_m. The quasi-static load strength was S_t = 1.963 MPa (in Table 5).

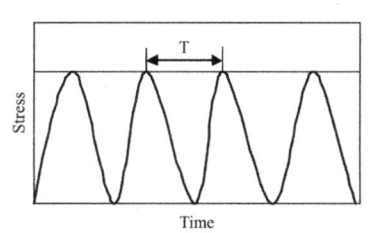

Fig. 2. Loading wave of fatigue test process

In fatigue tests t_m was 0.3, 0.4, 0.5, 0.6 and 0.7, and the loading frequency was 1, 10, 20, and 50 Hz. A continuous haversine loading curve describing the dependence between stress level (σ), applied in the fatigue test, and time (t), shown in Fig. 2, illustrates the fatigue loading process.

The v value can be calculated from the loading frequency (f) or cycle (T) and σ in fatigue tests according to equation:

$$v = \frac{\sigma}{T/2} = 2 f \sigma \quad (2)$$

The S_{dz} value is then calculated from eq. (1), and t_s can be expressed as:

$$t_s = \sigma / S_{dz} \quad (3)$$

The direct tension fatigue tests of the AC-13C were carried out at 15 °C for the beam specimens of the asphalt mixture. Results of the tests are summarized in Table 7.

Table 7. Results of the direct tension fatigue tests for AC-13C carried out at 15 °C

f, Hz	t_m	σ MPa	v MPa/s	S_{dz} MPa	t_s	N_f, cycles Sample 1	Sample 2
1	0.4	0.78	1.57	2.814	0.28	1 518	1 330
	0.5	0.98	1.96	2.943	0.33	510	541
	0.6	1.18	2.35	3.053	0.39	250	280
	0.7	1.37	2.74	3.149	0.44	163	112
10	0.3	0.59	11.76	4.219	0.14	30 820	35 231
	0.4	0.78	15.68	4.471	0.18	22 313	18 887
	0.5	0.98	19.60	4.676	0.21	7 883	5 807
	0.6	1.18	23.52	4.850	0.24	3 058	3 478
	0.7	1.37	27.44	5.003	0.27	1 712	1 388
20	0.3	0.59	23.52	4.850	0.12	117 293	106 538
	0.4	0.78	31.36	5.139	0.15	37 717	28 197
	0.5	0.98	39.20	5.375	0.18	9 627	8 234
	0.6	1.18	47.04	5.575	0.21	5 027	7 375
	0.7	1.37	54.88	5.751	0.24	3 036	4 066
50	0.3	0.59	58.80	5.831	0.10	198 472	132 897
	0.4	0.78	78.40	6.178	0.13	56 327	49 754
	0.5	0.98	98.00	6.462	0.15	16 231	19 430
	0.6	1.18	117.60	6.703	0.18	9 863	8 853
	0.7	1.37	137.20	6.914	0.20	3 763	4 084

The fatigue regression curves describing dependence of N_f on t_m and t_s (for various f value), shown in Figs. 3 and 4, were generated through the regression analysis according to equation:

$$N_f = k(1/t)^n \quad (4)$$

where: $t - t_m$ or t_s.

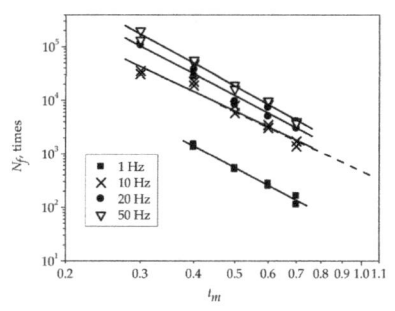

Fig. 3. Fatigue curves based on nominal stress ratio (t_m) under various loading frequencies (f)

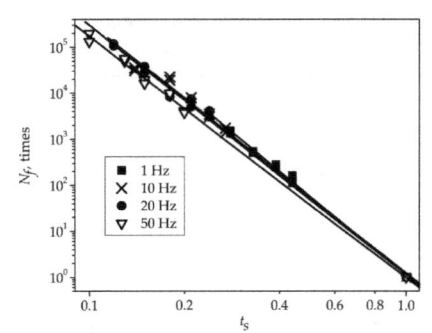

Fig. 4. Fatigue curves based on real stress ratio (t_s) under various loading frequencies (f)

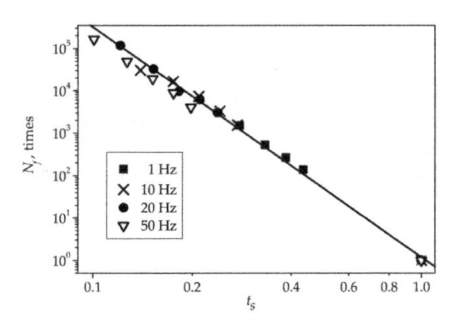

Fig. 5. Unified fatigue curves based on real stress ratio (t_s) under various loading frequencies (f)

The regression parameters based on t_m and t_s of fatigue equations are summarized in Table 8.

Table 8. Fitting results of fatigue equation parameters based on nominal (t_m) and real (t_s) stress ratios

		f, Hz			
		1	10	20	50
t_m	k	29.819	537.03	620.869	926.83
	n	4.245	3.55	4.305	4.333
	R^2	0.998	0.974	0.991	0.999
t_s	k	1.046	1.192	1.021	1.028
	n	5.734	5.427	5.514	5.236
	R^2	0.999	0.994	0.999	0.999

According to Fig. 4 and Table 8, the fatigue curve based on t_s crossed the strength failure point ($t_s = 1$, $N_f = 1$), and the parameters k in fatigue equation should be „1". Among the regression results excluding 10 Hz, the parameters k in every fatigue equation were all close to "1". Parameters k corresponding to 10 Hz were too large, which may have been caused by the results error related to $t_s = 0.14$. The fatigue equation based on t_s can be extended to $N_f = 1$. Therefore, the fatigue equation based on t_s revealed the internal relation between strength failure and fatigue failure.

In double logarithmic coordinates, the fatigue curves are straight lines for t_s and t_m (Figs. 3 and 4). However, the slope of true stress ratio is larger, and the intersection of the horizontal axis is close to one, which means that the fatigue equation also reflects the strength of asphalt mixture failure characteristics. The intersection of the horizontal axis for t_m is larger than one, which is clearly not in accordance with the actual case. Therefore, the fatigue equation represented by t_s is much more accurate than that represented by t_m. And moreover, the test results can be lengthened to both ends of the extension until they cross the axis.

At the same time, the difference of n among fatigue equations based on t_s in various f is slight, so fatigue test results under various f can be uniform to a curve with t_s, as shown in Fig. 5.

The fatigue curves based on t_s for various f can be uniform to a straight line (Fig. 5), which indicates that the effects of different loading frequencies and loading rates on the fatigue characteristics are equivalent.

The normalized fatigue equation based on t_s for various f of the asphalt mixture is:

$$N_f = \left(\frac{1}{t_s}\right)^n = \left(\frac{S_{dz}}{\sigma}\right)^n = \left(\frac{S_{dz}}{\sigma}\right)^{5.426} \quad (5)$$

$$R^2 = 0.993$$

Asphalt fatigue curve based on the real stress ratio for various degrees of aging

The asphalt mixture fatigue test results of the other aging degrees (1, 3, 5, and 7 days) were analyzed with the same method as above (see Fig. 6).

According to Fig. 6, when N_f for various degrees of aging is fitted with t_s, the fatigue curve shows a good linear relationship in double logarithmic coordinates, and

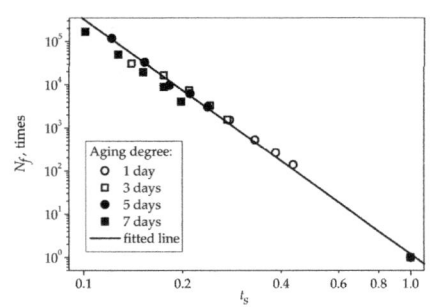

Fig. 6. Summary fatigue curves of asphalt mixture at different degree of aging

it can be extended to the point ($t_s = 1$, $N_f = 1$), without any change in the linear relationship.

The results show that all the aging asphalt mixture fatigue equations can be extended to the same point — the strength failure point — (1, 1) based on t_s. The tensile strength structure coefficient calculation is in line with its definition using t_s. This research, to some extent, makes up for the deficiencies in current asphalt pavement design specifications in China.

CONCLUSIONS

— The loading rate has a significant effect on the strength of an asphalt mixture, and in a certain range of loading rates, the strength increases with the loading rate and changes according to power function.

— According to the change rule between strength and loading rates, this paper proposes the concept and determining method for the real stress ratio, which is the basis of the approach to build the new, more accurate fatigue equation.

— In double logarithmic coordinates, the fatigue life versus the real stress ratio or nominal stress ratio gave straight lines. The fatigue equation curve can be extended to the strength failure points when the fatigue life is one represented by the real stress ratio. It also reveals the mutual relationship of fatigue failure and strength failure.

— The fatigue curves based on real stress ratios for various frequencies can be uniform to a straight line, which indicates that the effects of different loading frequencies and loading rates on the fatigue characteristics are equivalent.

— When the fatigue lives of different degrees of aging asphalt mixtures were fitted with the real stress ratios, the fatigue curves showed a good linear relationship in double logarithmic coordinates, and the fatigue curves can be extended to the condition of $t_s = 1$, $N_f = 1$, without any change in the linear relationship.

ACKNOWLEDGMENTS

This work was supported by the National Natural Science Foundation of China (51208066, 51038002), Specialized Research Fund for the Doctoral Program of Higher Education (20114316120001), Application and Basic Research Projects of Ministry of Transport (2012-319-825-150), Transportation Science and Technology Plan Projects of Henan Province (2013K28), Transportation Science and Technology Plan Projects of Hunan Province (201102), Funding Projects of Hunan Province Outstanding Doctorate Dissertation (YB2012B031), Open Fund of Key Laboratory of Road Structure and Material of Guangxi (2014gxjgclkf-002) and Key Laboratory of Highway Engineering (Changsha University of Science & Technology), Ministry of Education (kfj120101).

REFERENCES

[1] Abu Al-Rub R.K., Darabi M.K., Kim S.-M. et al.: *Constr. Build. Mater.* **2013**, *41*, 439.
http://dx.doi.org/10.1016/j.conbuildmat.2012.12.044
[2] Kim Y.-R., Lee H.-J.: *KSCE J. Civ. Eng.* **2003**, *7*, 389.
http://dx.doi.org/10.1007/BF02895837
[3] Tao Ma, Xiao-ming Huang, Enad Mahmoud et al.: *Int. J. Min. Met. Mater.* **2011**, *18*, 460.
http://dx.doi.org/10.1007/s12613-011-0463-4
[4] Xiao F., Newton D., Putman B. et al.: *Mater. Struct.* **2013**, *46*, 1987. http://dx.doi.org/10.1617/s11527-013-0031-7
[5] Yao Zu-kang: *Highway* **2003**, No. 2, 43.
[6] "Specification for design of highway asphalt pavement (JTG D50-2006)", China Communications Press, Beijing 2006, pp. 26—80.
[7] Chen Li-jie, Jiang Tie-qiang, Xie Li-yang: *J. Mech. Strength.* **2006**, *28*, 761.
[8] Kim J., West R.C.: *J. Eng. Mech.* **2010**, *36*, 496.
http://dx.doi.org/10.1061/(ASCE)EM.1943-7889.0000094
[9] Zhanping You, Sanjeev Adhikari, Kutay M.E.: *Mater. Struct.* **2009**, *42*, 617. http://dx.doi.org/10.1617/s11527-008-9408-4
[10] Gonzalez J.M., Miquel canet J., Oller S., Miro R.: *Comp. Mater. Sci.* **2007**, *38*, 543.
http://dx.doi.org/10.1016/j.commatsci.2006.03.013
[11] Lundstrom R., Isacsson U., Ekblad J.: *J. Mater. Sci.* **2003**, *38*, 4941.
http://dx.doi.org/10.1023/B:JMSC.0000004417.98590.7a
[12] Zheng Jian-long, Lv Song-tao: *China J. Highway Transport* **2009**, *22*, No. 5, 21.
[13] Kechao Qiu, Huisu Chen, Haiping Ye et al.: *Int. J. Fatigue* **2013**, *51*, 116.
http://dx.doi.org/10.1016/j.ijfatigue.2013.01.001
[14] Zoa Ambassa, Fatima Allou, Christophe Petit et al.: *Constr. Build. Mater.* **2013**, *43*, 443.
http://dx.doi.org/10.1016/j.conbuildmat.2013.02.017
[15] Youngguk Seo, Kim Y.R.: *J. Civ. Eng.* **2008**, *12*, 237.
http://dx.doi.org/10.1007/s12205-008-0237-3
[16] Xiang Shu, Baoshan Huang, Dragon Vukosavljevic: *Constr. Build. Mater.* **2008**, *22*, 1323.
http://dx.doi.org/10.1016/j.conbuildmat.2007.04.019
[17] Qiang Li, Hyun Jong Lee, Tae Woo Kim: *Constr. Build. Mater.* **2012**, *27*, 605.
http://dx.doi.org/10.1016/j.conbuildmat.2012.07.001
[18] Moreno F., Rubio M.C.: *Mater. Design.* **2013**, *47*, 61.
http://dx.doi.org/10.1016/j.matdes.2012.12.048

Received 27 VI 2014.

Normalization method for asphalt mixture fatigue equation under different loading frequencies

LÜ Song-tao(吕松涛), ZHENG Jian-long(郑健龙)

National Engineering Laboratory of Highway Maintenance Technology,
Key Laboratory of Highway Engineering (Ministry of Education), School of Traffic and
Transportation Engineering, Changsha University of Science and Technology, Changsha 410114, China

© Central South University Press and Springer-Verlag Berlin Heidelberg 2015

Abstract: In order to analyze the effect of different loading frequencies on the fatigue performance for asphalt mixture, the changing law of asphalt mixture strengths with loading speed was revealed by strength tests under different loading speeds. Fatigue equations of asphalt mixtures based on the nominal stress ratio and real stress ratio were established using fatigue tests under different loading frequencies. It was revealed that the strength of the asphalt mixture is affected by the loading speed greatly. It was also discovered that the fatigue equation based on the nominal stress ratio will change with the change of the fatigue loading speed. There is no uniqueness. But the fatigue equation based on the real stress ratio doesn't change with the loading frequency. It has the uniqueness. The results indicate the fatigue equation based on the real stress ratio can realize the normalization of the asphalt mixture fatigue equation under different loading frequencies. It can greatly benefit the analysis of the fatigue characteristics under different vehicle speeds for asphalt pavement.

Key words: road engineering; asphalt pavement; fatigue equation; loading speed; loading frequency; strength; stress ratio

1 Introduction

Fatigue failure is one of the most common failure modes of asphalt pavement, and the fatigue performance of asphalt mixtures has become an important research issue all over the world [1−2]. Researchers have carried out many in-depth studies and acquired valuable information on the fatigue performance of asphalt mixture, focusing on the stress−strain relationship, damage, and energy dissipation [3−7].

Currently, most of the research considering the effects of vehicle speeds on the fatigue failure characteristics of asphalt pavement adopts fatigue tests under different loading frequencies to simulate the real-world conditions, and different researchers propose different correlations between the loading frequency and vehicle speed [8−9]. Meanwhile, during the structural design of asphalt pavement, most researchers choose the experimental results of material fatigue tests under a fixed loading frequency for computation and analysis. This frequency is usually the one corresponding to the average vehicle speed [8], without further consideration on the experimental results under other loading frequencies. Therefore, the effects of other vehicle speeds on the fatigue failure rate of pavement are not considered, and a certain degree of un-scientificity during the parameter selection procedure of asphalt pavement structure design is introduced artificially.

Asphalt mixture is a typical viscoelastic material [10−12]. Its mechanical properties, such as strength and stiffness, are affected by the temperature and loading speed [13−14]. Its fatigue properties are also affected and different fatigue loading frequencies correspond to different loading speeds [15−17]. According to the literature available, there are few research results that focus on the quantitative evaluation of the effects of vehicle speed on fatigue characteristic of asphalt pavement; while the vehicle speed has great influence on the fatigue failure of pavement. The lower the vehicle

---

Foundation item: Projects(51208066,51038002) supported by the National Natural Science Foundation of China; Project(20114316120001) supported by Specialized Research Fund for the Doctoral Program of Higher Education, China; Project(2012-319-825-150) supported by Application and Basic Research Projects of Ministry of Transport, China; Project(2013K28) supported by Transportation Science and Technology Plan Projects of Henan Province, China; Project(201102) supported by Transportation Science and Technology Plan Projects of Hunan Province, China; Project(YB2012B031) supported by Funding Projects of Hunan Provincial Outstanding Doctorate Dissertation, China; Project(2014gxjgclkf-002) supported by Open Fund of Key Laboratory of Road Structure and Material of Guangxi Province China; Project(kfj120101) supported by Open Fund of the Key Laboratory of Highway Engineering (Changsha University of Science and Technology), China
Received date: 2014−07−01; **Accepted date:** 2014−10−28
Corresponding author: LÜ Song-tao, Associate Professor, PhD; Tel: +86−13975197481; E-mail: lstcs@126.com

speed, the greater the fatigue failure effect of the pavement. Conversely, a higher vehicle speed has less effect on the fatigue failure of pavement. However, due to the limitation of pavement grade, design standards, traffic safety, and mechanical properties of vehicles, the vehicle speed cannot be improved without limits. In China, the design speed for expressways and 1st class highways is 60−120 km/h, and for 2nd, 3rd, and 4th class highway is 20−80 km/h, with similar standards overseas. Generally, the speed of vehicles operating on pavement with a variety of grades covers a wide range, and even on pavements with the same grade, the speed of different vehicles varies greatly.

The traditional fatigue equation of asphalt mixture refers to the one under a particular loading frequency. Different loading frequencies correspond to different loading speeds. The fatigue strength is not equal under different loading speeds of asphalt mixture. It causes that the fatigue equations under different loading frequencies are not the same. So, the fatigue loading frequency affects the fatigue equation parameters of asphalt mixture directly.

Fatigue tests under a single frequency are unable to characterize the influence of various vehicle speeds on the fatigue performance of asphalt pavement. So, strength tests at different loading speeds were carried out in this work to reveal the law of the strength of asphalt mixture changing with the loading speed. A conventional S−N fatigue equation and a fatigue equation adopting the speed-related stress ratio are established using fatigue tests under different loading frequencies. The different loading frequencies corresponded to different conventional S−N fatigue curves, and the fatigue curve implementing the speed-related stress ratio under different frequencies is represented as a line in a log–log plot. Therefore, the normalization of asphalt mixture fatigue equation under different loading frequencies is realized, and it provides convenience and theoretical basis to analyze the effects of vehicle speeds.

2 Design of raw materials and mix proportions of asphalt mixture

Previous researches have proved that the SBS modified asphalt mixture has favorable anti-fatigue performance at the temperature ranging from −30 to 20 °C, because the addition of the SBS modifier improves the anti-fatigue performance [18]. In order to study the strength and fatigue performance of asphalt mixture, SBS modified asphalt mixture AC-13C was selected as the research mixture with basalt as the aggregate. The experimental results of raw materials and the designed gradation of mineral aggregate are listed in Tables 1−3.

Table 1 Test results of SBS (I-D) modified asphalt

Test item	Test result	Technical requirement
Penetration (25 °C, 100 g, 5 s)/0.1mm	55	30−60
Penetration index	0.525 (R^2=0.997)	≥0
Ductily (5 cm/min, 5 °C)/cm	32	≥20
Softening point, $T_{R\&B}$/°C	78	≥60
Kinematic viscosity (135 °C)/(Pa·s)	2.35	≤3
Flash point/°C	271	≥230
Solubility/%	99.94	≥99
Elastic recovery(25 °C)/%	80	≥75
Dissociation of storage stability, softening point difference after 48 h/°C	1.8	≤2.5
Residuum after TFOT (or RTFOT) — Quality change/%	0.2	≤±1.0
Residuum after TFOT (or RTFOT) — Residual penetration ratio (25 °C)/%	74	≥65
Residuum after TFOT (or RTFOT) — Residual ductility (5 °C)/cm	18	≥15

Table 2 Test results of bulk density of aggregate

Grain size/mm	13.2	9.5	4.75	2.36	1.18
Density/(g·cm^{-3})	2.735	2.732	2.731	2.720	2.717
Grain size/mm	0.6	0.3	0.15	0.075	Mineral powder
Density/(g·cm^{-3})	2.720	2.720	2.719	2.720	2.758

Table 3 Mineral aggregate gradation of AC-13C fine-grain asphalt mixture

Sieve size/mm	Passing rate/% Upper limit	Passing rate/% Lower limit	Synthesized gradation/%
16	100	100	100
13.2	100	90	95.5
9.5	85	68	74.5
4.75	68	38	48.8
2.36	50	24	34.2
1.18	38	15	23.7
0.6	28	10	15
0.3	20	7	11.1
0.15	15	5	8.8
0.075	8	4	5.9

The mix design of the asphalt mixture was carried out based on the Marshall proportion test method with the optimum asphalt-aggregate ratio determined as 5.25%. The test results of the density and void content under the optimum asphalt-aggregate ratio are listed in Table 4.

Table 4 Results of Marshall test with optimum asphalt-aggregate ratio

Asphalt-aggregate ratio/%	Bulk specific density/(g·cm^{-3})	Air void/%	Void filled with asphalt/%	Void in mineral aggregate/%	Marshall stability/kN	Flow value (0.1 mm)
5.2	2.455	5.2	67.2	16.1	15.7	27.9

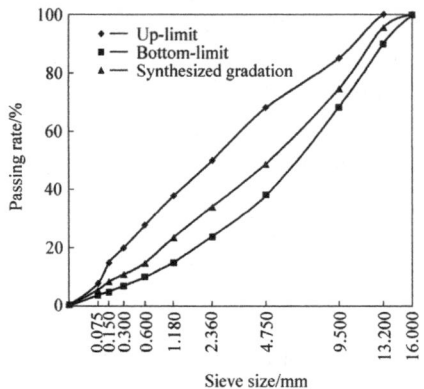

Fig. 1 Aggregate gradation of asphalt mixture

3 Test results and related analyses of asphalt mixture strength at different loading speeds

During the strength test of the asphalt mixture, the direct tensile strength test was adopted as the stress form since it is the simplest. According to the forming method of rutting plates in the Marshall dynamic stability test, the asphalt mixture was first mixed and wheel ground into plate specimens with dimensions of 300 mm×300 mm×50 mm; after they were cooled, they were cut into small beam specimens with dimensions of 25 cm× 5 cm×5 cm.

Fig. 2 Small beam specimens of asphalt mixture

The standard direct tensile strength test was carried out first using the MTS-Landmark material test system which was produced in America. The experimental temperature was 15 °C, and the specimens were placed in an environmental chamber for 24 h before the experiment to ensure the temperature homogeneity in the specimens. The loading speed was chosen as 2 mm/min, which is the most commonly used test speed in China.

The direct tensile strength test was repeated 3 times under each condition, and the results are listed in Table 5. The average value, 1.963 MPa, was selected as the final result of the standard strength test.

Table 5 Test results of standard direct tensile strength

Test number	Tensile strength/MPa	Average/MPa	Standard deviation	Variable coefficient
1	2.101			
2	1.894	1.963	0.120	0.061
3	1.894			

After that, 14 different loading speeds including 0.0037–37 MPa/s were selected for direct tensile strength tests. The test results are listed in Table 6.

Table 6 Test results of direct tensile strength at different loading speeds

Number	Loading speed/ (MPa·s^{-1})	Specimen area/mm^2	Failure load/N	Strength/MPa
1	0.0037	2695.7	2276	0.844
2	0.037	2688.2	3749	1.395
3	0.37	2727.2	5453	2.000
4	1.85	2662.8	7548	2.835
5	3.70	2676.6	7910	2.955
6	7.40	2799.6	10757	3.842
7	10.80	2778.3	11892	4.280
8	13.72	2915.4	13888	4.589
9	17.77	2813.1	13027	4.695
10	21.00	2869.8	13550	4.722
11	24.80	2818.7	13927	4.941
12	29.60	2703.0	13969	5.168
13	33.30	2625.1	13119	4.998
14	37.00	2703.1	14129	5.227

As displayed in Table 6, the strength of the asphalt mixture is obviously affected by the loading speed. Within the loading speed range tested, the maximum value of 5.227 MPa is six times the minimum value of 0.844 MPa. The direct tensile strength value in Table 6 at different loading speeds is plotted in Fig. 3.

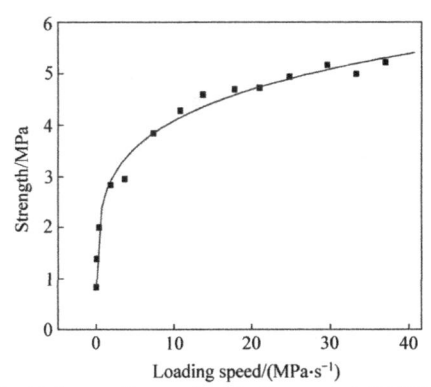

Fig. 3 Direct tensile strength vs loading speed of AC-13C at 15 °C

Using the nonlinear fit between loading speed and direct tensile strength, the regression relationship between them can be obtained by

$$S_v = 2.583 v^{0.2}, R^2 = 0.984 \quad (1)$$

where S_v is the direct tensile strength, v is the loading speed and R is the relation coefficient.

According to the linear fitting result, the loading speed has great influence on the strength of the asphalt mixture and they follow a power function change law. The strength value corresponding to the loading speed in the fatigue test is defined as the fatigue speed related strength.

When conducting fatigue tests of asphalt mixture, the loading frequency of 10 Hz is commonly used [2, 6–7, 9]. Thus, the loading cycle and unloading cycle are 0.1 s in total, among which the loading procedure counts for 0.05 s, half of the total time. In China, the tire ground pressure is set as 0.7 MPa in the asphalt pavement design. Then, for fatigue tests carried out with the stress of 0.7 MPa, the corresponding loading speed is 0.7 MPa/0.05 s=14 MPa/s. Based on Table 6 and Eq. (1), it can be calculated inversely that the loading speed corresponding to the standard strength test result of 1.963 MPa (2 mm/min) is just 0.35 MPa/s. That is to say, the loading speed of 2 mm/min is equivalent to the loading speed of 0.35 MPa/s, which is 14/0.35=40, less than that of 14 MPa/s corresponding to 0.7 MPa. Also, the strength corresponding to the loading speed of 14 MPa/s is calculated as 4.379 MPa, which is 1.970, larger than that of 1.963 MPa. Therefore, it can be proved that using the standard strength test to determine the stress ratio of conventional S–N fatigue equation is erroneous, since it is just a man-made strength ratio that does not consider the effects of loading speeds and lacks actual mechanical significance.

4 Fatigue equation of asphalt mixture under different loading frequencies considering effects of loading speeds

The stress ratio is determined based on the standard strength test results during the establishment of the conventional S–N fatigue equation; while the standard strength test is usually carried out at a fixed loading speed. Since the loading speed in the standard strength test does not correspond to that in the fatigue test procedure, there is no relationship among loading speeds under different loading frequencies. Therefore, this stress is defined as the nominal stress ratio $t_{nominal}$, during the determination of which the standard strength test of the asphalt mixture should be carried out first. According to Table 5, the standard strength S_t is 1.963 MPa.

Corresponding to the previous strength tests, the direct tensile fatigue test, which has the simplest stress condition, was also carried out during the fatigue test of the asphalt mixture. The loading control mode is stress control. The fatigue life is the loading times when the specimen was fractured. The test temperature was set as 15 °C, and the specimens were placed in an environmental chamber for 24 h in order to obtain a uniform temperature distribution. The fatigue test was also conducted in the constant temperature environmental cabinet with a temperature of 15 °C. The nominal stress ratio was set as 0.3, 0.4, 0.5, 0.6 and 0.7, and the loading frequency was set as 1, 10, 20 and 50 Hz. The fatigue load was a continuous haversine load with the waveform shown in Fig. 4.

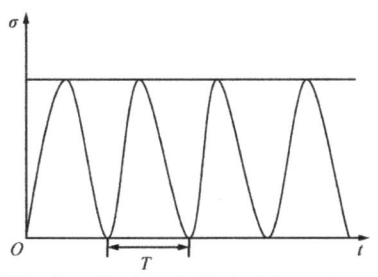

Fig. 4 Waveform of loads applied during fatigue tests

The fatigue loading speed during fatigue tests can be calculated according to the loading frequency f with period of T and stress σ, as shown in Eq. (2).

$$v = \frac{\sigma}{T/2} = 2f\sigma \quad (2)$$

Then, based on the correspondence between the strength and loading speed indicated by Eq. (1), the fatigue speed related strength S_{vf} can be determined.

The real stress ratio t_{real} is defined as the ratio of stress level "σ" to the fatigue speed related strength "S_{vf}" under its corresponding loading speed.

$$t_{real} = \sigma / S_{vf} \qquad (3)$$

where σ is the stress amplitude applied during fatigue test and its value is the product of the nominal stress ratio and standard strength; S_{vf} is the fatigue speed related strength under the loading speed corresponding to the loading frequency and stress level.

A small beam direct tensile fatigue test was conducted on the previously mentioned AC-13C asphalt mixture using the MTS-Landmark materials test system. The real stress ratio and fatigue life under different loading frequencies and stress levels are summarized in Table 7.

For the vehicles on the actual asphalt road, the loading speed is usually in the range of 4–84 MPa/s. In order to satisfy the research needs, the range of loading speed for fatigue test is slightly wider than the normal one. Based on regression analysis on the fatigue test results in Table 7 using the unified equation form of $N_f=k(1/t)^n$, the fatigue regression curves respectively represented by the nominal stress ratio and real stress ratio under different loading frequencies were obtained as shown in Fig. 5 and Fig. 6.

The regression parameters k, n, k', n' of the fatigue equation are summarized in Table 8.

As shown in Fig. 5, different loading frequencies correspond to different conventional S–N fatigue curves. This is theoretically caused by the fact that during the determination of the stress ratio in the conventional S–N fatigue equation, the strength value obtained using the standard strength test is chosen. This strength value is obtained under a fixed loading speed and has nothing to do with the loading frequency and the stress level. Meanwhile, during the standard strength test, the loading speed is much lower than that in the half circulation of the fatigue test, i.e. the loading procedure which is related to the loading frequency and the stress level. Actually, the true strength during fatigue tests is much greater than the nominal strength obtained via standard strength tests and its fatigue curve does not pass through the strength failure point at which both the stress ratio and fatigue life are 1. If the fatigue equation extends to both ends, a relatively large deviation will be caused and increase with the degree of extension.

According to the fatigue equation shown in Fig. 6,

Table 7 Summary of real stress ratio and fatigue life under different loading frequencies and stress

Loading frequency/Hz	Nominal stress ratio	Stress level/MPa	Loading speed/(MPa·s⁻¹)	Fatigue speed related strength/MPa	Real stress ratio	Fatigue life 1	Fatigue life 2
1	0.4	0.78	1.57	2.814	0.28	1518	1330
	0.5	0.98	1.96	2.943	0.33	510	541
	0.6	1.18	2.35	3.053	0.39	250	280
	0.7	1.37	2.74	3.149	0.44	163	112
10	0.3	0.59	11.76	4.219	0.14	30820	35231
	0.4	0.78	15.68	4.471	0.18	22313	18887
	0.5	0.98	19.60	4.676	0.21	7883	5807
	0.6	1.18	23.52	4.850	0.24	3058	3478
	0.7	1.37	27.44	5.003	0.27	1712	1388
20	0.3	0.59	23.52	4.850	0.12	117293	106538
	0.4	0.78	31.36	5.139	0.15	37717	28197
	0.5	0.98	39.20	5.375	0.18	9627	8234
	0.6	1.18	47.04	5.575	0.21	5027	7375
	0.7	1.37	54.88	5.751	0.24	3036	4066
50	0.3	0.59	58.80	5.831	0.10	198472	132897
	0.4	0.78	78.40	6.178	0.13	56327	49754
	0.5	0.98	98.00	6.462	0.15	16231	19430
	0.6	1.18	117.60	6.703	0.18	9863	8853
	0.7	1.37	137.20	6.914	0.20	3763	4084

equation is simple and clear.

The exponent n' of each fatigue regression equation based on the real stress ratio under different loading frequencies has little variation from each other. Therefore, the fatigue test results under different loading frequencies can be uniformed by taking advantage of the real stress ratio of the loading speed and regressed as a single curve, as shown in Fig. 6.

As it can be observed from Fig. 7 that the fatigue curves based on the real stress ratio under different frequencies can be regressed as a single curve, indicating that the influence of the loading frequency and loading speed on the fatigue performance of asphalt mixture is equivalent and the normalization of the asphalt mixture fatigue equation under different loading frequencies is achieved.

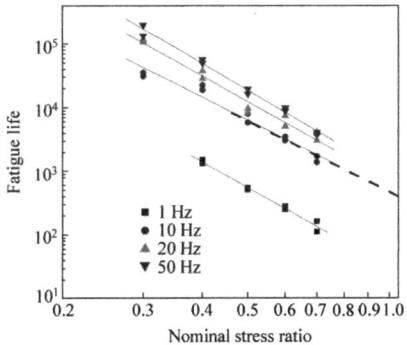

Fig. 5 Fatigue curves based on nominal stress ratio

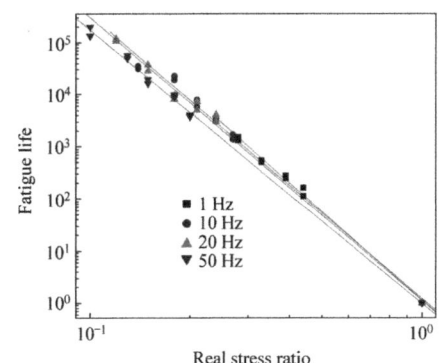

Fig. 6 Fatigue curves based on real stress ratio

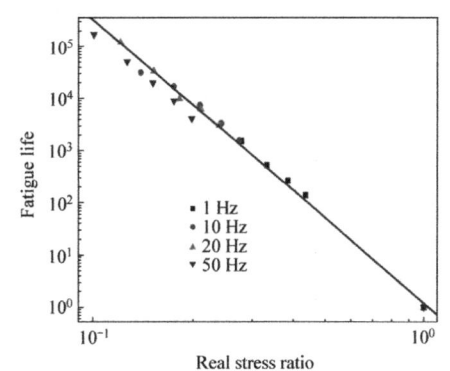

Fig. 7 Normalized fatigue curve based on real stress ratio under different loading frequencies

Table 8 Fitting results of fatigue equation parameters based on nominal and real stress ratios

Loading frequency/Hz	Nominal stress ratio			True stress ratio		
	k	n	R^2	k'	n'	R^2
1	29.819	4.245	0.998	1.046	5.734	0.999
10	537.03	3.55	0.974	1.192	5.427	0.994
20	620.869	4.305	0.991	1.021	5.514	0.999
50	926.83	4.333	0.999	1.028	5.236	0.999

which is established based on the real stress ratio of the speed related strength, the fatigue curves under various loading frequencies are very close to each other and all of them pass through the strength failure point (1, 1). That is to say, the fatigue equation represents the characteristic of the strength failure of asphalt mixture. It reveals the internal connection between the strength failure and the fatigue failure. Therefore, the fatigue equation represented by the real stress ratio is much more accurate than the one represented by the nominal stress ratio. The test result is able to extend to both ends. What's more, the expression form of this fatigue

The unified fatigue equation of asphalt mixture under different frequencies based on the real stress ratio is

$$N_f = (\frac{1}{t_{real}})^{n'} = (\frac{S_{vf}}{\sigma})^{n'} = (\frac{S_{vf}}{\sigma})^{5.426} \qquad (4)$$

5 Conclusions

1) Loading speed has a significant impact on the strength of asphalt mixture.

2) The fatigue equation based on the real stress ratio reveals the internal connection between the strength failure and fatigue failure for asphalt mixture.

3) The fatigue equation represented by the real stress ratio is able to prolong to both ends. But the nominal one cannot be prolonged.

4) The fatigue equation based on the real stress ratio can realize the normalization of the asphalt mixture fatigue equation under different loading frequencies.

5) The fatigue equation based on the real stress ratio

provides an analytical method to evaluate the fatigue failure of asphalt pavement for the different vehicle speeds.

References

[1] SAAD A Q, IBRAHEM S. Prediction of bituminous mixture fatigue life based on accumulated strain [J]. Construction and Building Materials, 2007, 21 (6): 1370–1376.

[2] SHU Xiang, HUANG Bao-shan, DRAGON V. Laboratory evaluation of fatigue characteristics of recycled asphalt mixture [J]. Construction and Building Materials, 2008, 22(7): 1323–1330.

[3] CASTRO M, SA´NCHEZ J A. Estimation of asphalt concrete fatigue curves—A damage theory approach [J]. Construction and Building Materials, 2008, 22(6): 1232–1238.

[4] LI Qiang, HYUN J L, TAE W K. A simple fatigue performance model of asphalt mixtures based on failure energy [J]. Construction and Building Materials, 2012, 27(1): 605–611.

[5] LI Ning, MOLENAAR A A A, van de VEN M F C, WU Shao-peng. Characterization of fatigue performance of asphalt mixture using a new fatigue analysis approach [J]. Construction and Building Materials, 2013, 45(2): 45–52.

[6] GE Zhe-sheng, WANG Hao, WANG Yang-yang, HU Xiao-qian. Evaluating fatigue behavior of asphalt mixtures under alternate tension–compression loading model using new alternate biaxial splitting method [J]. Construction and Building Materials, 2014, 54(11): 106–112.

[7] ALIREZA K K, MAHMOUD A. Laboratory evaluation of strain controlled fatigue criteria in hot mix asphalt [J]. Construction and Building Materials, 2013, 47(10): 1497–1502.

[8] ZOA A, FATIMA A, CHRISTOPHE P, ROBRET M E. Fatigue life prediction of an asphalt pavement subjected to multiple axle loadings with viscoelastic FEM [J]. Construction and Building Materials, 2013, 43(6): 443–452.

[9] GHAZI G A K, KHALID A G. The combined effect of loading frequency, temperature, and stress level on the fatigue life of asphalt paving mixtures using the IDT test configuration [J]. International Journal of Fatigue, 2014, 59(3): 254–261

[10] JAESEUNG K, RANDY C W. Application of the viscoelastic continuum damage model to the indirect tension test at a single temperature [J]. Journal of Engineering Mechanics, 2010, 36(4): 496–505.

[11] GONZALEZ J M, MIQUEL C J, OLLER S, MIRO R. A viscoplastic constitutive creep model with strain rate variables for asphalt mixtures-numerical simulation [J]. Computational Materials Science, 2007, 38(4): 543–560.

[12] ARABANI M, KAMBOOZIA N. The linear visco-elastic behaviour of glasphalt mixture under dynamic loading conditions [J]. Construction and Building Materials, 2013, 41(2): 594–601.

[13] YOU Zhan-ping, SANJEEV A, EMIN K M. Dynamic modulus simulation of the asphalt concrete using the X-ray computed tomography images [J]. Materials and Structures, 2009, 42(5): 617–630.

[14] LUNDSTROM R, ISACSSON U, EKBLAD J. Investigations of stiffness and fatigue properties of asphalt mixtures [J]. Journal of Materials Science, 2003, 38(24): 4941–4949.

[15] KECHAO Q, CHEN Hui-su, YE Hai-ping, HONG Jin-xiang, SUN Wei, JIANG Jin-yang. Thermo-mechanical coupling effect on fatigue behavior of cement asphalt mortar [J]. International Journal of Fatigue, 2013, 51(2): 116–120.

[16] YONG R K, HYUN J L. Evaluation of the effect of aging on mechanical and fatigue properties of sand asphalt mixtures [J]. KSCE Journal of Civil Engineering, 2013, 7(4): 389–398.

[17] YE Qun-shan, WU Shao-peng, LI Ning. Investigation of the dynamic and fatigue properties of fiber-modified asphalt mixtures [J]. International Journal of Fatigue, 2009, 31(10): 1598–1602.

[18] TAE W K, JONGEUN B, HYUN J L, CHOI J Y. Fatigue performance evaluation of SBS modified mastic asphalt mixtures [J]. Construction and Building Materials, 2013, 48(11): 908–916.

(Edited by YANG Hua)

基于劈裂试验的沥青混合料拉压模量同步测试方法

吕松涛，李亦鹏，刘超超，郑健龙

(长沙理工大学 公路养护技术国家工程实验室，湖南 长沙 410114)

摘要：为了较真实地表征沥青混合料的抗拉、抗压变形能力，提高其拉、压模量的测试效率与科学性，开展了沥青混合料直接拉伸、无侧限抗压以及基于劈裂试验的拉、压回弹模量试验。根据二维应力状态下的胡克定律，利用微积分原理，通过对试样中心水平径向和竖直径向应变函数进行积分，推导出劈裂试验中拉伸模量和压缩模量的解析算法，揭示了2种模量与荷载大小、试样尺寸、应变片长度、测试得到的拉压回弹应变和泊松比的定量关系。按劈裂试验方法同步测得的劈裂压缩模量与单轴压缩模量比较接近，偏差在2%之内；由于应力状态和应力水平的差别，劈裂拉伸模量与直接拉伸模量存在一定偏差，但亦在可接受的范围内。研究结果表明：沥青混合料存在明显的拉、压差异性，基于劈裂试验的沥青混合料拉、压模量同步测试方法能够提高沥青混合料拉、压模量的测试效率与科学性，可为沥青路面结构设计提供科学的设计参数。

关键词：道路工程；沥青混合料；劈裂试验；拉伸模量；压缩模量；同步测试

中图分类号：U416.217　　**文献标志码**：A

Synchronous Testing Method for Tensile and Compressive Moduli of Asphalt Mixture Based on Splitting Test

LU Song-tao, LI Yi-peng, LIU Chao-chao, ZHENG Jian-long

(National Engineering Laboratory of Highway Maintenance Technology, Changsha University of Science & Technology, Changsha 410114, Hunan, China)

Abstract: In order to truly characterize the ability of tensile and compressive deformation of asphalt mixture, and improve the test efficiency and scientificity of its tensile and compression moduli, the direct tensile and unconfined compressive moduli tests were carried out. Meanwhile, the tensile and compressive moduli in splitting tests were also carried out. The analytical algorithms of the tensile and compressive moduli were derived by integrating the functions of the horizontal and vertical radial strain at the center of the specimen during the splitting test, which based on the Hooke's law in the two-dimensional stress states and the principle of calculus. The quantitative relationship between two kinds of moduli with load magnitude, specimen size, strain gauge length, tensile and compressive resilient strain and Poisson's ratio was obtained. The splitting compressive modulus was close to the uniaxial compressive modulus tested by splitting testing method. Its deviation was within 2%. There existed a small deviation between splitting

---

* 中国公路学报，2017, 30(10): 1-16.

tensile modulus and direct tensile modulus because of the difference of stress states and stress levels, but the deviation was within the acceptable range. The results show that there is a significant difference between tensile and compressive characteristics of asphalt mixture. The synchronous testing method for tensile and compressive moduli based on splitting test can improve the testing efficiency and scientificity of asphalt mixture. The results can provide scientific parameters for the structural design of asphalt pavement.

Key words: road engineering; asphalt mixture; splitting test; tensile modulus; compressive modulus; synchronous test

0 引言

现阶段中国沥青路面设计方法采用结构层材料各向同性假设的弹性层状体系理论,在路面结构设计时简单采用无侧限抗压回弹模量作为设计参数[1]。美国AASHTO路面结构设计指南采用间接拉伸弹性模量;壳牌采用沥青混合料的弯拉模量;澳大利亚的路面结构设计指南采用弯曲和间接拉伸模量[2-3]。然而经大量试验证明,半刚性基层材料和沥青混合料均表现出拉、压模量不等的各向异性性质,而且一般抗压模量远大于抗拉模量[4]。在路面结构层实际受力中,一般同时存在拉应力区与压应力区;而且,一般处于上部受压、下部受拉的应力状态[5]。因此在进行路面力学计算时,简单地采用较大的抗压回弹模量作为设计参数,将导致高估路面材料的力学性能,并使得设计计算结果存在较大误差,严重影响实际路面的使用性能与寿命[6-7]。

现行沥青路面设计规范中采用沥青混合料抗压回弹模量,且要求按此模量计算得出的层底应力应小于等于容许拉应力,而该容许拉应力则是通过沥青混合料劈裂试验测得的劈裂强度除以抗拉强度结构系数而得。因此,有学者就提出抗压回弹模量与劈裂强度这2个参数的选取就存在着不对应关系[8],这也是当前沥青路面设计规范存在的一个不足之处,需进行修改完善。

现行路面材料试验规程中材料模量的测试方法主要有:抗压回弹模量测试,劈裂回弹模量测试,弯拉回弹模量测试。抗压回弹模量测试主要分为顶面法或承载板法,两者均是在无侧限单向受压状态下进行试验;弯拉回弹模量试验,虽然考虑到了路面结构层材料实际处于上部受压、下部受拉的应力状态,但模量计算的理论是基于混合料拉、压模量相同的假设,且没有考虑剪切作用对挠度的影响,导致计算出的弯拉模量误差较大,不能准确地反映材料的真实力学性能;劈裂回弹模量是一种间接拉伸试验,其试件中部的拉、压两向应力状态与路面结构层真实应力状态较为接近[9]。

现行路面材料试验规程中材料模量的测试方法均是以拉、压模量相同的各向同性假设为前提的。针对该测试方法带来与实际的材料特性存在较大出入的问题,本文在材料均质的假定前提下,考虑材料的拉、压差异性,利用微积分原理,对现有劈裂模量试验加以改进,推导出劈裂试验中拉伸模量、压缩模量与水平径向应变片的平均拉伸回弹应变、竖直径向应变片的平均压缩回弹应变的定量关系式;这使得可以通过劈裂模量试验同步测试得到劈裂拉伸模量和劈裂压缩模量,并提高了测试的科学性与效率。

1 劈裂试验中拉伸模量、压缩模量计算公式的理论推导

岩土领域对劈裂试验有比较早和比较深的研究。Erarslan等[10]、Kourkoulis等[11-12]求得了巴西圆盘受抛物线型载荷下的应力和位移场,并考虑了不同加载角度和载荷类型对圆盘内应力和位移分布的影响;黄耀光等[13]利用二维弹性理论,根据应力场叠加法求得圆盘内的应力近似解析解,并依据Griffith强度破坏准则[14],推导出岩石抗拉强度的理论计算公式;宫凤强等[15]结合圆盘对心受力的理论弹性解和实际试验中便于测量的物理参数,利用微积分原理,推导出岩石拉伸模量和总位移变形量之间的定量关系,并给出巴西劈裂试验中拉伸模量的解析算法。

劈裂试验加载示意和试件受力示意分别如图1,2所示。圆盘内任意一点$T(x,y)$的应力状态为

$$\left.\begin{aligned}\sigma_x &= \frac{2P}{\pi L}\left[\frac{\sin^2(\theta_1)\cos(\theta_1)}{r_1} + \frac{\sin^2(\theta_2)\cos(\theta_2)}{r_2}\right] - \frac{2P}{\pi DL}\\ \sigma_y &= \frac{2P}{\pi L}\left[\frac{\cos^3(\theta_1)}{r_1} + \frac{\cos^3(\theta_2)}{r_2}\right] - \frac{2P}{\pi DL}\\ \tau_{xy} &= \frac{2P}{\pi L}\left[\frac{\sin(\theta_1)\cos^2(\theta_1)}{r_1} - \frac{\sin(\theta_2)\cos^2(\theta_2)}{r_2}\right]\end{aligned}\right\} \quad (1)$$

附 录

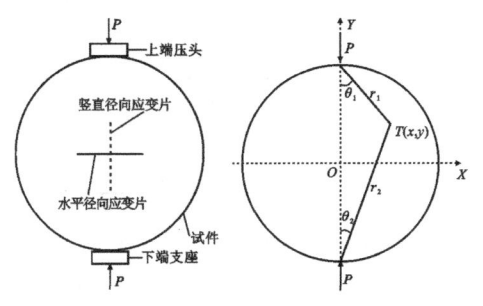

图 1 劈裂试验加载示意
Fig. 1 Loading Diagram of Splitting Test

图 2 试样受力示意
Fig. 2 Force Diagram of Sample

式中:σ_x,σ_y 分别表示圆盘内任意一点 $T(x,y)$ 的 x 方向和 y 方向的正应力;τ_{xy} 表示圆盘内任意一点 $T(x,y)$ 的剪应力;P 为劈裂试验压头施加的荷载;L 为劈裂试件的厚度;D 为劈裂试件的直径;θ_1,θ_2 与 r_1,r_2 的含义见图 2。

苏联学者 Мусхелишьили[16] 采用复变函数的方法,给出了巴西圆盘内任意一点的应力解析解;叶剑红等[17]以平面应力状态为基础,根据弹性理论中 Airy 应力函数和线弹性叠加原理,同样给出了巴西圆盘内任意一点应力的直角坐标形式的解析式,两者方法不同,但得到的应力场解析解完全吻合。

如图 2 所示,根据平面应力问题的弹性力学解析解和 OX 轴、OY 轴的几何特征,可得 OX 轴、OY 轴上任一点的应力状态如下:

在 OX 轴方向上

$$\left.\begin{array}{l}\sigma_x(x) = \dfrac{2P}{\pi DL}\left[1 - \dfrac{16D^2 x^2}{(4x^2+D^2)^2}\right]\\ \sigma_y(x) = \dfrac{2P}{\pi DL}\left[1 - \dfrac{4D^4}{(4x^2+D^2)^2}\right]\\ \tau_{xy}(x) = 0\end{array}\right\} \quad (2)$$

在 OY 轴方向上

$$\left.\begin{array}{l}\sigma_x(y) = \dfrac{2P}{\pi DL}\\ \sigma_y(y) = \dfrac{2P}{\pi DL}\left(1 - \dfrac{D^2}{R^2 - y^2}\right)\\ \tau_{xy}(y) = 0\end{array}\right\} \quad (3)$$

式中:$\sigma_x(x)$,$\sigma_y(x)$ 分别表示 OX 轴上任一点的拉应力和压应力;$\sigma_x(y)$,$\sigma_y(y)$ 分别表示 OY 轴上任一点的拉应力和压应力;$\tau_{xy}(x)$,$\tau_{xy}(y)$ 分别表示 OX 和 OY 轴上任一点的剪应力;R 为劈裂试件半径。

根据二维应力状态下的胡克定律,考虑拉、压模量的差异性,有

$$\left.\begin{array}{l}\varepsilon_x(x) = \dfrac{\sigma_x(x)}{E_x} - \dfrac{\mu\sigma_y(x)}{E_y}\\ \varepsilon_y(y) = \dfrac{\sigma_y(y)}{E_y} - \dfrac{\mu\sigma_x(y)}{E_x}\end{array}\right\} \quad (4)$$

式中:$\varepsilon_x(x)$ 为 OX 轴上任一点的拉应变;$\varepsilon_y(y)$ 为 OY 轴上任一点的压应变;E_x 为劈裂试验 x 方向的拉伸模量;E_y 为劈裂试验 y 方向的压缩模量;μ 为泊松比。

将式(2)、(3)代入式(4)得:
OX 轴上任一点的拉应变为

$$\varepsilon_x(x) = \dfrac{2P}{\pi DL}\left\{\dfrac{1}{E_x}\left[1 - \dfrac{16D^2 x^2}{(4x^2+D^2)^2}\right] - \dfrac{\mu}{E_y}\left[1 - \dfrac{4D^4}{(4x^2+D^2)^2}\right]\right\} \quad (5)$$

OY 轴上任一点的压应变为

$$\varepsilon_y(y) = \dfrac{2P}{\pi DL}\left[\dfrac{1}{E_y}\left(1 - \dfrac{D^2}{R^2 - y^2}\right) - \dfrac{\mu}{E_x}\right] \quad (6)$$

根据图 3 所示,由微分学可知,将试样中心(亦是应变片中点)到应变片端部 $l/2$(l 为应变片长度)处之间的距离均匀地分为 n 小段,横、纵向每段的长度依次记为:$x_1,x_2,\cdots,x_n$;$y_1,y_2,\cdots,y_n$。显然有

$$\sum_{i=1}^{n} x_i = \sum_{i=1}^{n} y_i = \dfrac{l}{2} \quad i = 1,2,\cdots,n \quad (7)$$

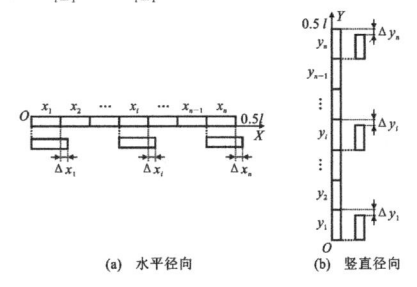

(a) 水平径向   (b) 竖直径向

图 3 水平径向和竖直径向上应变片变形计算示意
Fig. 3 Calculation Diagram of Strain Gauge Deformation in Horizontal and Vertical Radial Direction

当 n 越大,x_i 和 y_i 的长度就越短,则该段的应力和应变可视为均匀不变的,i 段上横、纵向微变形为

$$\left.\begin{array}{l}\Delta x_x(i) = \varepsilon_x(i)x_i \quad i = 1,2,\cdots,n\\ \Delta y_y(i) = \varepsilon_y(i)y_i \quad i = 1,2,\cdots,n\end{array}\right\} \quad (8)$$

应变片在水平径向的总变形 Δu 和竖直径向的总变形 Δv 分别视为是 $0 \sim l/2$ 上变形的 2 倍,即

$$\left.\begin{array}{l}\Delta u = 2\sum_{i=1}^{n}\Delta x_x(i) = 2\sum_{i=1}^{n}\varepsilon_x(i)x_i\\ \Delta v = 2\sum_{i=1}^{n}\Delta y_y(i) = 2\sum_{i=1}^{n}\varepsilon_y(i)y_i\end{array}\right\} \quad (9)$$

由式(4)可知,在水平和竖直方向上的应变函数在应变片范围内是连续的,再由积分学近似地有

$$\left.\begin{aligned}\Delta u &= 2\int_0^{\frac{l}{2}}\varepsilon_x(x)\mathrm{d}x \\ \Delta v &= 2\int_0^{\frac{l}{2}}\varepsilon_y(y)\mathrm{d}y\end{aligned}\right\} \quad (10)$$

将式(4)代入式(10)并求定积分得(应变片段的总变形取正值)

$$\left.\begin{aligned}\Delta u &= \frac{4P}{\pi L}\left[\left(\frac{\mu}{E_y}-\frac{1}{E_x}\right)\arctan\left(\frac{l}{D}\right)+\left(\frac{\mu}{E_y}+\frac{1}{E_x}\right)\frac{Dl}{l^2+D^2}+\left(\frac{1}{E_x}-\frac{\mu}{E_y}\right)\frac{l}{2D}\right] \\ \Delta v &= \frac{4P}{\pi L}\left[\left(\frac{1}{E_y}-\frac{\mu}{E_x}\right)\frac{l}{2D}-\frac{1}{E_y}\ln\left(\frac{D-l}{D+l}\right)\right]\end{aligned}\right\} \quad (11)$$

根据式(11)解关于拉伸模量 E_x、压缩模量 E_y 的方程,得

$$\left.\begin{aligned}E_x &= \frac{4P}{\pi L}\frac{ab+cd\mu^2}{b\Delta u-\mu d\Delta v} \\ E_y &= \frac{4P}{\pi L}\frac{ab+cd\mu^2}{\mu c\Delta u+a\Delta v}\end{aligned}\right\} \quad (12)$$

其中

$$\left.\begin{aligned}a &= \frac{Dl}{D^2+l^2}-\arctan\left(\frac{l}{D}\right)+\frac{l}{2D} \\ b &= \frac{l}{2D}-\ln\left(\frac{D-l}{D+l}\right) \\ c &= \frac{l}{2D} \\ d &= \frac{Dl}{D^2+l^2}+\arctan\left(\frac{l}{D}\right)-\frac{l}{2D} \\ \Delta u &= \varepsilon_h l \\ \Delta v &= \varepsilon_v l\end{aligned}\right\} \quad (13)$$

式中:ε_h 为水平径向应变片测得的平均拉伸回弹应变;ε_v 为竖直径向应变片测得的平均压缩回弹应变。

按式(12)、(13)即可得到劈裂试验中的拉伸、压缩回弹模量。

2 配合比设计及试件制备

从前述的理论推导过程可以看出,本文所得的基于劈裂试验的拉、压模量同步测试方法并未对混合料的具体类型加以限定,因此,该方法可适用于不同类型的混合料(既适用于沥青混合料,亦适用于半刚性基层材料)。

本文选用细粒式沥青混合料 AC-13C 作为研究对象,胶结料为 SBS 改性沥青,集料为玄武岩。沥青三大指标试验结果见表1,矿料级配表2,最佳油石比下的马歇尔试验结果见表3。沥青混合料

表1 SBS(I-D)改性沥青性能指标
Tab. 1 Performance Indexes of SBS(I-D) Modified Asphalt

试验项目	试验结果	技术要求
针入度(25 ℃,100 g,5 s)/0.1 mm	56	30~60
延度(5 cm·min⁻¹,5 ℃)/cm	34	≥20
软化点 $T_{R\&B}$/℃	79.5	≥60

表2 AC-13C 密级配沥青混合料矿料级配
Tab. 2 Gradation of AC-13C Dense Grading Asphalt Mixture

筛孔尺寸/mm	16	13.2	9.5	4.75	2.36	1.18	0.6	0.3	0.15	0.075
通过率/%	100.0	95.0	74.0	48.5	34.0	23.5	15.0	11.0	8.5	6.0

表3 最佳油石比下马歇尔试验结果
Tab. 3 Results of Marshall Test at Optimal Asphalt Content

油石比/%	毛体积相对密度/(g·cm⁻³)	空隙率/%	饱和度/%	矿料间隙率/%	稳定度/kN	流值/0.1 mm
5.2	2.445	4.5	67.2	16.1	12.7	27.9

的各项技术指标均满足《公路沥青路面施工技术规范》(JTG F40—2004)的要求。

按此最佳油石比,首先旋转压实成型直径为 150 mm、高为 100 mm 的圆柱体沥青混合料试件,再将试件进行钻芯和上、下表面切割得到直径为 100 mm、高为 60 mm 的标准试件,其尺寸误差不超过 2 mm;并选取表面均匀、密实的试件进行劈裂模量试验。

3 考虑拉、压差异的沥青混合料劈裂试验与计算结果

3.1 由劈裂试验测拉、压劈裂模量的试验过程

沥青混合料是一种典型的黏弹性材料,在不同的温度、不同的加载速度和不同的应力状态下会表现出不同的力学性能[18-19]。因此,为了准确分析沥青混合料劈裂试验中的拉、压差异性,本文的劈裂试验采用相同的加载速度(0.4 MPa·s⁻¹)和相同的试验温度(15 ℃)。

试验采用 MTS 多功能材料测试系统进行,在经典的巴西劈裂试验基础上,将试件前、后中心位置分别粘贴水平径向和竖直径向的应变片,加载示意如图1所示,劈裂模量试验如图4所示。

在进行劈裂模量试验前,需做相同加载速度和温度(15 ℃)条件下的劈裂强度试验,本文得到的破坏荷载为 $P_m = 10.32$ kN。模量试验程序中 7 级荷载大小分别为:$0.1P_m$,$0.2P_m$,$0.3P_m$,$0.4P_m$,$0.5P_m$,$0.6P_m$,$0.7P_m$。试验按应力控制模式以 0.4

附　录

MPa·s^{-1}的加载速度进行加载（经过截面尺寸换算后，其加载速度为361.9 kN·min^{-1}）。

本试验的加载、卸载是在多功能材料测试系统（MTS）上进行的，MTS实时采集荷载的大小，应变采集仪实时采集试件水平径向拉应变与竖直径向压应变。

图4　劈裂模量试验
Fig.4　Splitting Modulus Test

具体的加载、卸载试验步骤如下：

（1）以361.9 kN·min^{-1}的速率加载至$0.2P_m$进行预压，并保持1 min,然后以相同的速率卸荷至0,观察拉、压应变采集的数据曲线是否正常，发现不正常时，须重新进行一次预压。

（2）以361.9 kN·min^{-1}的速率加载至第1级荷载$0.1P_m$,然后以相同的速率卸荷至0,并保持30 s;接着依次进行第2~7级荷载的加载、卸载过程，步骤与第1级荷载相同。

对于荷载的确定，以每级循环的最大荷载作为该级的作用荷载P_i;对于水平径向回弹拉应变和竖直径向回弹压应变的确定，以每级荷载开始卸荷时刻的应变与卸荷后保持30 s时刻的应变的差值作为该级荷载作用下的拉、压回弹应变。

3.2　劈裂模量试验结果

MTS执行的回弹模量测试程序和应变采集系统是同步进行的，二者采集的试验数据分别如图5、6所示。

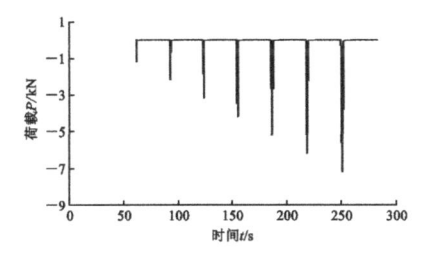

图5　MTS实时采集的逐级荷载
Fig.5　Real Time Data Acquisition of Step Load in MTS

本文劈裂试验试件的尺寸为：直径$D=100$ mm、厚度$L=60$ mm;应变片长度为$l=40$ mm;泊松比取$\mu=0.35$。

从应变采集系统采集的数据来看，由于第1级

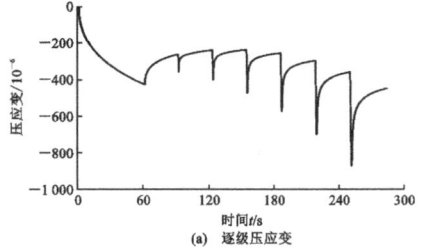

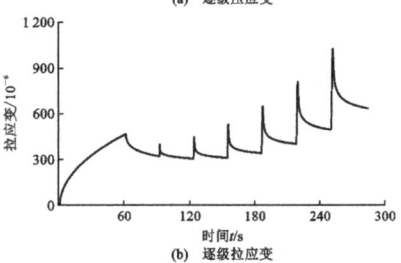

图6　应变采集仪实时采集的逐级应变
Fig.6　Real Time Acquisition of Step Strain Based on Strain Gauging Instrument

循环的回弹变形受预压阶段变形的影响，其数据参考价值较低，故从第2级循环开始计算各级的拉伸、压缩模量。根据前述的荷载、应变确定方法，得到各级荷载及其对应的回弹应变如表4所示。

表4　各级荷载水平的拉伸、压缩回弹模量结果
Tab.4　Tensile and Compressive Moduli in Each Loading Level

荷载等级	荷载P_i/kN	压应变/10^{-6}	拉应变/10^{-6}	拉伸模量/MPa	压缩模量/MPa
2	2.274	516	205	1 862	2 251
3	3.360	655	260	2 170	2 620
4	4.224	810	340	2 001	2 642
5	5.294	1 089	411	2 256	2 501
6	6.232	1 237	478	2 238	2 583
7	7.223	1 393	654	1 653	2 580
平均值				2 105	2 519

将上述试验数据结果和试件的尺寸代入式(12)、(13),计算得到各级荷载水平下的拉伸、压缩回弹模量见表4。

本文参考《公路工程沥青及沥青混合料试验规程》(JTG E20—2011)中静态回弹模量确定的原点修正方法，取2~7级回弹模量的平均值作为最终所测得的回弹模量，则根据试验结果，其劈裂拉伸回弹模量为2 105 MPa,劈裂压缩回弹模量为2 519 MPa。

上述过程为一个劈裂试件的拉伸、压缩回弹模量计算分析过程。本文进行了10组平行劈裂回弹

模量试验,测得的劈裂拉伸、劈裂压缩回弹模量试验结果汇总如表 5 所示。

表 5 劈裂拉伸、压缩回弹模量试验结果汇总
Tab. 5 Summary of Results of Tensile and Compressive Moduli in Splitting Tests

试件序号	拉伸模量/MPa	压缩模量/MPa
1	2 105	2 519
2	2 097	2 553
3	2 141	2 479
4	2 006	2 469
5	2 199	2 638
6	2 052	2 534
7	2 138	2 487
8	2 067	2 601
9	2 155	2 492
10	2 014	2 510
平均值	2 097	2 528
标准差	63	55
变异系数/%	3.0	2.2
保证率/%	≥90	≥90

从表 5 可以看出:

(1)通过劈裂试验得到的沥青混合料压缩回弹模量大于其拉伸回弹模量,这与传统的试验结果相一致。

(2)由于对试验全过程进行了精细化的控制,采用基于劈裂试验的拉、压模量同步测试方法所得的试验结果比较稳定、离散性小,其中拉伸模量变异系数为 3.0%、压缩模量的变异系数为 2.2%。对于路面材料试验来讲,完全能够满足试验要求,同时从试验数据的离散性方面亦证明了该方法的可行性。

3.3 与传统直接拉伸模量、单轴压缩模量的对比分析

为了进一步验证本文劈裂模量试验方法的科学合理性,考虑到沥青混合料的黏弹性特性,本文也同步进行了相同加载速度(0.4 MPa·s^{-1})和试验温度(15 ℃)条件下的直接拉伸模量、单轴压缩模量试验,以作对比分析。直接拉伸模量和单轴压缩模量的试验结果如表 6 所示。

本文将由劈裂试验得到的拉、压模量分别称为劈裂拉伸模量和劈裂压缩模量。不同拉伸回弹模量与压缩回弹模量的对比如图 7 所示。

不难看出,由本文劈裂模量试验方法计算得到的劈裂压缩回弹模量与单轴压缩试验测得的抗压回弹模量十分接近,偏差为 1.5%;劈裂拉伸回弹模量与直接拉伸试验测得抗回弹模量存在一定偏差,偏差为 14.7%。究其原因是由于相比于一维应力状态的直接拉伸试验,劈裂试验方法中的测试点处

表 6 直接拉伸、单轴压缩回弹模量试验结果汇总
Tab. 6 Summary of Results of Direct Tensile and Uniaxial Compressive Moduli Test

试件序号	拉伸模量/MPa	压缩模量/MPa
1	1 760	2 539
2	1 785	2 486
3	1 819	2 498
4	1 801	2 615
5	1 775	2 671
6	1 820	2 597
7	1 772	2 473
8	1 763	2 608
9	1 806	2 630
10	1 789	2 546
平均值	1 789	2 566
标准差	22	68
变异系数/%	1.2	2.6
保证率/%	≥90	≥90

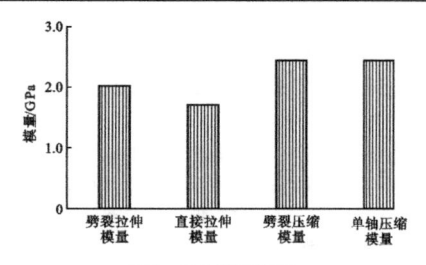

图 7 四种模量的对比
Fig. 7 Comparison of Four Kinds of Moduli

于二维应力状态,应力状态不同导致拉伸模量试验结果存在偏差,但亦在可接受的范围内。在路面实际的应力状态中,拉、压应力同在的情况是比较常见的,大量研究表明,不同受力方式的试验方法中沥青混合料具有不同的弹性模量值[7-8],而劈裂试验中的试件应力状态与其在实际沥青路面中的应力状态比较接近[4-5,8]。本文所提出的基于劈裂试验方法得到的劈裂拉、压回弹模量,不同于常规的直接拉伸与无侧限抗压回弹模量,因此,用劈裂拉、压模量更能真实地反映沥青路面的抗变形能力。

4 结 语

(1)本文结合劈裂试验试样中心拉伸、压缩模量的弹性力学解和应变片测得的水平径向拉伸回弹应变和竖直径向压缩回弹应变,基于二维胡克定律和微积分原理,提出了基于劈裂试验同步测得沥青混合料拉、压模量的试验原理和计算方法,极大地提高

了试验测试的效率与科学性。

(2)按该劈裂试验方法测得的平均劈裂拉伸回弹模量为 2 097 MPa,平均劈裂压缩回弹模量为 2 528 MPa。劈裂压缩回弹模量与单轴压缩试验测得的抗压回弹模量十分接近,偏差不超过2%;由于应力状态和应力水平的差别,劈裂拉伸回弹模量与直接拉伸试验测得的抗拉回弹模量存在一定偏差,但亦在可接受的范围内。

(3)在路面实际的应力状态中,拉、压同在的情况是比较常见的,劈裂试验时试件的应力状态与路面结构的真实应力状态比较接近。本文所提出的基于劈裂试验方法得到的劈裂拉伸回弹模量,不同于常规的直接拉伸回弹模量,更能真实地反映沥青路面的抗变形能力,其对沥青路面结构设计具有重要的参考意义。

(4)本文仅开展了一种沥青混合料的劈裂拉、压回弹模量测试,还需开展不同级配类型沥青混合料以及半刚性基层材料的相关试验,扩大该试验方法的适用范围,并为沥青路面结构设计提供合适的设计参数。

参考文献:
References:

[1] JTG D50—2006,公路沥青路面设计规范[S].
JTG D50 — 2006, Specifications for Design of Highway Asphalt Pavement[S].

[2] 姚祖康.沥青路面结构设计[M].北京:人民交通出版社,2011.
YAO Zu-kang. Asphalt Pavement Structure Design [M]. Beijing: China Communications Press,2011.

[3] 沈金安.国外沥青路面设计方法汇总[M].北京:人民交通出版社,2004.
SHEN Jin-an. Collection of Foreign Asphalt Pavement Design Method[M]. Beijing: China Communications Press,2011.

[4] 马林,张肖宁.基于间接拉伸试验模式的沥青混合料动态模量[J].华南理工大学学报:自然科学版,2008,36(10):86-91.
MA Lin, ZHANG Xiao-ning. Dynamic Modulus of Asphalt Mixture Based on Indirect Tensile Test Mode [J]. Journal of South China University of Technology: Natural Science Edition,2008,36(10):86-91.

[5] 马林,张肖宁.间接拉伸与单轴压缩模式沥青混合料动态模量比较分析[J].公路交通科技,2009,26(10):11-17.
MA Lin, ZHANG Xiao-ning. Comparison of HMA Dynamic Modulus Between Indirect Tension and Uniaxial Compression Test Modes[J]. Journal of Highway and Transportation Research and Development,2009,26(10):11-17.

[6] 郑健龙.基于结构层寿命递增的耐久性沥青路面设计新思想[J].中国公路学报,2014,27(1):1-7.
ZHENG Jian-long. New Structure Design of Durable Asphalt Pavement Based on Life Increment[J]. China Journal of Highway and Transport,2014,27(1):1-7.

[7] 张蕾,陈静云,乔英娟.间接拉伸试验条件下沥青混合料变形特性[J].辽宁工程技术大学学报:自然科学版,2008,27(6):856-858.
ZHANG Lei, CHEN Jing-yun, QIAO Ying-juan. Deformation Behaviors of Asphalt Mixture Under Indirect Tensile Experiment. [J] Journal of Liaoning Technical University: Natural Science, 2008, 27 (6): 856-858.

[8] 罗作芬,郑传超.沥青混合料劈裂回弹模量的研究[J].河北工业大学学报,2010,39(3):107-111.
LUO Zuo-fen, ZHENG Chuan-chao. Research on the Resilient Modulus of the Asphalt Mixture Under Splitting Loading[J]. Journal of Hebei University of Technology,2010,39(3):107-111.

[9] 陈少幸,虞将苗,李海军,等.沥青混合料模量不同测试方法的比较分析[J].公路交通科技,2008,25(8):6-9.
CHEN Shao-xing, YU Jiang-miao, LI Hai-jun, et al. Comparative Analysis of Different Test Methods on Asphalt Mixture Modulus[J]. Journal of Highway and Transportation Research and Development,2008,25(8):6-9.

[10] ERARSLAN N, LIANG Z Z, WILLIAMS D J. Experimental and Numerical Studies on Determination of Indirect Tensile Strength of Rocks[J]. Rock Mechanics and Rock Engineering,2012,45(5):739-751.

[11] KOURKOULIS S K, MARKIDES C F, CHATZISTERGOS P E. The Brazilian Disc Under Parabolically Varying Load: Theoretical and Experimental Study of the Displacement Field [J]. International Journal of Solids and Structures,2012,49(7):959-972.

[12] KOURKOULIS S K, MARKIDES C F, CHATZISTERGOS P E. The Standardized Brazilian Disc Test as a Contact Problem [J]. International Journal of Rock Mechanics and Mining Sciences,2013,57(1):132-141.

[13] 黄耀光,王连国,陈家瑞,等.平台巴西劈裂试验确定岩石抗拉强度的理论分析[J].岩土力学,2015,36(3):739-748.

(下转第16页)

[11] CHEVALIER B, COMBE G, VILLARD P. Experimental and Discrete Element Modeling Studies of the Trapdoor Problem: Influence of the Macro-mechanical Frictional Parameters[J]. Acta Geotechnica, 2012, 7(1):15-39.

[12] IGLESIA G R, EINSTEIN H H, WHITMAN R V. Investigation of Soil Arching with Centrifuge Tests[J]. Journal of Geotechnical and Geoenvironmental Engineering, 2014, 140(2):189-201.

[13] CHEN Y M, CAO W P, CHEN R P. An Experimental Investigation of Soil Arching Within Basal Reinforced and Unreinforced Piled Embankments[J]. Geotextile and Geomembrance, 2008, 26(2):164-174.

[14] RUI R, TOL A F V, XIA Y Y, et al. Investigation of Soil-arching Development in Dense Sand by 2D Model Tests[J]. Geotechnical Testing Journal, 2016, 39(3):415-430.

[15] JENCK O, DIAS D, KASTNER R. Two-dimensional Physical and Numerical Modeling of a Pile-supported Earth Platform over Soft Soil[J]. Journal of Geotechnical and Geoenvironmental Engineering, 2007, 133(3):295-305.

[16] JENCK O, DIAS D, KASTNER R. Soft Ground Improvement by Vertical Rigid Piles Two-dimensional Physical Modelling and Comparison with Current Design Methods[J]. Soils and Foundations, 2008, 45(6):15-30.

[17] ROTHENBURG L, BATHURST R J. Micromechanical Features of Granular Assemblies with Planar Elliptical Particles[J]. Geotechnique, 1992, 42(1):79-95.

[18] FUKUMOTO Y, SAKAGUCHI H, MURAKAMI A. The Role of Rolling Friction in Granular Packing[J]. Granular Matter, 2013, 15(2):175-182.

[19] FERELLEC J F, MCDOWELL G R. Modelling of Ballast-geogrid Interaction Using the Discrete-element Method[J]. Geosynthetics International, 2012, 19(6):470-479.

[20] 常 在,杨 军,程晓辉. 砂土强度和剪胀性的颗粒力学分析[J]. 工程力学, 2010, 27(4):95-104.
CHANG Zai, YANG Jun, CHENG Xiao-hui. Granular Mechanical Analysis of the Strength and Dilatancy of Sands[J]. Engineering Mechanics, 2010, 27(4):95-104.

[21] 胡 港. 桩承式路堤土拱演化——模型试验分析与 DEM 模拟[D]. 武汉:武汉理工大学, 2015.
HU Gang. Evolution of Arching in Piled Embankments—The Analysis of Model Experiments and DEM Simulation[D]. Wuhan: Wuhan University of Technology, 2015.

[22] HAYNES W M. CRC Handbook of Chemistry and Physics[M]. Boca Raton: CRC Press, 2014.

（上接第7页）

HUANG Yao-guang, WANG Lian-guo, CHEN Jia-rui, et al. Theoretical Analysis of Flattened Brazilian Splitting Test for Determining Tensile Strength of Rocks[J]. Rock and Soil Mechanics, 2015, 36(3):739-748.

[14] SATOCH Y. Position and Load of Failure in Brazilian Test a Numerical Analysis by Griffith Criterion[J]. Journal of the Society of Materials Science, 1987, 36(410):1219-1224.

[15] 宫凤强,李夕兵,ZHAO J. 巴西圆盘劈裂试验中拉伸模量的解析算法[J]. 岩石力学与工程学报, 2010, 29(5):881-891.
GONG Feng-qiang, LI Xi-bing, ZHAO J. Analytical Algorithm to Estimate Tensile Modulus in Brazilian Disk Splitting Tests[J]. Chinese Journal of Rock Mechanics and Engineering, 2010, 29(5):881-891.

[16] Мусхелишвили Н И. 数学弹性力学的几个基本问题[M]. 赵惠元,译. 北京:科学出版社, 1958.
Мусхелишвили Н И. Some Basic Problems in Mathematic Elastic Mechanics[M]. Translated by ZHAO Hui-yuan. Beijing: Science Press, 1958.

[17] 叶剑红,杨 洋,常中华,等. 巴西劈裂试验应力场解析解应力函数解法[J]. 工程地质学报, 2009, 17(4):528-532.
YE Jian-hong, YANG Yang, CHANG Zhong-hua, et al. Airy Stress Function Method for Analytic Solution of Stress Field During Brazilian Disc Test[J]. Journal of Engineering Geology, 2009, 17(4):528-532.

[18] LU Song-tao, LUO Zhao-hui, XIE Juan. Fatigue Performance of Aging Asphalt Mixtures[J]. Polimery, 2015, 60(2):126-131.

[19] LU Song-tao, ZHENG Jian-long. Normalization Method for Asphalt Mixture Fatigue Equation Under Different Loading Frequencies[J]. Journal of Central South University, 2015, 22(7):2761-2767.

养生期水泥稳定碎石强度、模量及疲劳损伤特性

吕松涛[1,2]，郑健龙[1,2]，仲文亮[1,2]

(1. 长沙理工大学 公路养护技术国家工程实验室，湖南 长沙 410114；
2. 长沙理工大学 公路工程教育部重点实验室，湖南 长沙 410114)

摘要：为了揭示养生期水泥稳定碎石强度、模量及疲劳损伤特性，有效减少施工期水泥稳定碎石基层产生的疲劳损伤，进行了不同龄期下水泥稳定碎石材料的无侧限抗压强度、抗压回弹模量、弯拉强度及弯拉疲劳特性研究，揭示了无侧限抗压强度、抗压回弹模量和弯拉强度随龄期的变化规律，建立了不同龄期下无侧限抗压强度与抗压回弹模量之间的相互转换关系，以及不同龄期下水泥稳定碎石材料的疲劳方程与疲劳损伤演化模型。研究结果表明，龄期对水泥稳定碎石的强度、模量与疲劳损伤性能影响显著，龄期越短，荷载对水泥稳定碎石材料产生的损伤越大，施工期造成的疲劳损伤将直接导致路面运营期的疲劳寿命大大缩减，为保证运营期的路面使用寿命，应严格控制短龄期情况下重载车辆的通行，包括施工车辆。

关键词：道路工程；水泥稳定碎石；室内试验；加载龄期；强度；模量；疲劳损伤

中图分类号：U416.217　　**文献标志码**：A

Characteristics of Strength, Modulus and Fatigue Damage for Cement Stabilized Macadam in Curing Period

LU Song-tao[1,2], ZHENG Jian-long[1,2], ZHONG Wen-liang[1,2]

(1. State Engineering Laboratory of Highway Maintenance Technology, Changsha University of Science & Technology, Changsha 410114, Hunan, China; 2. Key Laboratory of Highway Engineering of Ministry of Education, Changsha University of Science & Technology, Changsha 410114, Hunan, China)

Abstract: In order to reveal the characteristics of strength, modulus and fatigue damage for cement stabilized macadam in curing period and reduce the fatigue damage of cement stabilized macadam base course during the construction, the researches on performances of unconfined compressive strength, compressive resilient modulus, flexural strength and flexural fatigue during different ages were carried out. The change rules of unconfined compressive strength, compressive resilient modulus and flexural strength with ages were revealed. The transformation relationship between the unconfined compressive strength and the compressive resilient modulus, and fatigue equation and fatigue damage evolution model on cement stabilized macadam under different ages were established. The results show that the influence of age on strength, modulus and fatigue damage performances of cement stabilized macadam is significant. The shorter the age is, the greater the damage caused by load to cement stabilized macadam is. Fatigue damage during

*中国公路学报，2015, 28(9): 9-15, 45.

the construction period will directly reduce the fatigue life in pavement operation periods greatly. In order to ensure the pavement service life in operation period, the passage of the overloading vehicles should be controlled strictly in short age state, including the construction vehicles.

Key words：road engineering; cement stabilized macadam; indoor test; loading age; strength; modulus; fatigue damage

0 引言

半刚性基层（底基层）材料的力学性能显著地受其龄期的影响。中国现行沥青路面设计规范、施工技术规范及试验规程在对半刚性基层（底基层）材料的力学性能进行描述时均对其龄期进行了规定，如在进行沥青路面结构设计时对水泥稳定类和石灰稳定类基层（底基层）结构分别采用的是90 d和180 d的无侧限抗压回弹模量和劈裂强度，在进行混合料配合比设计及工地质量控制时采用的是7 d的无侧限抗压强度[1-5]。

在半刚性基层（底基层）沥青路面的实际施工过程中，及时的保湿养生可以避免基层材料的干燥收缩裂缝[6]，但由于受施工季节及工期所限，赶工期的现象也比较常见，许多高速公路在半刚性底基层养生7 d后即进行基层的铺筑，养生时间远未到结构设计参数取值时的90 d或180 d，且在路面交竣工验收时，路表弯沉检测的标准值是按结构设计时确定的路面结构厚度与材料模量（水泥稳定类90 d、石灰稳定类180 d）计算的路表弯沉值[2]。

以上客观事实会直接导致以下问题：

（1）半刚性基层材料配合比设计参数（无侧限抗压强度）与结构设计参数（无侧限抗压回弹模量）不匹配，导致材料设计与结构设计脱节。

（2）半刚性基层材料的强度与刚度随龄期的增长而增长，铺筑7 d后或在较短的龄期（未达到90 d或180 d）下即进行上层结构的铺筑，养生车辆、运料车辆、摊铺机、压路机等施工设备必然会对还未形成足够强度、刚度的下承层产生破坏作用，在施工期即产生了路面结构的内部损伤。

（3）在路面交竣工验收时，路表弯沉检测的标准值是按无损状态、确定龄期（水泥稳定类90 d、石灰稳定类180 d）条件下的材料模量计算所得的，而没有考虑施工期路面结构产生的损伤与半刚性基层所处实际龄期，事实上实测路表总弯沉并不能保证半刚性基层刚好处于90 d或180 d的龄期，这就造成材料设计参数的工作状态与交竣工验收时结构所处状态不匹配的现象，从而导致验收标准的确定方法存在一定的不科学性。

基于上述问题，本文以水泥稳定碎石基层材料为研究对象，通过开展其不同龄期下的强度、模量、疲劳等试验研究，揭示不同龄期条件下水泥稳定碎石基层材料的强度、模量及疲劳损伤特性，为实现设计参数、施工控制参数与验收标准的动态统一，提高半刚性基层设计、施工、交竣工验收的科学性提供理论依据。

1 试件成型与试验准备

水泥稳定碎石原材料选用的水泥为兴安海螺普通硅酸盐水泥PC32.5，集料采用杨家桥碎石厂生产的石灰岩集料，经检测，其技术指标均满足相关规范规程要求。采用的矿料级配如表1所示。

表1 水泥稳定碎石矿料合成级配

Tab. 1 Synthetic Gradation of Cement Stabilized Macadam

筛孔孔径/mm	合成级配各筛孔的通过率/%
26.5	100.0
19	92.5
16	85.5
13.2	77.0
9.5	62.7
4.75	34.4
2.36	21.2
1.18	17.0
0.6	11.5
0.3	8.2
0.15	5.1
0.075	3.6

根据表1确定的矿料合成级配，进行水泥稳定碎石的室内配合比设计试验，最终设计结果为：水泥稳定碎石的外掺水泥剂量（质量分数）为4.5%，最大干密度为2.350 g·cm^{-3}，最佳含水量为4.5%。

据此，按照相关试验规程和规范要求，制作的无侧限抗压强度及抗压回弹模量试件尺寸为：150 mm（直径）×150 mm（高）的圆柱体试件。弯拉强度及弯拉疲劳试件的尺寸为：400 mm（长）×100 mm（宽）×100 mm（高）的梁式试件。试件成型均采用

附 录

静压成型的试验方法,成型后,试件在标准的养生室内(温度 20 ℃±2 ℃,湿度不小于 95%)进行不同龄期下的养生。

达到规定的龄期即进行强度、模量及疲劳试验,试验均采用美国生产的材料测试系统(MTS-Landmark)进行。

2 不同龄期下抗压强度与模量变化规律

2.1 不同龄期下无侧限抗压强度变化规律

将成型的圆柱体试件在标准养生条件下分别养生至 3,7,14,28,60,90 d 后,按照试验规程规定的试验方法进行无侧限抗压强度试验,试验加载速率为 1 mm·min⁻¹,试件破坏形状如图 1 所示。

图 1 试件无侧限抗压强度破坏形状
Fig. 1 Sample Failure Shape of Unconfined Compressive Strength

不同龄期下水泥稳定碎石无侧限抗压强度试验结果如表 2 所示。

表 2 不同龄期下的无侧限抗压强度试验结果
Tab. 2 Test Results of Unconfined Compressive Strength Under Different Ages

龄期 t/d	S_c/MPa	$\bar{S}_c$/MPa
3	3.1,3.1,2.7,3.2,3.2,2.4,2.6,3.0,2.6,1.8,2.8	2.8
7	3.4,4.3,3.5,4.0,3.2,4.2,4.1,3.9,3.4,3.9	3.8
14	5.0,4.7,3.9,4.0,4.1,4.2,4.8,4.1,4.2,4.6,4.3	4.3
28	5.1,4.7,4.9,4.4,3.4,4.3	4.6
60	5.5,5.2,5.3,5.4,5.7,5.9	5.5
90	5.5,5.8,5.6,6.3,6.9,5.9	5.7

注:S_c 为无侧限抗压强度;$\bar{S}_c$ 为无侧限抗压强度平均值。

将表 2 中不同龄期下的强度试验结果平均值进行拟合,拟合结果如图 2 所示。

拟合函数关系为

$$S_c = 2.02 + 1.91\lg(t) \quad R^2 = 0.98 \quad (1)$$

式中:R 为相关系数。

从表 2 及图 2 的拟合结果可以看出:

(1)水泥稳定碎石 7 d 的无侧限抗压强度平均值为 3.8 MPa,满足《公路路面基层施工技术规范》(JTJ 034—2000)中关于高速公路水泥稳定碎石基层强度 3~5 MPa 的要求。

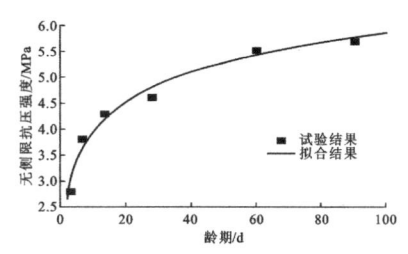

图 2 无侧限抗压强度随龄期变化规律
Fig. 2 Change Rule of Unconfined Compressive Strength with Ages

(2)无侧限抗压强度随龄期的增长而增大。在龄期的初期,强度随龄期的增长速度比较快,28 d 龄期后增长速度变缓,90 d 强度基本趋于稳定,这与文献[7]、[8]中的研究结论一致,也与规范所确定的以 90 d 的龄期为设计参数取值的标准龄期的初衷一致。

2.2 不同龄期下抗压回弹模量变化规律

按前述相同的养生方法,将试件分别养生至 3,7,14,28,60,90 d 后,按照文献[5]、[9]规定的试验方法进行抗压回弹模量试验,试验结果见表 3。

表 3 不同龄期下的抗压回弹模量试验结果
Tab. 3 Test Results of Compressive Resilient Modulus Under Different Ages

t/d	E_c/MPa	$\bar{E}_c$/MPa
3	1 830,1 515,1 573,1 370,1 515,1 573,1 370	1 572
7	1 919,1 946,2 294,2 126	2 071
14	2 564,2 493,2 344,2 397,2 379	2 435
28	3 004,3 243,2 806,2 793,3 306	3 067
60	3 556,3 974,4 026,3 860	3 854
90	4 222,4 204,4 107,4 571,4 127	4 246

注:E_c 为抗压回弹模量;$\bar{E}_c$ 为抗压回弹模量平均值。

将表 3 中的不同龄期下的抗压回弹模量平均值试验结果进行拟合,拟合结果如图 3 所示,拟合函数关系如式(2)所示,即

$$E_c = 0.54 + 1.83\lg(t) \quad R^2 = 0.98 \quad (2)$$

从表 3 及图 3 拟合结果可以看出:

(1)水泥稳定碎石 90 d 的抗压回弹模量平均值为 4 246 MPa,该试验结果与《公路沥青路面设计规范》(JTG D50—2006)在进行结构层层底拉应力时给出的模量范围(3 000~4 200 MPa)接近。

(2)抗压回弹模量随龄期的变化规律与无侧限抗压强度随龄期的变化规律类似,均随着龄期的增长而增大。在龄期的初期,抗压回弹模量随龄期的

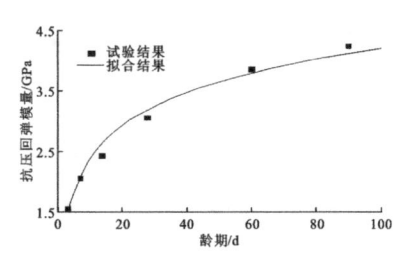

图 3 抗压回弹模量随龄期变化规律
Fig. 3 Change Rule of Compressive Resilient Modulus with Ages

增长速度比较快,28 d 龄期后增长趋势变缓,90 d 的抗压回弹模量基本趋于稳定,这与规范所确定的以 90 d 龄期为设计参数(回弹模量)取值的标准龄期的初衷是一致的。

2.3 无侧限抗压强度与抗压回弹模量的相互关系

在进行半刚性基层材料的配合比设计及施工阶段采用的控制指标是无侧限抗压强度,而在进行路面结构设计时选取的材料设计参数是抗压回弹模量,二者存在不匹配性,为了通过一个指标定量地评价另一个指标,需建立无侧限抗压强度与抗压回弹模量二者之间的相互转换关系。

将表 2 及表 3 中所示的相同龄期下的无侧限抗压强度与抗压回弹模量进行回归,可得到二者之间的相互转换关系,计算分析结果如图 4 及式(3)所示。

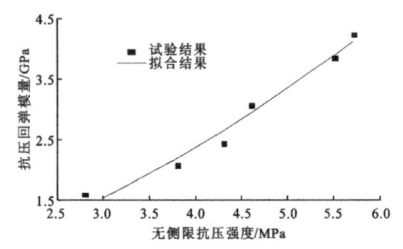

图 4 无侧限抗压强度与抗压回弹模量的对应关系
Fig. 4 Corresponding Relationship Between Unconfined Compressive Strength and Compressive Resilient Modulus

$$E_c = 0.27 S_c^{1.57} \quad R^2 = 0.97 \quad (3)$$

结合式(1)～(3)即可得到不同龄期情况下无侧限抗压强度与抗压回弹模量之间的相互转换关系。确定了材料配合比设计及施工质量控制时的无侧限抗压强度指标,即可得到结构设计时材料所处结构层的模量(刚度)指标,则可对结构服役期路面结构的抗变形能力有预期把握。同样地,确定了结构设计时的半刚性基层材料的模量值,则对材料配合比设计和施工质量控制时的无侧限抗压强度指标进行预期控制与约定,即通过二者的相互转换关系,为实现材料配合比设计参数与结构设计参数的统一、路面结构设计与施工质量控制的统一提供了理论与方法依据。

3 不同龄期下水泥稳定碎石的疲劳损伤特性

施工过程中,现行施工技术规范对半刚性基层养生时间的要求比较短[2],其规定是"新建半刚性基层铺筑后应及时进行养生和保护,浇洒透层或铺筑下封层,并尽快铺筑沥青面层",所以许多高速公路在建设过程中,由于受工期所限,半刚性基层的强度与刚度(模量)还未达到稳定状态时即开始进行上一结构层的铺筑。

从前面不同龄期下的水泥稳定碎石材料强度与模量的试验结果可以看出,龄期达到 90 d 后,水泥稳定碎石材料强度与模量才能达到稳定状态,才能满足路面结构设计时对抗压回弹模量的要求。若在较短的龄期内进行面层施工,水泥稳定碎石基层材料并不能充分形成稳定的强度与刚度,在此期间若不封闭交通,养生车辆及施工重载车辆必将对短龄期条件下的低强度、低模量半刚性基层产生较大的疲劳破坏作用。许多研究者对水泥稳定碎石的疲劳破坏性能进行了研究,也得到了许多有价值的结论[10],但研究大多针对某一固定龄期下的材料疲劳性能,不同龄期疲劳性能的研究还比较少见。若养生及施工重载车辆在半刚性基层未达到 90 d 龄期时就通行,就会对路面造成较大的施工期损伤,直接导致运营期路面使用寿命的衰减,而且目前这一现象还比较普遍,为了探究养生期施工车辆对水泥稳定碎石的疲劳破坏作用,需开展不同龄期下水泥稳定碎石的疲劳损伤特性研究。

3.1 不同龄期下弯拉强度试验结果分析

在进行弯拉疲劳试验之前首先进行弯拉强度试验。将成型好的 400 mm(长)×100 mm(宽)×100 mm(高)的梁式试件在标准养生室内分别养生至 7、14、28、90 d 共 4 个龄期,然后按照《公路工程无机结合料稳定材料试验规程》(JTG E51—2009)T0851—2009 的试验方法进行不同龄期下的三分点弯拉强度试验,其加载速率为 50 mm·min⁻¹,所得试验结果如表 4 所示。

附 录

表 4 不同龄期下的弯拉强度试验结果
Tab. 4 Test Results of Flexural Strength Under Different Ages

t/d	破坏荷载 F/kN	弯拉强度 S_t/MPa
7	4.17	1.251
	3.68	1.104
	3.93	1.179
14	4.43	1.329
	3.83	1.149
	4.59	1.377
28	5.14	1.542
	5.72	1.716
	5.69	1.707
90	6.48	1.944
	6.32	1.896
	6.77	2.031
	6.63	1.989

将表 4 所示的不同龄期下的强度试验结果进行拟合,拟合结果如图 5 所示。

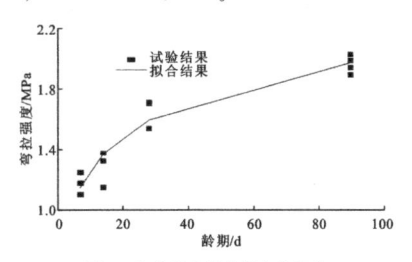

图 5 弯拉强度随龄期变化规律

Fig. 5 Change Rule of Flexural Strength with Ages

拟合函数关系为

$$S_t = 0.52 + 0.75 \lg(t) \quad R^2 = 0.97 \quad (4)$$

从表 4 及图 5 可以看出,水泥稳定碎石的弯拉强度随龄期的变化规律与无侧限抗压强度随龄期的变化规律类似,均随龄期的增长而增大,且在龄期的初期,弯拉强度随龄期的增长速度比较快,28 d 龄期后增长速度变缓,90 d 的强度基本趋于稳定。

3.2 不同龄期下弯拉疲劳试验结果分析

水泥稳定碎石弯拉疲劳试验同样采用材料试验系统进行,荷载采用连续半正矢波荷载,加载频率采用 10 Hz,疲劳试验采用应力控制的方式进行,以试件断裂作为材料疲劳失效判据。

龄期设定为 7,14,28,90 d 共 4 个龄期,试件采用前述的 400 mm(长)×100 mm(宽)×100 mm(高)梁式试件,对各龄期下的试件分别进行不同应力比下的三分点加载疲劳试验,每个应力比下均进行了 5 组平行试验。水泥稳定碎石由于最大公称粒径比较大,试件成型过程中难免存在一定的不均匀性,导致疲劳试验结果有一定的离散性,剔除离散性比较大的试验点后,试验结果如表 5 所示。

将表 5 的疲劳试验结果利用常见的 S-N 疲劳方程 $N_f = k[1/(\sigma/S_t)]^n$ 进行拟合(σ 为应力,σ/S_t 为应力比),拟合结果如图 6 及表 6 所示(N_f 为疲劳寿命)。

各龄期的疲劳方程拟合结果汇总如表 6 所示。

从图 6 及表 6 的分析结果可以看出:在相同的应力比情况下,长龄期的疲劳寿命比短龄期的大,随着龄期的增加,水泥稳定碎石的抗疲劳性能逐渐提

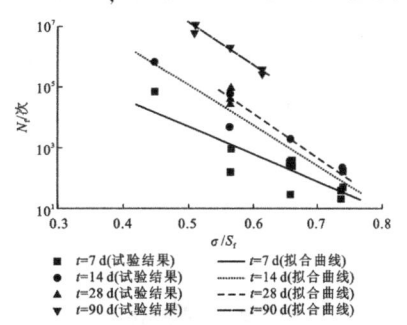

图 6 不同龄期下疲劳试验结果拟合曲线

Fig. 6 Fitting Curves of Fatigue Test Results Under Different Ages

表 5 不同龄期下的疲劳试验结果
Tab. 5 Test Results of Fatigue Under Different Ages

σ/S_t (t=7 d)	N_f/次	σ/S_t (t=14 d)	N_f/次	σ/S_t (t=28 d)	N_f/次	σ/S_t (t=90 d)	N_f/次
0.4	129 499	0.4	932 017	0.4		0.45	11 294 222,7 229 042
0.5	629,3 065	0.5	12 435,107 557	0.5	83 339,159 179,52 914	0.50	2 401 842,2 612 832
0.6	129,970,1 391	0.6	6 704,905,1 126,5 461	0.6	2 899,7 146	0.55	406 238,499 823
0.7	106,219,659	0.7	190,772	0.7	564		

表6 各龄期疲劳方程拟合结果汇总
Tab. 6 Fitting Results Summary of Fatigue Equations Under Different Ages

t/d	疲劳方程	R^2
7	$\lg(N_f)=0.75-9.43\lg(\sigma/S_f)$	0.71
14	$\lg(N_f)=0.33-14.03\lg(\sigma/S_f)$	0.88
28	$\lg(N_f)=0.52-14.27\lg(\sigma/S_f)$	0.90
90	$\lg(N_f)=1.80-14.92\lg(\sigma/S_f)$	0.98

高。同时，不同龄期下的水泥稳定碎石材料若要达到相同的疲劳寿命，在短龄期情况下，较小的应力比即较小的交通荷载作用下即可达到，而在长的龄期情况下，则对应相对较大的应力比即较大的交通荷载才能达到。可见，延长水泥稳定碎石的养生时间可以有效地提高其抗疲劳耐久性。

3.3 不同龄期下抗弯拉模量衰变规律分析

选定的抗弯拉模量衰变模型如式(5)所示，即

$$E(N)=E_0(1-\frac{N}{N_f})^q \qquad (5)$$

式中：$E(N)$ 为疲劳荷载作用到 N 时水泥稳定碎石的弯拉回弹模量；E_0 为初始回弹模量；N 为荷载循环次数；q 为模型指数，表征影响因素对模量衰变的敏感性。

由于试验仪器及材料本身存在的缺陷，重复荷载作用第1次时得到的抗弯拉模量值并不能准确表征材料的初始模量，因此参照沥青混合料疲劳损伤分析时初始回弹模量的取值方法[11-13]，选取第50个循环的稳定模量值作为初始回弹模量值 E_0。

典型的水泥稳定碎石抗弯拉模量衰变规律如图7所示，由图7可知，随着加载次数的增加，其模量逐渐衰减，到疲劳寿命的后期，其衰变速率急剧增大。

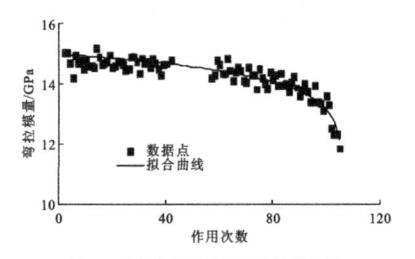

图7 典型的弯拉模量衰变规律曲线
Fig. 7 Typical Curve of Flexural Modulus Decay Law

按照式(5)所示的抗弯拉模量衰变模型，将不同龄期、不同应力比下的弯拉模量衰变试验结果进行拟合，汇总，结果如表7所示。

选取表7所示的应力比，其对应的应力水平值比较接近，均在0.8 MPa左右，其目的是为了分析

表7 不同龄期下弯拉模量衰变规律汇总
Tab. 7 Summary of Flexural Modulus Decay Law Under Different Ages

t/d	σ/S_f	σ/MPa	抗弯拉模量衰变方程
7	0.70	0.83	$E(N)=15\,000(1-N/N_f)^{0.045\,26}$
14	0.60	0.77	$E(N)=17\,000(1-N/N_f)^{0.023\,76}$
28	0.50	0.83	$E(N)=16\,400(1-N/N_f)^{0.008\,92}$
90	0.45	0.88	$E(N)=20\,907(1-N/N_f)^{0.000\,12}$

相同的交通荷载对不同龄期水泥稳定碎石的疲劳破坏作用。

在疲劳应力水平接近的情况下，抗弯拉模量衰变方程指数 q 在此表征的是龄期对模量衰变规律的敏感程度，其值越大，龄期对模量衰变规律的影响越敏感。由表7可以看出，龄期 t 不同，抗弯拉模量衰变方程的指数 q 亦不相同，随着龄期的增加其值越来越小，表明龄期对模量衰变的敏感性越来越小，说明在相同的交通荷载作用下，短龄期的模量衰减程度比较大，随着龄期的增加，其模量衰变程度越来越小，逐渐趋于稳定。将指数 q 与龄期 t 进行拟合，拟合结果如图8和式(6)所示。

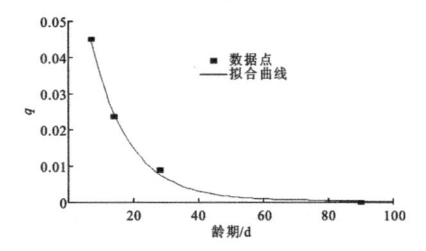

图8 抗弯拉模量衰变方程指数 q 随龄期 t 变化规律
Fig. 8 Change Rule of Index q of Flexural Modulus Decay Equation with Age t

拟合方程为

$$q(t)=0.08e^{(-t/11.63)} \quad R^2=0.99 \qquad (6)$$

根据表5的疲劳试验结果，将表7所选取应力比下的龄期 t 与其对应的疲劳寿命 N_f 进行拟合，拟合结果如图9和式(7)所示。

拟合方程为

$$\lg(N_f)=4.45\lg(t)-1.57 \quad R^2=0.99 \qquad (7)$$

从图9和式(7)可以看出，在相同的疲劳应力水平作用情况下，水泥稳定碎石的疲劳寿命随着龄期的增长而增加，龄期增长则其抗疲劳性能增强。

3.4 不同龄期下疲劳损伤规律分析

为了揭示施工车辆对养生期水泥稳定碎石的疲劳破坏作用，需对不同龄期下的水泥稳定碎石疲劳

图 9 疲劳寿命 N_f 随龄期 t 变化规律

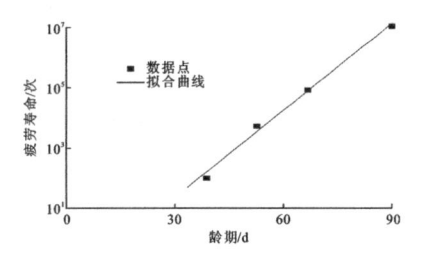

Fig. 9 Change Rule of Fatigue Life N_f with Age t

损伤过程进行分析。

定义水泥稳定碎石的抗弯拉模量衰变为其疲劳损伤变量,如式(8)所示,即

$$D(N)=1-\frac{E(N)}{E_0} \qquad (8)$$

式中:$D(N)$为荷载作用到N时材料产生的损伤。

根据前面模量衰变规律的分析结果,由于疲劳寿命N_f为龄期t的函数,抗弯拉模量衰变方程指数q亦为龄期t的函数,根据式(5)与式(8),则其损伤$D(N)$亦为龄期t的函数,即

$$D(N,t)=1-\frac{E(N)}{E_0}=1-\left[1-\frac{N}{N_f(t)}\right]^{q(t)} \qquad (9)$$

式(9)即为水泥稳定碎石的疲劳损伤方程。

根据式(6)、式(7)及式(9),将龄期t不同而疲劳应力水平接近条件下的疲劳损伤演化规律绘制于同一张图中,如图10所示。

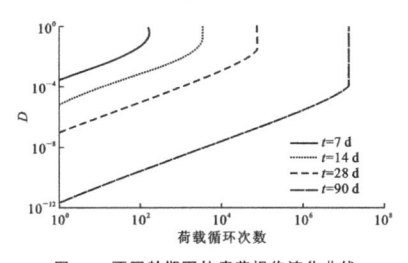

图 10 不同龄期下的疲劳损伤演化曲线

Fig. 10 Fatigue Damage Evolution Curves Under Different Ages

从图10可以明显地看出,在相同荷载及其作用次数情况下,龄期越短,损伤演化曲线越靠上,荷载产生的损伤越大。在较短的龄期条件下产生的损伤远远大于长龄期条件下产生的损伤,甚至在较少的作用次数下即可发生疲劳断裂破坏。这说明若水泥稳定碎石基层材料得不到充分的养生,强度与模量达不到规定的要求,则养护或施工车辆将对其造成非常大的疲劳损伤。这种施工期造成的疲劳损伤将直接导致路面运营期的疲劳寿命大大缩减。因此,为保证运营期的路面使用寿命,应严格控制半刚性基层强度与模量还没形成时重载车辆的通行,包括施工车辆。

4 结 语

(1)水泥稳定碎石基层材料的无侧限抗压强度、抗压回弹模量、弯拉强度受龄期影响显著,均随龄期的增长而增长,在90 d时趋于稳定。

(2)通过无侧限抗压强度与抗压回弹模量的相互转换关系,为实现材料配合比设计参数与结构设计参数的统一、路面结构设计与施工质量控制的统一提供了理论与方法上的依据。

(3)随着龄期的增加,水泥稳定碎石的抗疲劳性能逐渐提高,因此通过延长水泥稳定碎石的养生时间可以有效地提高其抗疲劳耐久性。

(4)水泥稳定碎石在较短的龄期条件下产生的损伤远远大于长龄期条件下产生的损伤。施工期造成的损伤将导致路面的疲劳寿命大大缩减。因此应严格控制短龄期情况下重载车辆的通行,包括施工车辆。

(5)本文揭示了龄期对水泥稳定碎石强度、模量及疲劳性能的影响规律,但未研究不同矿料级配类型对其路用性能的影响,而矿料级配类型对水泥稳定碎石的强度、模量及疲劳性能的影响非常显著,为了提高养生期半刚性基层材料抵抗荷载破坏的能力,对其级配的优化设计将是下一步的重要研究方向。

参考文献:

References:

[1] JTG D50—2006,公路沥青路面设计规范[S].
 JTG D50—2006,Specifications for Design of Highway Asphalt Pavement[S].

[2] GB 50092—96,沥青路面施工及验收规范[S].
 GB 50092—96,Code for Construction and Acceptance of Asphalt Pavements[S].

[3] JTG F40—2004,公路沥青路面施工技术规范[S].
 JTG F40—2004,Technical Specifications for Construction of Highway Asphalt Pavements[S].

[4] JTJ 034—2000,公路路面基层施工技术规范[S].
 JTJ 034—2000,Technical Specifications for Construction of Highway Roadbases[S].

[5] JTG E51—2009,公路工程无机结合料稳定材料试验规程[S].

(下转第45页)

[8] NIE J G, WANG Y H, ZHANG X G, et al. Mechanical Behavior of Composite Joints for Connecting Existing Concrete Bridges and Steel-concrete Composite Beams[J]. Journal of Constructional Steel Research, 2012, 75:11-20.

[9] HUCKELBRIDGE J R A, EL-ESNAWI H, MOSES F. Shear Key Performance in Multibeam Box Girder Bridges[J]. Journal of Performance of Constructed Facilities, 1995, 9(4):271-285.

[10] 杨勇,祝刚,周丕健,等. 钢板混凝土组合桥面板受力性能与设计方法研究[J]. 土木工程学报,2009, 42(12):135-141.
YANG Yong, ZHU Gang, ZHOU Pei-jian, et al. Experimental Study on the Mechanical and Design Method of Plain Steel Plate and Concrete Composite Bridge Decks[J]. China Civil Engineering Journal, 2009, 42 (12):135-141.

[11] 杨勇,周现伟,薛建阳,等. 带钢板混凝土组合桥面板的组合梁疲劳性能试验研究[J]. 土木工程学报, 2012, 45(6):123-131.
YANG Yong, ZHOU Xian-wei, XUE Jian-yang, et al. Experiment Study on Fatigue Behavior of Composite Girders with Steel Plate-concrete Composite Bridge Decks[J]. China Civil Engineering Journal, 2012, 45(6):123-131.

[12] 杨勇,周丕健,聂建国,等. 钢板混凝土组合桥面板静力与疲劳性能试验[J]. 中国公路学报, 2009, 22(4):78-83.
YANG Yong, ZHOU Pei-jian, NIE Jian-guo, et al. Experiment on Static and Fatigue Behavior of Steel Plate-concrete Composite Bridge Decks[J]. China Journal of Highway and Transport, 2009, 22(4):78-83.

[13] 卫军,李沛,徐岳,等. 空心板铰缝协同工作性能影响因素分析[J]. 中国公路学报, 2011, 24(2):29-33.
WEI Jun, LI Pei, XU Yue, et al. Influencing Factor Analysis on Coordinated Working Performance of Hinge Joint in Hollow Slab[J]. China Journal of Highway and Transport, 2011, 24(2):29-33.

[14] PRIESTLEY M J N, SEIBLE F, CALVI G M. Seismic Design and Retrofit of Bridges[M]. Hoboken: Wiley-interscience Publication, 1996.

[15] JGJ 138—2001, 型钢混凝土组合结构技术规程[S].
JGJ 138—2001, Technical Specification for Steel Reinforced Concrete Composite Structures[S].

(上接第15页)
JTG E51—2009, Test Methods of Materials Stabilized with Inorganic Binders for Highway Engineering[S].

[6] 沙爱民. 半刚性基层的材料特性[J]. 中国公路学报, 2008, 21(1):1-5.
SHA Ai-min. Material Characteristics of Semi-rigid Base[J]. China Journal of Highway and Transport, 2008, 21(1):1-5.

[7] 庄少勤,刘朴,孙振平. 水泥稳定碎石变形性能及其影响因素[J]. 建筑材料学报, 2003, 6(4):356-363.
ZHUANG Shao-qin, LIU Pu, SUN Zhen-ping. Investigation on Deformation and Its Influencing Factors of Cement-stabilized Macadam Base[J]. Journal of Building Materials, 2003, 6(4):356-363.

[8] 孙兆辉,王铁斌,许志鸿,等. 水泥稳定碎石强度影响因素的试验研究[J]. 建筑材料学报, 2006, 9(3):285-290.
SUN Zhao-hui, WANG Tie-bin, XU Zhi-hong, et al. Trial Study on Influence Factors of Cement-stabilized Macadam Strength[J]. Journal of Building Materials, 2006, 9(3):285-290.

[9] 程箭,许志鸿,张超,等. 水泥稳定碎石设计参数研究[J]. 建筑材料学报, 2008, 11(6):673-677.
CHENG Jian, XU Zhi-hong, ZHANG Chao, et al. Research of Design Parameters of Cement-stabilized Macadam[J]. Journal of Building Materials, 2008, 11(6):673-677.

[10] 贾侃. 半刚性基层材料的疲劳特性研究[D]. 西安:长安大学, 2009.
JIA Kan. Study on the Fatigue Performance of Semi-rigid Base Course Materials[D]. Xi'an: Chang'an University, 2009.

[11] MATEOS A, GÓMEZ J A, HERNÁNDEZ R, et al. Application of the Logit Model for the Analysis of Asphalt Fatigue Tests Results[J]. Construction and Building Materials, 2015, 82:53-60.

[12] MANNAN U A, ISLAM M R, TAREFDER R A. Effects of Recycled Asphalt Pavements on the Fatigue Life of Asphalt Under Different Strain Levels and Loading Frequencies[J]. International Journal of Fatigue, 2015, 78:72-80.

[13] 吕松涛. 基于非线性疲劳损伤的沥青路面轴载换算[J]. 工程力学, 2012, 29(10):268-274.
LU Song-tao. Axle Load Conversion of Asphalt Pavement Based on Nonlinear Fatigue Damage[J]. Engineering Mechanics, 2012, 29(10):268-274.

附录 ·167·

基于非线性疲劳损伤的沥青路面轴载换算

吕松涛

(长沙理工大学交通运输工程学院道路结构与材料交通行业重点实验室(长沙), 长沙 410004)

摘 要: 为了建立沥青混合料的非线性疲劳损伤演化方程, 同时为完善沥青路面的轴载换算方法, 首先进行沥青混合料的配合比设计, 确定矿料级配及最佳油石比, 然后从损伤力学基本理论出发, 定义模量衰减为其疲劳损伤参量, 由此推导得到了疲劳损伤方程, 并以此方程对小梁直接拉伸疲劳试验结果进行拟合, 得到了模型参数和损伤随应力比的变化规律, 建立了沥青路面轴载换算新方法。结果表明: 沥青混合料的疲劳损伤演化具有明显的非线性, 用 Miner 线性疲劳损伤理论来描述沥青路面疲劳损伤演化过程不合适, 由此推导得到的轴载换算方法偏不安全, 建立在非线性疲劳损伤演化基础上的轴载换算方法考虑了加载历史和损伤历史的影响。

关键词: 道路工程; 沥青路面; 非线性疲劳损伤; 劲度模量; 轴载换算
中图分类号: U416.217　　**文献标志码:** A　　doi: 10.6052/j.issn.1000-4750.2011.05.0294

AXLE LOAD CONVERSION OF ASPHALT PAVEMENT BASED ON NONLINEAR FATIGUE DAMAGE

LÜ Song-tao

(Key Laboratory of Road Structure and Material of Ministry of Transport, School of Communication and Transportation Engineering, Changsha University of Science & Technology, Changsha 410004, China)

Abstract: In order to establish the non-linear fatigue damage evolution equation of asphalt mixture and the axial load conversion method of asphalt pavement, the aggregate gradation and optimum asphalt-aggregate ratios are determined by a proportion design of asphalt mixture. Then, the fatigue damage variable is defined by the modulus decay basing on the basic theory of damage mechanics. The fatigue damage equation was deduced. The direct tensile fatigue test results were fitted from using the fatigue damage equation. The regularities of model parameters and damage with a stress ratio are given out. The new axle load conversion method is established for asphalt pavement. The results indicate that the fatigue damage evolution has the apparent non-linear properties of asphalt mixture. The Miner linear fatigue damage theory is not suitable to describe the process of fatigue damage evolution for asphalt pavement. It is not safe to use the axial load conversion method deriving from the *Miner* equation. The new axial load conversion method basing on the nonlinear fatigue damage evolution can consider the influence of loading history and damage history.

Key words: road engineering; asphalt pavement; non-linear fatigue damage; stiffness modulus; axial load conversion

目前国内外沥青路面轴载换算方法普遍是基于 Miner 线性疲劳损伤理论及其累计理论建立的, 我国亦如此, Miner 准则存在着一个致命的缺陷, 即忽略了疲劳破坏过程中材料本身损伤的不断加剧所产生的非线性效应, 无法考虑应力幅值变化历史的影响, 用 Miner 理论来估算疲劳寿命其结果是不安全的, 与实际的路面结构疲劳损伤过程有较大的差别[1-3]。

---
*工程力学, 2012, 29(10): 268-274.

近些年来,国内外道路工作者对沥青混合料的疲劳损伤性能进行了大量的研究,从不同的理论(如不可逆热力学方法、现象学方法等)和试验(弯拉、劈裂、直接拉伸)分析角度出发、基于不同的损伤变量定义,得到了大量具有非常重要价值的沥青混合料非线性疲劳损伤方程,沥青混合料具有的非线性疲劳损伤特性已形成共识,理论研究已日趋成熟[3-10],目前存在的主要问题在于疲劳试验方法和试验数据量的积累方面,对沥青混合料的疲劳试验目前国内外还没有一个统一的试验方法,试件形状和尺寸也是五花八门,出现了百家争鸣的景象,同时造成了不同研究单位、不同研究者之间试验数据的可对比性比较差。总的研究趋势是要逐步和重复荷载作用下沥青路面的实际受力状态相接近,由于疲劳试验需要耗费大量的时间和费用,疲劳试验数据在数量的积累方面还存在大量的不足。

为此,本文通过在一定试验条件下的 AC-13C 沥青混合料疲劳试验,揭示其非线性疲劳损伤演化规律,建立一种能够考虑加载历史影响的沥青路面轴载换算方法,但若要达到设计规范适用的程度,还需要通过后续大量不同的沥青混合料、不同的试验方法下的疲劳试验来补充完善该换算方法,本文将起到抛砖引玉的作用。

1 原材料试验及配合比设计

1.1 沥青材料

试验所采用的结合料为中海油泰州 SBS(I-D)改性沥青,其技术指标满足《沥青路面施工技术规范》(JTG F40-2004)的技术要求,具体试验结果如表 1 所示。

表1 SBS(I-D)改性沥青试验结果
Table 1 Test results of SBS modified asphalt (I-D)

试验项目	试验结果	技术要求
针入度(25℃, 100g, 5s)/(0.1mm)	56	30~60
针入度指数 PI	0.533	≥0
延度(5cm/min, 5℃)/cm	34	≥20
软化点 $T_{R\&B}$/(℃)	79	≥60
运动粘度 135℃/(Pa·s)	2.31	≤3
闪点/(℃)	267	≥230
溶解度/(%)	99.92	≥99
弹性恢复 25℃/(%)	77	≥75
储存稳定性离析, 48h 软化点差/(℃)	1.5	≤2.5
TFOT/RTFOT 后残留物 质量变化/(%)	0.1	≤±1.0
TFOT/RTFOT 后残留物 25℃残留针入度比/(%)	73	≥65
TFOT/RTFOT 后残留物 残留延度(5℃)/cm	16	≥15

1.2 矿料密度及级配

本文采用的矿料为南京生产的玄武岩,由集料筛分和配合比设计得出的密度及各筛孔通过率见表 2 和表 3。

表2 集料密度
Table 2 Aggregate density

筛孔尺寸/mm	13.2	9.5	4.75	2.36	1.18	0.6	0.3	0.15	0.075	矿粉
密度/(g/cm³)	2.731	2.730	2.729	2.715	2.716	2.717	2.717	2.718	2.719	2.753

表3 AC-13C 密级配沥青混合料矿料级配
Table 3 Mineral aggregate gradation of AC-13C

筛孔尺寸/mm	16	13.2	9.5	4.75	2.36	1.18	0.6	0.3	0.15	0.075
通过率/(%)	100	95	74	48.5	34	23.5	15	11	8.5	6

1.3 马歇尔试验结果

进行沥青混合料配合比设计,确定的最佳油石比为 5.3%,最佳油石比下的马歇尔试验结果如表 4 所示,根据确定的 AC-13C 级配及最佳油石比,轮碾成型车辙板,然后切割成 50mm×50mm×250mm 小梁试件。

表4 最佳油石比下马歇尔试验结果
Table 4 Marshall test results under optimum asphalt-aggregate ratio

油石比/(%)	毛体积相对密度/(g/cm³)	空隙率VV/(%)	饱和度VFA/(%)	矿料间隙率VMA/(%)	稳定度/kN	流值/(0.1mm)
5.3	2.455	5.2	67.2	16.1	15.7	27.9

2 沥青混合料疲劳试验

2.1 沥青混合料疲劳试验方法

本次试验采用小梁直接拉伸的疲劳试验方法,荷载采用连续半正矢荷载,荷载波形如图 1 所示。

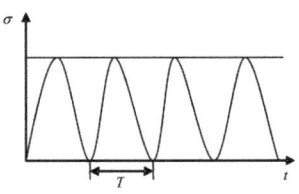

图1 加载波形
Fig.1 Load waveform

疲劳试验仪器采用从美国进口的 MTS-810 (Material Test System-810)材料试验系统进行,加载频率为 10Hz。

2.2 沥青混合料疲劳试验结果

为了确定沥青混合料不同应力比下对应施加的疲劳荷载大小,首先需要做抗拉强度试验,抗拉

附　录

强度及极限拉应变做 3 次平行试验取其平均值作为试验结果，试验温度为 15℃，抗拉强度试验结果为 0.798MPa。

进行不同应力比(0.3、0.4、0.5、0.6、0.7)下的沥青混合料小梁直接拉伸疲劳试验，试验温度为 15℃，加载频率为 10Hz。不同应力比下疲劳试验结果如表 5 所示。

表 5　不同应力比沥青混合料疲劳试验结果
Table 5　Fatigue test results at different stress ratios of HMA

应力比 r	应力水平 σ /MPa	疲劳寿命 N_f/次	
		试件 1	试件 2
0.3	0.59	30820	35231
0.4	0.78	22313	18887
0.5	0.98	7883	5807
0.6	1.18	3058	3478
0.7	1.37	1712	1388

3　沥青混合料疲劳损伤方程的建立

在同一温度，不同应力比条件下沥青混合料在考虑应力幅影响的情况下，一种常用的疲劳损伤演化方程为[11]：

$$\frac{dD}{dt} = c[1-(1-D)^{1+\beta}]^{\alpha}\left(\frac{\Delta\sigma}{1-D}\right)^{\beta} \quad (1)$$

式中：D 为损伤；$\Delta\sigma$ 为应力幅值；c、α 和 β 均为材料参数。

考虑一定加载频率(周期为 T)条件下的疲劳试验其作用次数 ΔN 与加载时间 Δt 的一一对应关系 $\Delta t = T\Delta N$，对式(1)进行积分，积分过程如下：

$$\int_0^N T\Delta\sigma^{\beta}dN = \int_0^D \frac{d[1-(1-D)^{1+\beta}]}{c(1+\beta)[1-(1-D)^{1+\beta}]^{\alpha}},$$

$$T\cdot\Delta\sigma^{\beta}N = \int_0^D \frac{1}{c(1+\beta)(1-\alpha)}d[1-(1-D)^{1+\beta}]^{1-\alpha} =$$

$$\frac{1}{c(1+\beta)(1-\alpha)}[1-(1-D)^{1+\beta}]^{1-\alpha},$$

$$[c(1+\beta)(1-\alpha)T\cdot\Delta\sigma^{\beta}N]^{1/(1-\alpha)} = 1-(1-D)^{1+\beta},$$

$$D = 1-\{1-[c(1+\beta)(1-\alpha)T\Delta\sigma^{\beta}N]^{1/(1-\alpha)}\}^{1/(\beta+1)}。$$

当 $N=N_f$ 时，$D=1$，所以：

$$D = 1-\left[1-\left(\frac{N}{N_f}\right)^{1/(1-\alpha)}\right]^{1/(\beta+1)} \quad (2)$$

根据损伤力学理论和应变等效假设，对于沥青混合料小梁疲劳试件，损伤后的本构关系仍可表示为：

$$E_0 = \frac{\sigma_t}{(1-D_N)\varepsilon_{t(N)}} = \frac{E_N}{(1-D_N)} \quad (3)$$

则：

$$D_N = 1-\frac{E_N}{E_0} \quad (4)$$

式中：E_0 为初始劲度模量，试验结果分析时取第 50 次荷载循环时的模量值[4]；σ_t 为疲劳试验施加的应力幅值；E_N 为荷载作用 N 次后试件劲度模量；$\varepsilon_{t(N)}$ 为荷载作用 N 次后试件的应变幅值；D_N 为荷载作用 N 次后的损伤值。

式(4)即为基于劲度模量衰减定义的损伤变量表达式。

采用式(2)对不同应力比下的疲劳损伤演化曲线进行拟合，拟合结果如图 2~图 6 所示。

由疲劳损伤演化曲线可以看出：不同应力比下的沥青混合料疲劳损伤演化规律比较接近，即在疲劳损伤稳定发展阶段损伤增加比较缓慢，此阶段占整个疲劳破坏全过程的绝大部分，而在临近破坏阶段损伤急剧增大，直至破坏。

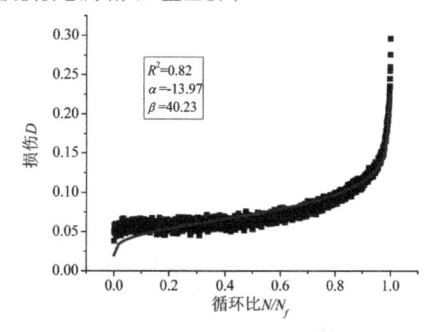

图 2　应力比 0.3 损伤演化规律
Fig.2　Damage evaluation rules at stress ratio 0.3

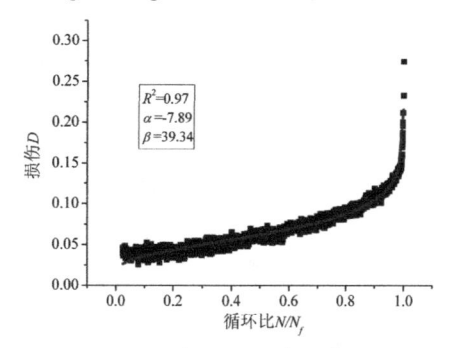

图 3　应力比 0.4 损伤演化规律
Fig.3　Damage evaluation rules at stress ratio 0.4

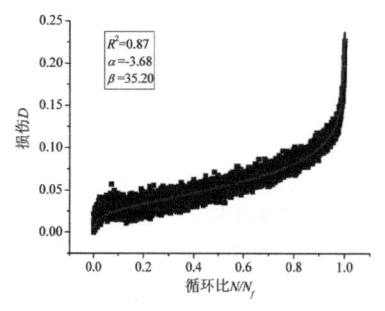

图 4 应力比 0.5 损伤演化规律
Fig.4 Damage evaluation rules at stress ratio 0.5

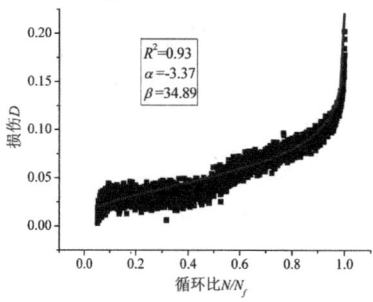

图 5 应力比 0.6 损伤演化规律
Fig.5 Damage evaluation rules at stress ratio 0.6

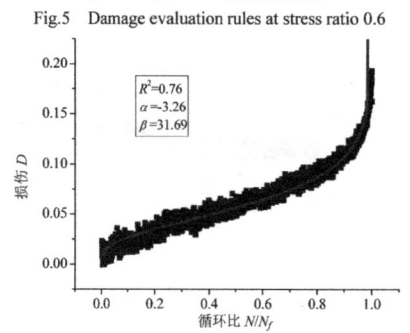

图 6 应力比 0.7 损伤演化规律
Fig.6 Damage evaluation rules at stress ratio 0.7

疲劳损伤参数 α、β 拟合结果如表 6 所示。

表 6 疲劳损伤参数 α、β 表
Table 6 Parameters of fatigue damage α、β

参数	应力比				
	0.3	0.4	0.5	0.6	0.7
α	−13.97	−7.89	−3.68	−3.37	−3.26
β	40.23	39.34	35.20	34.89	31.6
R^2	0.82	0.97	0.87	0.93	0.96

分别将疲劳损伤演化参数 α、β 对应力比 r 进行拟合，拟合结果如图 7 和式(5)、式(6)所示，图 7(a)表征系数 α 随应力比 r 的变化规律，图 7(b)表征参数 β 随应力比 r 的变化规律。

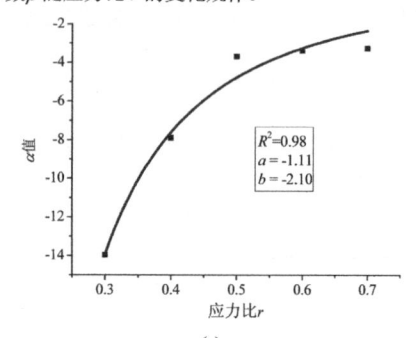

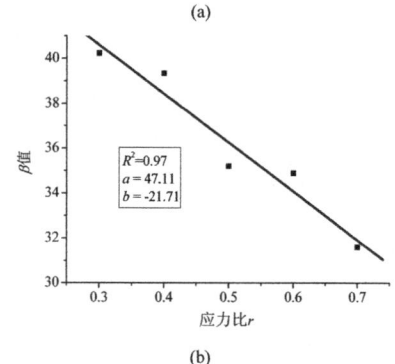

图 7 疲劳损伤演化参数 α、β 与应力比 r 拟合曲线
Fig.7 Fitting curve between parameters of fatigue damage evaluation α、β with r

$$\alpha(r) = -1.156 r^{-2.097}, \quad R^2 = 0.976 \quad (5)$$

$$\beta(r) = 47.107 - 21.71 r, \quad R^2 = 0.971 \quad (6)$$

将上述拟合结果代入疲劳损伤演化方程即式(2)可得不同应力比 r 下的疲劳损伤演化规律表达式：

$$D = 1 - \left[1 - \left(\frac{N}{N_f}\right)^{\frac{1}{1-\alpha(r)}}\right]^{\frac{1}{\beta(r)+1}} \quad (7)$$

由式(5)~式(7)计算得到的不同应力比下的疲劳损伤演化值如表 7 所示。

表 7 不同应力比下的疲劳损伤演化值表
Table 7 Fatigue damage evaluation at different stress ratio

循环比 N/N_f	应力比 r				
	0.3	0.4	0.5	0.6	0.7
0	0	0	0	0	0
0.1	0.0449	0.0358	0.0294	0.0249	0.0206
0.2	0.0525	0.0436	0.0373	0.0329	0.0288
0.3	0.0587	0.0500	0.0440	0.0398	0.0350
0.4	0.0645	0.0561	0.0504	0.0465	0.0421
0.5	0.0705	0.0624	0.0571	0.0536	0.0495

附　录

（续表）

循环比 N/N_f	应力比 r				
	0.3	0.4	0.5	0.6	0.7
0.6	0.0770	0.0694	0.0644	0.0614	0.0569
0.7	0.0847	0.0776	0.0732	0.0707	0.0669
0.8	0.0947	0.0883	0.0846	0.0830	0.0801
0.85	0.1014	0.0955	0.0923	0.0913	0.0891
0.9	0.1105	0.1052	0.1028	0.1021	0.1013
0.95	0.1255	0.1213	0.1200	0.1191	0.1163
0.99	0.1585	0.1566	0.1540	0.1520	0.1506
$(N_f-1)/N_f$	0.2774	0.2643	0.2642	0.2447	0.2404
1	1	1	1	1	1

表7作图如图8所示。

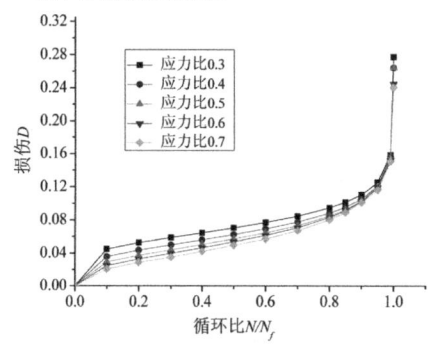

图8　损伤演化规律汇总图
Fig.8　Summary of Damage evolution

由上述分析可以看出，在循环比-损伤坐标系中，应力比越小，损伤演化曲线越靠上，即在循环比 N/N_f 一定的情况下，损伤随应力比的增大而减小。

4　沥青路面轴载换算推导

目前道路工程界广泛应用的是 Miner 线性疲劳损伤模型，当式(2)中 α 和 β 均为 0 时，则退化为 Miner 线性模型，即：

$$D(N) = \frac{N}{N_f} \quad (8)$$

式中：N 为荷载循环次数；N_f 为疲劳寿命。

Miner 模型认为相同的荷载条件下，随着加载次数 N 的增加，损伤 D 呈线性增加。

在多级加载情况下，设材料依次承受应力水平为 $\sigma_1, \sigma_2, \sigma_3, \cdots, \sigma_n$ 的循环荷载作用，经历的循环荷载作用次数分别为 $N_1, N_2, N_3, \cdots, N_n$，那么损伤累积值为：

$$D(N) = \sum_{i=1}^{n} \frac{N_i}{N_{f_i}} \quad (9)$$

式中，N_{f_i} 为应力 σ_i 单独作用时的疲劳寿命。

式(9)表明损伤的累积是线性的，即任意改变加载顺序，对当前损伤值没有影响。这显然不符合路面实际疲劳损伤演化规律，低估了材料或结构已有的损伤对轴载换算的影响，换算的结果将偏不安全，因此，需要建立一种能够考虑加载历史影响的沥青路面轴载换算方法。

基于弯沉等效、层底拉应力等效和疲劳损伤等效等的轴载等效换算方法都是以轴载对路面产生的效应等效为依据的[12-13]。当路面达到的破坏条件一定时，不同汽车轮轴荷载所需作用的重复次数是不同的。下面来推导非标准轴载作用次数 N_i 等效换算成标准轴载作用次数 N_s 的换算关系。

考虑到应力比 r 与应力水平 σ_i 的一一对应关系，在此轴载换算时将前述的应力比 r 均替换为应力水平 σ_i。设在标准应力水平 σ_s 作用下的疲劳寿命为 N_{f_s}，在非标准应力水平 σ_i 作用下的疲劳寿命为 N_{f_i}。基于疲劳损伤等效的沥青路面轴载换算时，假定路面结构的初始损伤相等，任意荷载 σ_i 作用 N_i 次对路面结构造成的损伤 $D(N_i)$ 与标准荷载 σ_s 作用 N_s 次对路面结构造成的损伤 $D(N_s)$ 相等，即：

$$D(N_i) = D(N_s) \quad (10)$$

将式(7)代入式(10)，由应力比 r 与应力水平 σ_r 的一一对应关系，令 $\alpha_r = \alpha(r) = \alpha'(\sigma_r)$，则有：

$$1 - \left(\frac{N_i}{N_{f_i}}\right)^{\frac{1}{1-\alpha_i}} = \left[1 - \left(\frac{N_s}{N_{f_s}}\right)^{\frac{1}{1-\alpha_s}}\right]^{\frac{1+\beta_i}{1+\beta_s}} \quad (11)$$

对式(2)求导，得：

$$\frac{dD(N)}{dN} = \frac{\left[1 - \left(\frac{N}{N_f}\right)^{\frac{1}{1-\alpha}}\right]^{\frac{-\beta}{\beta+1}} \left(\frac{N}{N_f}\right)^{\frac{\alpha}{1-\alpha}}}{(\beta+1)(1-\alpha)N_f} \quad (12)$$

式(12)即为疲劳损伤演化方程，在局部范围内也是疲劳损伤的增量表达形式，即：

$$\Delta D(N) = \frac{\left[1 - \left(\frac{N}{N_f}\right)^{\frac{1}{1-\alpha}}\right]^{\frac{-\beta}{\beta+1}} \left(\frac{N}{N_f}\right)^{\frac{\alpha}{1-\alpha}}}{(\beta+1)(1-\alpha)N_f} \Delta N \quad (13)$$

同时基于疲劳损伤等效，轴载换算时任意荷载 σ_i 作用第 N_i+1 次对路面结构造成的损伤增量与标准荷载 σ_s 作用第 $N_s+\Delta N_s$ 次内对路面结构造成的损伤增量相等，即：

$$D(N_i+1) - D(N_i) = D(N_s + \Delta N_s) - D(N_s) \quad (14)$$

式(14)表明在疲劳过程中任意荷载 σ_i 作用 1 次相当于标准荷载 σ_s 作用 ΔN_s 次,此即为二者的换算关系。

由式(13)、式(14)得:

$$\frac{\left[1-\left(\dfrac{N_s}{N_{f_s}}\right)^{\frac{1}{1-\alpha_s}}\right]^{\frac{-\beta_s}{\beta_s+1}}\left(\dfrac{N_s}{N_{f_s}}\right)^{\frac{\alpha_s}{1-\alpha_s}}}{(\beta_s+1)(1-\alpha_s)N_{f_s}}\Delta N_s =$$

$$\frac{\left[1-\left(\dfrac{N_i}{N_{f_i}}\right)^{\frac{1}{1-\alpha_i}}\right]^{\frac{-\beta_i}{\beta_i+1}}\left(\dfrac{N_i}{N_{f_i}}\right)^{\frac{\alpha_i}{1-\alpha_i}}}{(\beta_i+1)(1-\alpha_i)N_{f_i}} \quad (15)$$

将式(11)代入式(15),又根据传统 S-N 疲劳方程 $N_f = K(1/\sigma)^n$,则:

$$\Delta N_s = \frac{(\beta_s+1)(1-\alpha_s)}{(\beta_i+1)(1-\alpha_i)}\left(\frac{\sigma_i}{\sigma_s}\right)^n\left[1-\left(\frac{N_s}{N_{f_s}}\right)^{\frac{1}{1-\alpha_s}}\right]^{\frac{\beta_s-\beta_i}{\beta_s+1}} \cdot$$

$$\left\{1-\left[1-\left(\frac{N_s}{N_{f_s}}\right)^{\frac{1}{1-\alpha_s}}\right]^{\frac{\beta_i+1}{\beta_s+1}}\right\}^{\alpha_i}\left(\frac{N_s}{N_{f_s}}\right)^{\frac{-\alpha_s}{1-\alpha_s}} \quad (16)$$

将式(7)代入式(16),得:

$$\Delta N_s = \frac{(\beta_s+1)(1-\alpha_s)}{(\beta_i+1)(1-\alpha_i)}\left(\frac{\sigma_i}{\sigma_s}\right)^n (1-D_s)^{(\beta_s-\beta_i)} \cdot$$

$$[1-(1-D_s)^{1+\beta_i}]^{\alpha_i}[1-(1-D_s)^{1+\beta_s}]^{-\alpha_s} \quad (17)$$

式中,D_s 为路面结构或材料当前的损伤状态。

式(17)即为非标准荷载 σ_i 作用 1 次相当于标准荷载 σ_s 作用 ΔN_s 次的等效换算关系,式(17)中前三项表明等效换算关系与荷载 σ_i 大小有关,后三项表明等效换算关系还与材料或结构所处的损伤状态和荷载 σ_i 大小有关,综上说明该等效换算关系与材料或结构所处的损伤状态(即加载历史)有关,考虑了加载历史和损伤历史的影响,符合实际情况。

5 结论

(1) 沥青混合料的疲劳损伤演化过程具有明显的非线性特性,基于 Miner 线性疲劳损伤理论建立的轴载换算方法不合适。

(2) 定义劲度模量衰减为损伤变量,建立了沥青混合料非线性疲劳损伤演化方程,不同应力比下的疲劳损伤演化规律比较接近,即在疲劳损伤稳定发展阶段损伤增加比较缓慢,而在临近破坏阶段损伤急剧增大,直至破坏。

(3) 基于沥青混合料非线性疲劳损伤方程及 Miner 方程的不足,推导出能考虑加载历史和损伤历史影响的沥青路面轴载换算公式。

参考文献:

[1] 吕松涛. 老化沥青混合料粘弹性疲劳损伤特性研究[D]. 长沙: 长沙理工大学, 2008.
LÜ Songtao. Research on viscoelastic fatigue damage of aged asphalt mixture [D]. Changsha: Changsha University of Science & Technology, 2008. (in Chinese)

[2] 姚祖康. 对国外沥青路面设计指标的评述[J]. 公路, 2003(3): 18－25.
Yao Zukang. Comment of foreign asphalt pavement design index [J]. Highway, 2003(3): 18－25. (in Chinese)

[3] 郑健龙, 吕松涛. 沥青混合料非线性疲劳损伤模型[J]. 中国公路学报, 2009, 22(5): 21－28.
Zheng Jianlong, Lü Songtao. Nonlinear fatigue damage model for asphalt mixtures [J]. China Journal of Highway and Transport, 2009, 22(5): 21－28. (in Chinese)

[4] 唐雪松, 蒋持平, 郑健龙. 沥青混合料疲劳过程的损伤力学分析[J]. 应用力学学报, 2000, 17(4): 92－99.
Tang Xuesong, Jiang Chiping, Zheng Jianlong. Damage mechanical analysis for fatigue failure process of bituminous mixtures [J]. Chinese Journal of Applied Mechanics, 2000, 17(4): 92－99. (in Chinese)

[5] Shu Xiang, Huang Baoshan, Dragon Vukosavljevic. Laboratory evaluation of fatigue characteristics of recycled asphalt mixture [J]. Construction and Building Materials, 2007(19): 1－9.

[6] Kim Jaeseung, West Randy C. Application of the viscoelastic continuum damage model to the indirect tension test at a single temperature [J]. Journal of Engineering Mechanics, 2010, 36(4): 496－505.

[7] Lundstrom R, Isacsson U, Ekblad J. Investigations of stiffness and fatigue properties of asphalt mixtures [J]. Journal of Materials Science, 2003, 38: 4941－4949.

[8] Seo Y, Kim Y R. Using acoustic emission to monitor fatigue damage and healing in asphalt concrete [J]. Journal of Civil Engineering, 2008, 12(4): 237－243.

[9] Saad Abo-Qudais, Ibrahem Shatnawi. Prediction of bituminous mixture fatigue life based on accumulated strain [J]. Construction and Building Materials, 2007, 21: 1370－1376.

[10] Castro Ma, Sánchez J A. Estimation of asphalt concrete fatigue curves-A damage theory approach [J]. Construction and Building Materials, 2007, 12: 1−7.

[11] 杨光松. 损伤力学与复合材料损伤[M]. 北京: 国防工业出版社, 1995: 62−63.
Yang Guangsong. Damage mechanics and composite material damage [M]. Beijing: National Defence Industrial Press, 1995: 62−63. (in Chinese)

[12] 李海军, 黄晓明. 重载条件下沥青路面按弯沉等效的轴载换算[J]. 公路交通科技, 2004, 21(7): 5−8.
Li Haijun, Huang Xiaoming. Axle load conversion formula based on deflection equivalent for semi-rigid base asphalt pavement under heavy-load [J]. Journal of Highway and Transportation Research and Development, 2004, 21(7): 5−8. (in Chinese)

[13] 王辉, 武和平. 沥青路面按弯沉等效轴载换算的研究[J]. 中国公路学报, 2003, 16(1): 19−21.
Wang Hui, Wu Heping. Research on axle exchange based on deflection equivalent for asphalt pavement [J]. China Journal of Highway and Transport, 2003, 16(1): 19−21. (in Chinese)

(上接第267页)

[11] 梁建国, 方亮. 砖砌体墙的屈服准则及其抗剪强度计算[J]. 土木工程学报, 2010, 43(6): 42−47.
Liang Jianguo, Fang Liang. Yield criterion and calculation of shear strength for brick masonry walls [J]. China Civil Engineering Journal, 2010, 43(6): 42−47. (in Chinese)

[12] 砖石结构设计规范抗震设计研究组. 无筋墙体的抗震剪切强度[J]. 建筑结构学报, 1984, 5(6): 1−11.
The Seismic Research Group of Code for Design of Masonry Structures. Seismic shear strength of unreinforced masonry walls [J]. Journal of Building Structures, 1984, 5(6): 1−11. (in Chinese)

[13] ENV1996-1-1, Eurocode6: Design of masonry structures-Part 1-1:General rules for buildings [S]. Rules for reinforced and unreinforced masonry. Comite European de Normalisation: 1995.

[14] GB50003-2001, 砌体结构设计规范[S]. 北京: 中国建筑工业出版社, 2002.
GB50003-2001, Code for design of masonry structures [S]. Beijing: The Standards of People's Republic of China, 2002. (in Chinese)

[15] GB50011-2001, 建筑抗震设计规范[S]. 北京: 中国建筑工业出版社, 2001.
GB50011-2001, Code for seismic design of buildings [S]. Beijing: The Standards of People's Republic of China, 2001. (in Chinese)

考虑加载速度影响的沥青混合料疲劳方程

吕松涛

(长沙理工大学交通运输工程学院道路结构与材料交通行业重点实验室(长沙)，长沙 410004)

摘　要： 为了建立沥青混合料强度与疲劳行为之间的联系，通过不同加载速率下的沥青混合料直接拉伸强度试验，揭示了强度随加载速率的幂函数变化规律；基于不同加载速率下的强度值，得到了与疲劳加载速率对应的沥青混合料疲劳真实应力比；通过疲劳试验，创建了基于名义应力比和真实应力比的沥青混合料疲劳方程，基于名义应力比的疲劳方程后延后与横坐标的交点远比 1 大，不具有后延性，而基于真实应力比的疲劳方程可以后延到疲劳寿命为 1 的强度破坏点，统一了强度破坏与疲劳破坏行为；据此推导了沥青路面抗拉强度结构系数计算新方法；研究结果可为我国公路沥青路面设计规范的修订提供理论依据。

关键词： 道路工程；沥青路面；疲劳；加载速率；应力比；抗拉强度结构系数

中图分类号： U416.217　　**文献标志码：** A　　doi: 10.6052/j.issn.1000-4750.2011.05.0273

FATIGUE EQUATION OF ASPHALT MIXTURE CONSIDERING THE INFLUENCE OF LOADING RATE

LÜ Song-tao

(Key Laboratory of Road Structure and Material of Ministry of Transport, School of Communication and Transportation Engineering, Changsha University of Science & Technology, Changsha 410004, China)

Abstract: In order to establish the relationship between the strength and fatigue behavior of asphalt mixture, the direct tensile strength tests under different loading rates are presented and the power function rule between the strength and loading rate is revealed. Basing on the strength values under different loading rates, the real stress ratios corresponding to the fatigue loading rates of asphalt mixture are obtained. The asphalt mixture fatigue equations based on nominal and real stress ratio are created by fatigue tests. The intersection of fatigue curve characterized by the nominal stress ratio and abscissa axis is much larger than 1. The fatigue curve based on a nominal stress ratio cannot be extended. But the fatigue curve characterized by a real stress ratio can be extended to the strength failure point, whose fatigue life is 1. The strength and fatigue failure behavior are unified. The structure coefficient of tensile strength of asphalt pavement is deduced. The results of the research provide a theoretical foundation for revising the specifications for the design of highway asphalt pavement in our country.

Key words: road engineering; asphalt pavement; fatigue; loading rate; stress ratio; structure coefficient of tensile strength

　　现行沥青路面设计规范在使用 S-N 疲劳方程时将疲劳方程后延到 $N_f=1$，认为此时根据疲劳方程计算得到的强度就是其极限抗拉强度，并由此来计算抗拉强度结构系数，缺乏足够的论据和试验验证。

疲劳方程是疲劳试验结果经过回归分析后得出的，它有一定的试验条件和适用范围。例如 Pell 指出他的双对数直线关系式的适用范围为 $N_f=10^4 \sim 10^8$，超出这一范围，便不一定存在此关系，而是否可以外

---

*工程力学，2012, 29(8): 276-281.

延，需要通过试验进行验证[1-2]，通常范围外与范围内的关系曲线呈折线状。在低循环疲劳情况下的疲劳曲线并不呈现出明显线性关系，而是向下弯向上凸的，由此将疲劳方程后延到 $N_f=1$ 得到的极限抗拉强度值是不合适的[3]。

分析问题出现的主要原因是沥青混合料室内疲劳试验应力比大小确定时其强度参考值是由恒定加载速率的标准强度试验确定的，沥青混合料是一种典型的粘弹性材料，其刚度指标与强度指标均受到加载速度与温度的显著影响[4-7]，由于标准强度试验加载速率远小于疲劳试验 1/2 循环内的加载速率(与应力水平和加载频率有关)，国内外在研究沥青混合料的疲劳特性时都很少有人考虑加载速度对强度的影响，实际上疲劳试验时的真实强度远高于标准强度试验所得到的名义强度[8-14]。这样一来就会和疲劳加载速率对应的强度值有较大差别，传统疲劳试验应力比确定时的强度取值由标准强度试验得到，定义此应力比为名义应力比，定义与疲劳加载速率对应的强度值确定的应力比为真实应力比，即传统疲劳试验分析时采用的应力比为名义应力比而非真实应力比，因此将基于名义应力比建立的疲劳方程后延到 $N_f=1$ 所得到的强度值也就非其极限抗拉强度值，由此计算抗拉强度结构系数不合适。

1 沥青混合料原材料及配合比设计

为了开展沥青混合料强度及疲劳特性研究，本文以细粒式沥青混合料 AC-13C 为研究对象，胶结料采用 SBS 改性沥青，集料采用玄武岩，原材料及配合比设计试验结果如表 1~表 4 所示。

表 1 SBS(I-D)改性沥青试验结果
Table 1 SBS(I-D) modified asphalt test results

试验项目	试验结果	技术要求
针入度(25℃, 100g, 5s)/(0.1mm)	56	30~60
针入度指数 PI	0.533(R^2=0.997)	≥0
延度(5cm/min, 5℃)/cm	34	≥20
软化点 $T_{R\&B}$/(℃)	79	≥60
运动粘度 135℃/(Pa·s)	2.31	≤3
闪点/℃	267	≥230
溶解度/(%)	99.92	≥99
弹性恢复 25℃/(%)	77	≥75
储存稳定性离析, 48h 软化点差/(℃)	1.5	≤2.5
TFOT(或 RTFOT)后残留物	质量变化/(%)	0.1	≤±1.0
	残留针入度比(25℃)/(%)	73	≥65
	残留延度(5℃)/cm	16	≥15

表 2 集料毛体积密度试验结果
Table 2 Bulk density of basalt aggregate tests result

粒径/mm	密度/(g/cm³)	粒径/mm	密度/(g/cm³)
13.2	2.731	0.6	2.717
9.5	2.730	0.3	2.717
4.75	2.729	0.15	2.718
2.36	2.715	0.075	2.719
1.18	2.716	矿粉	2.753

表 3 AC-13C 密级配沥青混合料矿料设计级配
Table 3 Design gradation of AC-13C

筛孔尺寸/mm	规范上限/(%)	规范下限/(%)	通过率/(%)
16	100	100	100
13.2	100	90	95
9.5	85	68	74
4.75	68	38	48.5
2.36	50	24	34
1.18	38	15	23.5
0.6	28	10	15
0.3	20	7	11
0.15	15	5	8.5
0.075	8	4	6

表 4 最佳油石比下马歇尔试验结果
Table 4 Marshall tests result under optimum asphalt-aggregate ratio

油石比/(%)	毛体积相对密度/(g/cm³)	空隙率 VV/(%)	饱和度 VFA/(%)	矿料间隙率 VMA/(%)	稳定度/kN	流值/(0.1mm)
5.3	2.455	5.2	67.2	16.1	15.7	27.9

2 沥青混合料直接拉伸强度随加载速度变化规律

将沥青混合料拌合成型为 30cm×30cm×5cm 的板状试件，然后将其切割成 25cm×5cm×5cm 的小梁试件备用。试验仪器采用 MTS-810 材料试验系统，每个应力周期的力、位移值都由数据采集系统进行自动地采集，通过适当的计算可求出对应的应力、应变，数据采集系统的时间间隔可根据具体的试验条件要求进行设定；试验温度为 15℃，试件进行试验前在环境箱保温 24h。

首先进行标准的直接拉伸强度试验，加载速率为 5mm/min，做 3 次平行试验，取其平均值为 1.963MPa，试验结果如表 5 所示。

表 5 标准的直接抗拉强度试验结果
Table 5 Standard direct tensile strength test results

试验编号	抗拉强度 S_t/MPa	平均值/MPa	标准偏差	变异系数
1	2.101			
2	1.894	1.963	0.120	0.061
3	1.894			

然后选择 0.0037MPa/s~37MPa/s 的 14 种不同加载速率进行直接拉伸强度试验，试验结果见表 6。

表 6　不同加载速率下的直接拉伸强度试验结果
Table 6　Direct tensile strength test results under different loading rates

序号	加载速率 v/(MPa/s)	试件面积/mm²	破坏荷载/N	强度 S_{dz}/MPa
1	0.0037	2695.7	2276	0.844
2	0.0370	2688.2	3749	1.395
3	0.3700	2727.2	5453	2.000
4	1.8500	2662.8	7548	2.835
5	3.7000	2676.6	7910	2.955
6	7.4000	2799.6	10757	3.842
7	10.8000	2778.3	11892	4.279
8	13.7200	2915.4	13888	4.589
9	17.7700	2813.1	13027	4.695
10	21.0000	2869.8	13550	4.722
11	24.8000	2818.7	13927	4.941
12	29.6000	2703.0	13969	5.168
13	33.3000	2625.1	13119	4.998
14	37.0000	2703.1	14229	5.227

由表 6 中的试验结果不难发现，加载速度对沥青混合料的强度影响非常显著，在试验的加载范围内，强度最大值是最小值的 6 倍多。

在进行沥青混合料疲劳试验时，通常选择 10Hz 的加载频率，假如在 1MPa 的应力水平下进行疲劳试验，其加载过程中速度为 20MPa/s，由表 6 根据标准强度试验结果 1.963MPa 可反算出其对应的加载速度仅相当于 0.35MPa/s，二者加载速度相差 20/0.35=57 倍；由表 6 可计算出加载速度 20MPa/s 所对应的强度为 4.689MPa，二者强度有 4.689/1.963=2.389 倍的差异，可见疲劳试验所采用的应力比是不真实的，疲劳方程中的应力比只是一个名义应力比。

将表 6 中的不同加载速率下的直接拉伸强度绘图如图 1 所示。

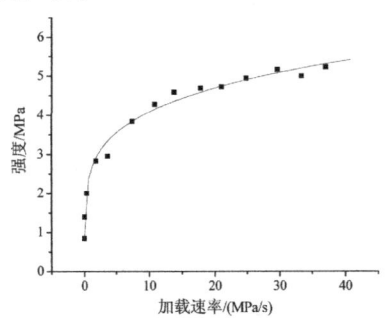

图 1　15℃条件下 AC-13C 直接拉伸强度随加载速率变化曲线

Fig.1　Direct tensile strength versus loading rate of AC-13C at 15℃

将加载速率与直接拉伸强度进行非线性拟合，可得二者的回归关系如下式所示：

$$S_{dz} = 2.583v^{0.2}, \quad R^2 = 0.984 \qquad (1)$$

由拟合结果可知，加载速率对沥青混合料强度有显著影响，二者呈幂函数规律变化，定义与疲劳试验加载速率对应的强度值为疲劳动载强度。

3　以真实应力比表征的沥青混合料的疲劳特性

建立沥青混合料传统 S-N 疲劳方程时是由固定加载速率下的标准强度值来确定应力比的，由于该强度值与疲劳试验过程的加载速率并非对应，因此定义此应力比为名义应力比 t_m，确定名义应力比时须首先进行固定加载速率下的沥青混合料标准静载强度试验，由表 5 得到的准静载强度 S_f=1.963MPa。

疲劳试验温度采用 15℃，试件进行试验前首先在环境箱保温 24h。名义应力比取 0.3、0.4、0.5、0.6 和 0.7 这 5 种，加载频率为 1Hz、10Hz、20Hz 和 50Hz 这 4 种，疲劳荷载采用连续半正矢荷载，波形如图 2 所示。

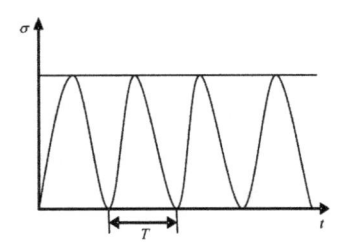

图 2　疲劳试验时施加的荷载波形

Fig.2　Loading wave of fatigue test

根据疲劳试验时的加载频率 f(周期为 T)和应力水平 σ 可以求出对应的加载速率，见下式：

$$v = \frac{\sigma}{T/2} = 2f\sigma \qquad (2)$$

再由式(1)可以求出对应的疲劳动载强度值 S_{dz}。

定义真实应力比 t_s 为不同应力水平与其对应加载速率下的疲劳动载强度的比值，即：

$$t_s = \sigma/S_{dz} \qquad (3)$$

式中：σ 为疲劳试验施加的应力水平；S_{dz} 为与加载频率和应力水平相对应加载速率下的疲劳动载强度。

附　录

在温度 15℃条件下对 AC-13C 沥青混合料进行小梁直接拉伸疲劳试验,不同频率和不同应力水平的疲劳试验结果汇总见表 7。

表 7　不同加载频率和名义应力比下的真实应力比及疲劳寿命
Table 7　Summary of real stress ratio and fatigue life under different loading frequency and stress level

加载频率 f/Hz	名义应力比 t_m	应力水平 σ/MPa	加载速率 v/(MPa/s)	动载强度 S_{dt}/MPa	真实应力比 t_s	疲劳寿命 N_f/次 试件 1	试件 2
1	0.4	0.78	1.57	2.814	0.28	1518	1330
	0.5	0.98	1.96	2.943	0.33	510	541
	0.6	1.18	2.35	3.053	0.39	250	280
	0.7	1.37	2.74	3.149	0.44	163	112
10	0.3	0.59	11.76	4.219	0.14	30820	35231
	0.4	0.78	15.68	4.471	0.18	22313	18887
	0.5	0.98	19.60	4.676	0.21	7883	5807
	0.6	1.18	23.52	4.850	0.24	3058	3478
	0.7	1.37	27.44	5.003	0.27	1712	1388
20	0.3	0.59	23.52	4.850	0.12	117293	106538
	0.4	0.78	31.36	5.139	0.15	37717	28197
	0.5	0.98	39.20	5.375	0.18	9627	8234
	0.6	1.18	47.04	5.575	0.21	5027	7375
	0.7	1.37	54.88	5.751	0.24	3036	4066
50	0.3	0.59	58.80	5.831	0.10	198472	132897
	0.4	0.78	78.40	6.178	0.13	56327	49754
	0.5	0.98	98.00	6.462	0.15	16231	19430
	0.6	1.18	117.60	6.703	0.18	9863	8853
	0.7	1.37	137.20	6.914	0.20	3763	4084

将表 7 中的疲劳试验结果利用统一方程形式 $N_f = k(1/t)^n$ 进行回归分析,分别得到不同加载频率下以名义应力比和真实应力比表示的疲劳回归曲线,如图 3 和图 4 所示。疲劳方程回归参数汇总如表 8 所示。

表 8　名义和真实应力比疲劳方程参数拟合结果表
Table 8　Fitting results of fatigue equation parameters based on nominal & real stress ratio

加载频率 f		1Hz	10Hz	20Hz	50Hz
名义应力比 t_m	k	29.819	537.030	620.869	926.830
	n	4.245	3.550	4.305	4.333
	R^2	0.998	0.974	0.991	0.999
真实应力比 t_s	k'	1.046	1.192	1.021	1.028
	n'	5.734	5.427	5.514	5.236
	R^2	0.999	0.994	0.999	0.999

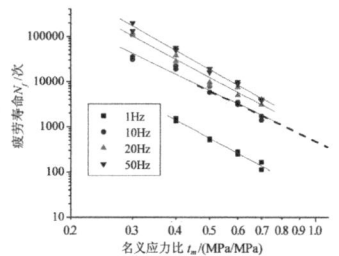

图 3　基于名义应力比的疲劳方程曲线
Fig.3　Fatigue curves based on nominal stress ratio

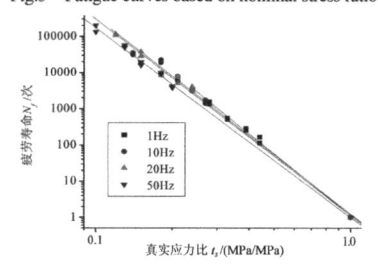

图 4　基于真实应力比的疲劳方程曲线
Fig.4　Fatigue curves based on real stress ratio

由图 4 和表 8 可以看出:基于真实应力比的疲劳曲线过(1,1)点,则疲劳方程参数 k' 应为 1,回归结果中除 10Hz 外,各疲劳回归方程的 k' 都比较接近 1,只有 10Hz 的 k' 偏大可能是其对应的真实应力比 0.14 时的疲劳试验结果误差所致。基于真实应力比的疲劳方程可以后延到 $N_f = 1$,$N_f = 1$ 对应的即是疲劳寿命为一次的强度破坏点,因此基于真实应力比的疲劳曲线揭示了强度破坏和疲劳破坏的内在联系。

由图 3 和图 4 可以发现无论是真实应力比表示的疲劳方程还是名义应力比表示的疲劳方程在双对数坐标下均为一直线方程,但以真实应力比表示的疲劳方程的斜率大,其与横坐标的交点接近于应力比为1的坐标位置，即疲劳方程同时反映了沥青混合料的强度破坏特征。而以名义应力比表示的疲劳方程与横坐标的交点远比应力比1要大，显然这不符合实际。可见以真实应力比表示的疲劳方程远比以名义应力比表示的疲劳方程准确，而且试验结果可向两端延拓，直至与坐标轴相交；而以名义应力表示的疲劳方程如向两端延拓则会导致较大的偏差，而且延拓的范围越大，其偏差也越大。

同时基于真实应力比不同频率的各疲劳回归方程的 n' 差别不大，因此可将不同频率下的疲劳试验结果利用真实应力比这一纽带进行统一，回归成一条曲线，如图5所示。

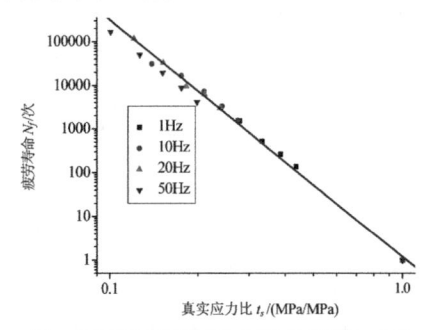

图 5 不同频率下基于真实应力比的疲劳统一曲线
Fig.5 Unified fatigue curves based on real stress ratio under different loading frequencies

由图5可知，基于真实应力比不同频率的疲劳曲线可以回归为一条直线，说明不同加载频率和不同加载速度对疲劳特性的影响是等价的。

则基于真实应力比建立的不同频率下沥青混合料统一疲劳方程为：

$$N_f = \left(\frac{1}{t_s}\right)^{n'} = \left(\frac{S_{dz}}{\sigma}\right)^{n'} = \left(\frac{S_{dz}}{\sigma}\right)^{5.426} \quad (4)$$

4 沥青路面抗拉强度结构系数计算新方法

我国现规范中沥青面层抗拉强度结构系数是通过劈裂疲劳试验得到的，推荐的疲劳方程为[2]：

$$N_f = 280\sigma^{-4.5} \text{ 或 } \sigma = 3.45 N_f^{-0.22} \quad (5)$$

抗拉强度结构系数定义为一次荷载作用下的极限抗拉强度与疲劳容许拉应力的比值，即：

$$K_s = \frac{\sigma_1}{\sigma_R} = \frac{3.45}{3.45 N_f^{-0.22}} = N_f^{0.22} \quad (6)$$

考虑间歇时间、裂缝传播速度、交通量折减和轮迹横向分布等各种室内外试验条件的差异等因素的修正公式为：

$$K_s = 0.09 N_e^{0.22}/A_c \quad (7)$$

式中：N_e 为设计年限内一个方向上一个车道累计当量轴次；A_c 为公路等级系数。

规范中采用的疲劳方程是基于名义应力比建立的，通过前面的分析，据此来进行抗拉强度结构系数计算是不合适的。

根据前面真实应力比 t_s 的定义，其为应力水平与其对应加载速率下的疲劳动载强度的比值；通过与抗拉强度结构系数 K_s 定义的比较可知：二者互为倒数关系，即：

$$\left.\begin{array}{l} K_s = \dfrac{\sigma_1}{\sigma_R} = \dfrac{S_{dz}}{\sigma} \\ t_s = \dfrac{\sigma}{S_{dz}} \end{array}\right\} \Rightarrow K_s = \frac{1}{t_s} = \frac{S_{dz}}{\sigma} \quad (8)$$

又根据式(4)，则式(8)可变为：

$$K_s = \frac{1}{t_s} = \frac{S_{dz}}{\sigma} = (N_f)^{\frac{1}{n'}} = (N_f)^{\frac{1}{5.426}} = N_f^{0.184} \quad (9)$$

式(9)即为基于真实应力比疲劳方程推导得到的沥青路面面层抗拉强度结构系数计算公式。

从前面的分析计算过程可以看出，基于真实应力比建立的疲劳方程能够后延到一次强度破坏点，据此进行抗拉强度结构系数推导计算符合其定义，是合适的也是合理的，一定程度上弥补了我国现行沥青路面设计规范在此计算推导方面的不足。

5 结论

通过对我国沥青路面常用的 AC-13C 沥青混合料进行大量的强度与疲劳试验，根据试验结果，利用现象学的分析方法，得到如下结论：

(1) 加载速率对沥青混合料直接拉伸强度有显著的影响，在一定加载速率范围内，直接拉伸强度随加载速率的增大而增大，二者呈幂函数规律变化。

(2) 根据直接拉伸强度随加载速率的变化规律，提出了真实应力比的概念及其确定方法和以真实应力比构建疲劳方程的新方法。

(3) 无论是真实应力比表示的疲劳方程还是名义应力比表示的疲劳方程在双对数坐标下均为一直线方程；采用真实应力比建立的疲劳方程曲线可

后延到疲劳寿命为 1 的强度破坏点, 疲劳方程同时反映了沥青混合料的强度破坏特征, 揭示了强度破坏和疲劳破坏的内在联系。而以名义应力比表示的疲劳方程与横坐标的交点远比应力比 1 要大, 显然这不符合实际。

(4) 以真实应力比表示的疲劳方程远比以名义应力比表示的疲劳方程准确, 而且试验结果可向两端延拓, 直至与坐标轴相交; 而以名义应力比表示的疲劳方程如向两端延拓则会导致较大的偏差, 而且延拓的范围越大, 其偏差也越大。

(5) 基于真实应力比表示的统一的疲劳方程能够表征不同加载频率下的沥青混合料疲劳特性, 反映了不同加载频率和不同加载速度对疲劳特性的影响是等价的。

(6) 基于真实应力比表示的疲劳方程得到了沥青路面抗拉强度结构系数计算新方法, 为完善现行沥青路面设计规范提供了理论依据。

参考文献：

[1] 姚祖康. 对我国沥青路面设计指标的评述[J]. 公路, 2003(2): 43-49.
Yao Zukang. A review on design criteria of asphalt pavements [J]. Journal of Highway, 2003(2): 43-49. (in Chinese)

[2] JTG D50-2006, 公路沥青路面设计规范[S]. 北京: 人民交通出版社, 2006: 26-80.
JTG D50-2006, Specification for design of highway asphalt pavement [S]. Beijing: China Communications Press, 2006: 26-80. (in Chinese)

[3] 陈立杰, 江铁强, 谢里阳. 低循环疲劳寿命预测的幂指函数模型[J]. 机械强度, 2006, 28(5): 761-765.
Chen Lijie, Jiang Tieqiang, Xie Liyang. Low cycle fatigue life prediction method based on power-exponent function model [J]. Journal of Mechanical Strength, 2006, 28(5): 761-765. (in Chinese)

[4] Kim Jaeseung, West Randy C. Application of the viscoelastic continuum damage model to the indirect tension test at a single temperature [J]. Journal of Engineering Mechanics, 2010, 36(4): 496-505.

[5] You Zhanping, Adhikari Sanjeev, Emin Kutay M. Dynamic modulus simulation of the asphalt concrete using the X-ray computed tomography images [J]. Materials and Structures, 2009, 42: 617-630.

[6] Gonzalez J M, Miquel canet J, Oller S, Miro R. A viscoplastic creep model with strain rate variables for asphalt mixtures-numerical simulation [J]. Computational Materials Science, 2007, 38: 543-560.

[7] Lundstrom R, Isacsson U, Ekblad J. Investigations of stiffness and fatigue properties of asphalt mixtures [J]. Journal of Materials Science, 2003, 38: 4941-4949.

[8] 郑健龙, 吕松涛. 沥青混合料非线性疲劳损伤模型[J]. 中国公路学报, 2009, 22(5): 21-28.
Zheng Jianlong, Lü Songtao. Nonlinear fatigue damage model for asphalt mixtures [J]. China Journal of Highway and Transport, 2009, 22(5): 21-28. (in Chinese)

[9] 平树江, 申爱琴, 李鹏. 长寿命路面沥青混合料疲劳极限研究[J]. 中国公路学报, 2009, 22(1): 34-38.
Ping Shujiang, Shen Aiqin, Li Peng. Study of fatigue limit of asphalt mixture for perpetual pavement. China Journal of Highway and Transport, 2009, 22(1): 34-38. (in Chinese)

[10] 张志祥, 吴建浩. 再生沥青混合料疲劳性能试验研究[J]. 中国公路学报, 2006, 19(2): 31-35.
Zhang Zhixiang, Wu Jianhao. Experimental research on fatigue characteristics of RAP mixtures [J]. China Journal of Highway and Transport, 2006, 19(2): 31-35. (in Chinese)

[11] Seo Y, Kim Y R. Using acoustic emission to monitor fatigue damage and healing in asphalt concrete [J]. Journal of Civil Engineering, 2008, 12(4): 237-243.

[12] Saad Abo-Qudais, Ibrahem Shatnawi. Prediction of bituminous mixture fatigue life based on accumulated strain [J]. Construction and Building Materials, 2007, 21: 1370-1376.

[13] Shu Xiang, Huang Baoshan, Vukosavljevic Dragon. Laboratory evaluation of fatigue characteristics of recycled asphalt mixture [J]. Construction and Building Materials, 2007(19): 1-9.

[14] Castro Ma, Sánchez J A. Estimation of asphalt concrete fatigue curves-A damage theory approach [J]. Construction and Building Materials, 2007, 12: 1-7.